Unwin Critical Library
GENERAL EDITOR: CLAUDE RAWSON

GREAT EXPECTATIONS

Great Expectations

Anny Sadrin

University of Dijon

London
UNWIN HYMAN
Boston   Sydney   Wellington

Published by the Academic Division of
Unwin Hyman Ltd
15/17 Broadwick Street, London W1V 1FP

Allen & Unwin Inc.,
8 Winchester Place, Winchester, Mass. 01890, USA

Allen & Unwin (Australia) Ltd,
8 Napier Street, North Sydney, NSW 2060, Australia

Allen & Unwin (New Zealand) Ltd in association with the
Port Nicholson Press Ltd,
60 Cambridge Terrace, Wellington, New Zealand

First published in 1988

British Library Cataloguing in Publication Data

Sadrin, Anny
    Great expectations. – (Unwin Critical Library).
1. Dickens, Charles, *1812–1870*. Great expectations
I. Title
823'.8   PR4560
ISBN 0–04–800051–5

Library of Congress Cataloging-in-Publication Data

Sadrin, Anny, 1935–
    Great expectations / Anny Sadrin.
p. cm. – (Unwin critical library)
Bibliography: p.
Includes index.
ISBN 0–04–800051–5 (alk. paper)
1. Dickens, Charles. 1812–1870. Great expectations. I. Title.
II. Series.
PR4560.S23 1988
823'. 8–dc19

Typeset in 10 on 12 point Sabon by
Computape (Pickering) Ltd, North Yorkshire
and printed in Great Britain by
Billing and Son, London and Worcester

For Paul

CONTENTS

GENERAL EDITOR'S PREFACE

Each volume in this series is devoted to a single major text. It is intended for serious students and teachers of literature, and for knowledgeable non-academic readers. It aims to provide a scholarly introduction and a stimulus to critical thought and discussion.

Individual volumes will naturally differ from one another in arrangement and emphasis, but each will normally begin with information on a work's literary and intellectual background, and other guidance designed to help the reader to an informed understanding. This is followed by an extended critical discussion of the work itself, and each contributor in the series has been encouraged to present in these sections his own reading of the work, whether or not this is controversial, rather than to attempt a mere consensus. Some volumes, including those on *Paradise Lost* and *Ulysses*, vary somewhat from the more usual pattern by entering into substantive critical discussion at the outset, and allowing the necessary background material to emerge at the points where it is felt to arise from the argument in the most useful and relevant way. Each volume also contains a historical survey of the work's critical reputation, including an account of the principal lines of approach and areas of controversy, and a selective (but detailed) bibliography.

The hope is that the volumes in this series will be among those which a university teacher would normally recommend for any serious study of a particular text, and that they will also be among the essential secondary texts to be consulted in some scholarly investigations. But the experienced and informed non-academic reader has also been in our minds, and one of our aims has been to provide him or her with reliable and stimulating works of reference and guidance, embodying the present state of knowledge and opinion in a conveniently accessible form.

C.J.R.
University of Warwick,
December 1979

A NOTE ON THE TEXT

We have at present no authoritative edition of *Great Expectations*. Neither the Clarendon nor the long-awaited Norton editions have come out yet. And there is so far no Unwin Hyman 'Companion' to this novel. My references are to the Penguin English Library edition, introduced, edited and annotated by Angus Calder. The text reprinted there is basically that of the first edition (1861), with occasional alterations. The cancelled ending is reproduced in an appendix. The notes are substantial and often very useful. The edition has the further advantage of being cheap and easily available.

ACKNOWLEDGEMENTS

I would like first of all to express my gratitude to Sylvère Monod, my former supervisor, now a friend, who agreed to be my first 'Dickensian' reader. His knowledge of Dickens, his generosity, his readiness to help and his critical acumen were all immensely precious and saved me from several errors.

To my friend and colleague, Terence McCarthy, I am also extremely grateful for his scrupulous reading of my typescript and for his very tactful suggestions, which have prevented linguistic infelicities and ought to prevent Podsnappian dismissals of the book as 'Not English!'.

I also wish to acknowledge my debt to Professor Robert L. Patten for the information and help he has given me and to Professor George J. Worth who kindly sent me his *Great Expectations* Bibliography hot from the press just in time for me to consult it while still in the throes of writing my critical survey.

Claude Rawson provided me throughout with encouragement. For his patience as general editor of the series and for his unfailing trust in this enterprise, he deserves my most heartfelt gratitude.

A special debt is also owed to the British Council for a grant that enabled me to undertake my early research in London.

Lastly, I cannot resist the pleasure of expressing my admiration for a man in whose company I have now spent more than twenty years and whose infinite variety custom cannot stale: I am referring, of course, to Charles Dickens.

A.S.
Dijon, May 1987

PRELIMINARY

CHAPTER 1

Genesis
and Publication

Dickens never tried to probe the mystery of creativeness. He just wrote books. And when he once set out to relate how one of them, *The Pickwick Papers*, had come into existence, all he found to say of its conception and execution was 'I thought of Mr. Pickwick, and wrote the first number':[1] a simple statement, intimating almost spontaneous generation, unless it suggests that Pickwick had always been there, in one of the 'many little drawers' of his creator's imagination, wanting all the time, like the seeds and flower-bulbs and pips in Pumblechook's premises, 'of a fine day to break out of those jails, and bloom'.[2]

Pickwick had early bloomed into immortality, when the young Boz had thought of him and 'The first ray of light which illumines the gloom' had converted his obscurity into 'a dazzling brilliancy'.[3] Little Pip was given his chance in the autumn both of Dickens's life and of the year 1860. Latecomer though he was, he must have been lurking in the novelist's unconscious ever since the days when Charles Huffam, aged six or seven, had been living in Kent, within walking distance of 'them misty marshes' and of the 'wicked Noah's ark[s]'[4] that then adorned the estuary of the Medway.[5]

But not only does *Great Expectations* take us back to familiar scenes of Dickens's early boyhood; it also gives new life to the dreams and dreads of childhood and adolescence re-explored by a grown man in the personal mode of an autobiography.

This is not to say that the story of Pip is the story of Charles. But the choice of writing a first-person narrative entailed personal involvement on the part of the writer that would have been less compulsive if he had resorted to traditional omniscience. Dickens was well aware of this. He knew what snares and difficulties would be attending the complex process of identification: the emotional turmoil, the insidious tricks of involuntary memory. As he recorded his hero's fictitious memoirs, some of his own recollections would creep in, inevitably, and he could not overlook the fact. This is made apparent in a letter he wrote to Forster just before embarking on his enterprise. There, he drew his friend's attention to possible similarities between his new story and *David Copperfield*, the nearest thing he had ever written to an autobiography:

> To be quite sure I had fallen into no unconscious repetitions, I read *David Copperfield* again the other day, and was affected by it to a degree you would hardly believe.[6]

We know, besides, from his correspondence and the revelations of his biographers, that the break-up of his marriage, in 1858, had left him a restless, dissatisfied man, nostalgic and self-pitying, with a growing sense of 'one happiness' he had 'missed in life'[7] and a tendency to brood over his past miseries. He often reverted in particular to the days when his family were all inmates of the Marshalsea and he, 'a common labouring-boy',[8] hired to a Strand manufacturer, had to stick labels on shoe-polish bottles in order to get a living 'in that universal struggle'.[9] To Forster he wrote in 1862:

> I must entreat you to pause for an instant, and go back to what you know of my childish days, and to ask yourself whether it is natural that something of the character formed in me then, and lost under happier circumstances, should have reappeared in the last five years. The never to be forgotten misery of that old time, bred a certain shrinking sensitiveness in a certain ill-clad ill-fed child, that I have found come back in the never to be forgotten misery of this later time.[10]

Thus in the right mood for confessional writings, at the beginning of 1860, he started contributing, under the title *The Uncommercial Traveller*, a new series of essays, 'often reminiscent in tone',[11] to *All the Year Round*, his weekly magazine. 'In addition to recounting current experiences', comments Leslie Staples in his introduction to these collected essays, 'he frequently drew upon his memories of the past, and not the least interesting feature of the papers is the autobiographical material that is to be found in many of them. Here

is much that he probably originally intended for the autobiography
that he never wrote, and much to supplement what we gather about
his early life in *David Copperfield*.'[12]

One of the best known, and justly celebrated, of these essays is the
one called 'Travelling Abroad' where the narrator, on his way from
Gravesend to Rochester, meets 'a very queer small boy' whom he
takes up with him in his 'travelling chariot'. As they drive past Gad's
Hill, the country residence that, after years of frustrated desire,
Dickens had eventually bought in 1856, the little boy indulges in
dreams only too familiar to his interlocutor:

> '... But *do* let us stop at the top of the hill, and look at the house
> there, if you please!'
> 'You admire the house?' said I.
> 'Bless you, sir,' said the very queer small boy, 'when I was not
> more than half as old as nine, it used to be a treat for me to be
> brought to look at it. And now, I am nine, I come by myself to
> look at it. And ever since I can recollect, my father, seeing me so
> fond of it, has often said to me, "If you were to be very persevering
> and were to work hard, you might some day come to live in it."
> Though that's impossible!' said the very queer small boy,
> drawing a low breath, and now staring at the house out of
> window with all his might.
> I was rather amazed to be told this by the very queer small boy;
> for that house happens to be *my* house, and I have reason to
> believe that what he said was true.[13]

Similarly, the reader of *Great Expectations* has reason to believe
that Pip is to his creator what the very queer small boy was to his
travelling companion and that, in a broad sense, his confessions are
true.

As a matter of fact, the germ of this novel[14] was one such little
sketch that Dickens wrote in September 1860 and first intended for
The Uncommercial Traveller. The manuscript, unfortunately, has
not been preserved (Dickens presumably destroyed it at once
without even showing it to Forster as he had first meant to do) and
we know little of it, except that it must have been written in the first
person like all the other essays of the series and that its author was
so taken up with its 'drollery'[15] that, even before he had finished it,
he considered reworking it into a full-length novel:

For a little piece I have been writing – or am writing; for I hope to finish it to-day – such a very fine, new, and grotesque idea has opened upon me, that I begin to doubt whether I had not better cancel the little paper, and reserve the notion for a new book. You shall judge as soon as I get it printed. But it so opens out before *me* that I can see the whole of a serial revolving on it, in a most singular and comic manner ... [16]

What he had in mind then was a serial in twenty monthly parts, his favourite mode of publication. Had he carried out his plan, the book would have been twice as long as it turned out to be under the new circumstances that soon compelled him to reconsider his project.

The reasons – 'perhaps fortunate', as Forster suggests[17] – that brought about this change of mind were no less than 'the state and prospects'[18] of *All the Year Round* itself, whose sales in recent weeks had been falling alarmingly. The sudden collapse in the circulation of the magazine and the ensuing financial crisis had been simultaneous with the publication, since 18 August, of a new leading serial, *A Day's Ride, A Life's Romance*, by Charles Lever: unmistakably, the coincidence pointed to a connection. On reading Lever's manuscript, Dickens had actually spotted at once its major weakness, a lack of purpose and drive; and, before getting it to print, he had felt it necessary to make deletions and alterations to what he considered a verbose, sprawling, uselessly digressive text: 'In the first portion', he had to tell Lever, 'I have made a few short cuts. They are but a sentence here and a sentence there, where I feel the getting at the action to be delayed.'[19] But editorial abridgement could not prevent the latent, and lasting, discursiveness of a story which, quite understandably, failed from the first to arouse the readers' interest. And, as the weeks went by, there was no sign of improvement.

This was all the more worrying as the current serial was the journal's main attraction. As former editor of *Household Words*, Dickens, in nine years of practice,[20] had learnt to associate an increase in the profits with the (at that time) occasional publication of serial novels in the columns of his magazine; and, when he launched *All the Year Round* in 1859,[21] he not unwisely thought that the best means of promoting its circulation would be to give priority of place to an original story. Accordingly, the first issue started with the opening chapters of *A Tale of Two Cities*, written for the occasion, and the result was so rewarding that when, seven months later, the novel reached its conclusion, an announcement was made establishing the serialization of fiction as a regular feature of the new periodical:

> We purpose always reserving the first place in these pages for a continuous original work of fiction, occupying about the same amount of time in its serial publication, as that which is just completed ... And it is our hope and aim, while we work hard at every other department of our journal, to produce, in this one, some sustained works of imagination that may become a part of English Literature.[22]

Ideally, a novel 'would make about 150 printed pages of All the Year Round', as Dickens specified to Edward Bulwer Lytton in December 1860, requesting a contribution. 'The publication of such 150 pages', he added, 'would occupy *about* thirty weeks.'[23] An instalment would therefore cover an average length of five pages in a twenty-four page issue. Needless to say, the welfare of the magazine was bound up with the popularity of each new serial, and Dickens was taking a risk in adopting this policy. For, as Ella Ann Oppenlander rightly points out, he was no professional editor of fiction and 'he was now committed to competing regularly in the manuscript market with experienced publishers'.[24]

So far, the risk had proved worth taking. *All the Year Round* had been an immediate success, reaching a much wider audience than its predecessor and bringing profits that 'exceeded the most sanguine expectations'.[25] Within three months the sales had amply repaid investments: 'So well has All the Year Round gone', Dickens wrote in July 1859, 'that it was yesterday able to repay me, with five per cent. interest, all the money I advanced for its establishment (paper, print &c. all paid, down to the last number), and yet to leave a good £500 balance at the banker's!'[26] and by the fifth number its circulation had trebled that of *Household Words*.[27] Additional income came from the sales of publication rights to American publishers, Thomas Cole Evans (only for a few months), then J. M. Emerson and Company of New York, to whom Evans had sold the *All the Year Round* publishing rights and who remained the publishers of the journal in the United States during its lifetime.[28] The agreement seems to have been mutually profitable and William H. Wills, Dickens's sub-editor,[29] could rejoice after two years that 'The American edition of *All the Year Round*' was 'rather a good thing netting from £600 to £700 a year'.[30] Dickens therefore had every right to be satisfied with his enterprise and to be proud of himself whether as businessman, first editor or chief contributor, not the least reason for such an astounding beginning being his self-appointment as first serialist.

The *Tale* had been followed by another very popular novel, Wilkie Collins's *The Woman in White*. This jigsaw-puzzle detective story, with its mastery of suspense and skilful experimenting in multiple narrative, appealed both to common and sophisticated readers and secured steady, even rising sales for another eight months. But then, with *A Day's Ride*, the circulation dropped almost instantaneously and the slump caught Dickens totally unprepared after such a booming start. The whole fabric of his journal, he realized, was endangered and quick steps had to be taken to boost the sales and rescue the property. In such an emergency, Dickens the editor could think of no better rescuer than Dickens the novelist. He knew he could rely on his talent, his energy and his goodwill, and on the prestige of his name. For anonymity was no longer the rule in *All the Year Round* as it had been in *Household Words*, and contributors were now introduced by name: 'the name is really of importance and great importance'[31] was Dickens's present conviction. So, if 'a new serial story by Mr Charles Dickens to be published shortly' were to be advertised in the coming weeks, he felt confident that his difficulties would soon be overcome. With no loss of time a decision was made: Dickens thought of Pip and wrote the first numbers . . .[32]

On 4 October, hardly a week after that day in late September when he had toyed with his 'grotesque idea' for a book in monthly parts, he informed Forster of his new intention:

Last week, I got to work on a new story. I had previously very carefully considered the state and prospects of All the Year Round, and, the more I considered them, the less hope I saw of being able to get back, *now*, to the profit of a separate publication in the old 20 numbers. However, I worked on, knowing that what I was doing would run into another groove. I called a council of war at the office on Tuesday. It was perfectly clear that the one thing to be done was, for me to strike in. I have therefore decided to begin a story, the length of the Tale of Two Cities, on the First of December – begin publishing, that is. I must make the most I can out of the book. When I come down, I will bring you the first two or three weekly parts. The name is, GREAT EXPECTA- TIONS. I think a good name?[33]

Lever, in turn, was duly advised of this regrettable, yet necessary decision. Dickens, in a letter which he said he hated, dreaded, couldn't write, expounded the case, and, though it is obvious he had no wish to give offence, his tone admitted of no objection:

We drop, rapidly and continuously, with The Day's Ride. Whether it is too detached and discursive in its interest for the audience and the form of publication, I can not say positively; but it does not *take hold*. The consequence is, that the circulation becomes affected, and that subscribers complain. I have waited week after week, for these three or four weeks, watching for any sign of encouragement. The least sign would have been enough. But all the tokens that appear, are in the other direction; and therefore I have been driven upon the necessity of considering how to act, and of writing to you.

There is but one thing to be done. I had begun a book which I intended for one of my long twenty number serials. I must abandon that design and forego its profits (a very serious con- sideration, you may believe), and shape the story for these pages. I must get into these pages, as soon as possible, and must con- sequently begin my story in the No. for the 1st of December. For as long a time as you continue afterwards, we must go on together.

This is the whole case. If the publication were to go steadily down, too long, it would be very, very, very difficult to raise again. I do not fear the difficulty at all, by taking this early and vigorous action. But without it there is not a doubt that the position would be serious.[34]

While Lever swallowed the pill and bitterly toiled on, Dickens, steeled with self-confidence, made headway with his new, self- appointed task. On 27 October, *Great Expectations* was advertised for the first time in *All the Year Round*. On 1 December, according to schedule, the first instalment made its appearance there, ousting

Lever's serial from the opening pages. The publication ran for a period of thirty-six weeks, ending on 3 August 1861. Dickens throughout contrived to do more than 'hold [his] ground', often working ahead of his 'old month's advance'[35] or usual safety-margin. According to Edgar Rosenberg, he even 'presumably managed to keep about two months ahead of publication in *All the Year Round*';[36] for it has also to be borne in mind that he had made an agreement with Harper and Company of New York, who were to serialize the novel in *Harper's Weekly* a week ahead of *All the Year Round*, which compelled him to send the proofs a fortnight in advance.[37] By mid April he had 'gotten well into Stage Three of the novel'[38] and he wrote this portion almost at a stroke. On 24 May he could tell Wilkie Collins: 'I hope – begin to hope – that somewhere about the 12th of June will see me out of the book'[39] and on 11 June, he had actually completed his novel in its original version and wrote to Macready: 'I have just finished my book of Great Expectations, and am the worse for wear ... But I hope that the book is a good book.'[40] Later in the month, acting on Bulwer Lytton's counsel, he re-wrote the conclusion and by 24 June the revised ending was ready to be sent to Bulwer for approval.[41] On 6 July, Chapman and Hall issued the first edition of the novel in book form.

The decision to contribute a story of his own to revive the magazine had been made quickly but not easily. Besides the inconvenience of hurting the pride of a contributor and spoiling the partnership, there were two major drawbacks: one technical, the other financial. Dickens, at least as a writer, had never had much taste for weekly deliveries. The hectic pace to be sustained was both energy and time consuming and left little room for other activities in the life of one who like himself had so many further commitments. Moreover, the need to portion out the story into tiny fragments, get at the action quickly, then keep it going with renewed interest week in week out, entailed very careful planning, allowed for no second thoughts and badly threatened to strait-jacket 'the Robber Fancy'. When writing *Hard Times*, a few years earlier, Dickens, with his fondness for 'meandering' and beating about the bush, for the leisurely methods he had been able to employ in *David Copperfield*, had already complained that he was cramped for room: 'The difficulty of space is CRUSHING',[42] he had written to Forster. By the time he embarked on *A Tale of Two Cities*, he had not reconciled himself to this rate of production and, taken up though he was with his new story, he found the writing of it very strenuous and very taxing on his nerves: 'the small portions thereof, drive me frantic',[43] he grumbled. When *Great Expectations* was nearing completion he again wrote to Forster: 'As to the planning out from week to week, nobody can imagine what the difficulty is, without trying.'[44] And as an editor he was always careful to warn prospective serialists against the 'difficulty and labour' of 'that specially trying mode of publication'.[45]

Giving up the idea of a twenty-number serial also implied financial sacrifices, as Dickens explained to Forster and Lever; and this was no small matter for a man whose standard of living, as Ada Nisbet puts it, 'was always several jumps ahead of his income'.[46] We must bear in mind that, at this stage of his life, the novelist had not only a large family to support, including notoriously improvident sons and poor relations,[47] but several establishments to keep going: his wife's, presumably Ellen Ternan's, and the recently purchased Gad's Hill, which had been a costly place to buy. Moreover, by improving it and building extensions, Dickens had made it even more expensive to keep.[48] It had been to pay for the house that he had 'revived' the old idea of the public readings which, ungenteel though the practice was in the eyes of Forster,[49] were to net him a lot of money, though not enough apparently to meet all his requirements. It is therefore quite natural that he should have felt reluctant to give up a project that he knew for certain would be lucrative. But he could even less afford to lose money than forgo the advantage of separate profits if he wanted to keep his magazine afloat and face all the expenses incurred in the editing, printing, publishing and dispatching of it. There was the rent to be paid for the offices in the Strand, payments to be made to the printers, stationery suppliers, advertisers and distributors in England and in the United States; there were salaries to be secured for the editing staff (himself and W. H. Wills, his sub-editor), and remunerations for the contributors. This represented an enormous budget and Dickens had no choice but to strike in as he did to avoid a financial catastrophe.

But the welfare of the magazine mattered even more to the man than to the journalist or to the manager, considering the circumstances under which it had been started. For *All the Year Round* was somehow a by-product of Dickens's marital disruption. When, after the separation, Kate's family had started spreading rumours that Ellen Ternan was his mistress, Dickens, imagining that all his countrymen were aghast at the news, and with his heart full of misgivings lest the chirping of the national cricket on the hearth should henceforth sound discordant to them, had, rather ill-advisedly, thought it necessary to make a public statement on his private life. The statement, printed in *Household Words* (12 June 1858),[50] had been duly reproduced in all the London newspapers with the one exception of *Punch*, whose editor, Mark Lemon (a friend of the novelist),[51] and publishers, Bradbury & Evans (Dickens's own printers and publishers), had tactfully refrained from scandalmongering. But their reticence was interpreted as an act of disloyalty by the novelist, who decided at once to sever all connections with those who, he thought, had let him down in utter disregard of a long-standing association. During the weeks and months that followed the event, his resentment did not slacken; to Evans's entreaties and overtures he remained unamenable, bent as he had been from the start on dissolving the partnership. His intention was either to buy his publishers' share of *Household Words* or, if they would not sell, to withdraw as editor, which he knew would be a death-blow to the magazine with which his name was so intimately associated. By mid November, Forster was appointed to negotiate on his behalf,[52] but the negotiations dragged on unsuccessfully and Dickens, who had no patience with delays, felt entitled after a time to speed things up by taking action single-handedly. He had meanwhile made up his mind to start a new miscellany in replacement of the old one, and, no sooner had he found a name for it[53] than he settled an agreement with his old associate W. H. Wills concerning matters of ownership and editorship. Then, without even warning Bradbury & Evans, he began advertising for the new journal: he even had the effrontery to use *Household Words* as a reference: 'Nine years of Household Words, are the best practical assurance that can be offered to the public, of the spirit and objects of ALL THE YEAR ROUND'[54] read the handbills that he started circulating throughout the country in March 1859. Learning of this 'unauthorized and premature public announcement of the cessation of *Household Words*',[55] Bradbury & Evans immediately reacted and brought an action against him. Two months later (16 May), by decision of the court of Rolls, *Household Words* was sold at public auction: Dickens purchased both the copyright and the stock of his former miscellany.[56] The last issue of *Household Words* appeared on 28 May, the first issue of *All the Year Round* as early as 30 April, so that the two magazines overlapped for a few weeks.

This new journal was therefore a challenge. In launching it, Dickens was writing a major chapter of his own life-story and was aware that he would have to make a success of it if he wished to prove to the world (and to himself) the validity of his grievances and the rightfulness of his cause. The prosperity of *All the Year Round* was as vital to him morally as it was financially; any crisis in the life of the magazine would be experienced as a personal crisis; any setback would be a personal humiliation. When he fell on evil days, it is therefore no wonder that he should have acted as promptly and efficiently as he did; and it is perhaps no accident either that the novel which was to save him from disgrace should have been entitled *Great Expectations*. In the intimations of prosperity and in the underlying apprehensions of failure borne by the title, it would be difficult indeed not to perceive echoes of the author's personal hopes and misgivings at such a crucial period of his sentimental and professional life. It has been suggested[57] that Dickens got his title from Sonnet 21 in Sir Philip Sidney's *Astrophel and Stella* ('that friendly foe,/Great expectation'); whether or not this is the case, the questions expressed by the poet are the very questions that the novelist was asking himself at that time of his life:

> For since mad March great promise made of me,
> If now the May of my yeares much decline,
> What can be hoped my harvest time will be?

Going back to square one at the age of 48 compelled him to look backward to March as much as forward to the harvest season and to reflect, like his narrator-hero, on all the ground he had covered since he was a boy with aspirations and expectations.

The plot itself is surely very remote from his misadventures whether past or present, but the general atmosphere of the book, the ironic overtones, the pervading sense of guilt, the twin themes of faithfulness and disloyalty, the vain quest for money and gentility, the misery of unrequited love were all of intensely emotional topicality. To press the similarities between writer and hero may be a dangerous and tiresome game; to overlook them would be a mistake. None of Dickens's writings can be dissociated from his real-life experience,[58] least of all this novel written under such compulsions. Personal involvement might even be put forward as one of the reasons why the writing was executed so speedily and with such gusto in spite of the usual complaints.[59]

Thus it is that in less than a year one of the greatest works in the English language came to be conceived and delivered. When, in July 1861, the novel appeared in book form, it was diversely reviewed, disparaged by a few for its 'melodramatic exaggeration',[60] greeted by many as 'the creation of a great artist', 'the imaginative book of the year',[61] and celebrated for its humour and for a welcome return to 'the old *Pickwick* style'.[62] But, whatever the appreciations of the professional critics, there was an undeniable sign that the book was a success, for, within a few weeks of its publication, it had to be reprinted no less than four times. Dickens anyway did not have to wait until then to form an opinion on the reception of his novel by the general public, for no sooner had he stepped in with his new story than the sales of *All the Year Round* rose gratifyingly,[63] while letters from his many correspondents assured him at each stage that they were 'faithfully' following the serial, which he could legitimately boast was 'a very great success'.[64] For all its disadvantages, serial publication had this considerable merit that it enabled writers to feel the pulse of their readers and to thrive on their praises should the occasion arise, which in this instance it did not fail to do.

NOTES: CHAPTER 1

1 See John Forster, *The Life of Charles Dickens* [1872–74], New edition with notes and an index by A. J. Hoppé (London: Dent, 1966), Vol. 1, p. 59.
2 *Great Expectations* (Harmondsworth: Penguin, 1965), ch. viii, p. 83.
3 *The Pickwick Papers*, ed. James Kinsley, Clarendon Dickens (Oxford, 1986), i, 1.
4 *Great Expectations*, op. cit., ch. v, p. 71.
5 The Hulks were moored off Upnor in the Medway estuary, north of Rochester. See T. W. Hill, 'Notes to *Great Expectations*', *Dickensian*, vol. 53 (Spring 1957), p. 122. Dickens lived in Chatham from 1817 to 1823.
6 See Forster, op. cit., Vol. 2, p. 285.
7 ibid., p. 197.
8 *Great Expectations*, op. cit., ch. viii, p. 89.
9 ibid., ch. i, p. 35.
10 Walter Dexter (ed.), *The Letters of Charles Dickens*, The Nonesuch Dickens (London, 1938), Vol. 3, p. 297, June 1862.

11   Edgar Johnson, *Charles Dickens: His Tragedy and Triumph* [1952] (London: Victor Gollancz, 1953), Vol. 2, p. 963.

12   *The Uncommercial Traveller*, The New Oxford Illustrated Dickens (London: Oxford University Press, 1958), p. vi.

13   ibid., p. 62.

14   See Forster, op. cit., Vol. 2, pp. 284–9 and Johnson, op. cit., Vol. 2, p. 964. For a discussion of this accepted view, see Edgar Rosenberg's 'A Preface to *Great Expectations*: the pale usher dusts his lexicons', *Dickens Studies Annual*, vol. 2 (1972), p. 315.

15   See Forster, op. cit., Vol. 2, p. 285.

16   Nonesuch *Letters*, Vol. 3, p. 182 [September] 1860, to Forster.

17   Forster, op. cit., Vol. 2, p. 284.

18   Nonesuch *Letters*, Vol. 3, p. 182, 4 October, to Forster.

19   ibid., p. 168, 25 July 1860, to Lever.

20   For further information on *Household Words*, see Anne Lohrli (comp.), *Household Words, A Weekly Journal 1850–1859 Conducted by Charles Dickens, Table of Contents, List of Contributors and Their Contributions* (Toronto: University of Toronto Press, 1973), pp. 1–50.

21   On *All the Year Round*, see Ella Ann Oppenlander (comp.), *Dickens' All the Year Round: Descriptive Index and Contributor List* (Troy, NY: The Whitston Publishing Company, 1984), pp. 1–61.

22   *All the Year Round*, Vol. 2, p. 95, 26 November 1859.

23   Nonesuch *Letters*, Vol. 3, p. 194, 4 December 1860, to Bulwer.

24   Oppenlander, op. cit., p. 24.

25   Letter from W. H. Wills to T. C. Evans, 19 May 1859, *All the Year Round* Letter-book, quoted by Oppenlander, op. cit., p. 49.

26   Nonesuch *Letters*, Vol. 3, p. 113, July 1859, to Forster.

27   cf. *Household Words*, vol. 19, p. 601, 28 May 1859: on the front page of this last issue, Dickens made an announcement entitled 'ALL THE YEAR ROUND' in which he stated: 'Since this was issued, the Journal itself has come into existence, and has spoken for itself five weeks. Its fifth Number is published to-day, and its circulation, moderately stated, trebles that now relinquished in HOUSEHOLD WORDS.' The circulation of *Household Words* must have averaged 40,000 copies a week (See Johnson, op. cit., Vol. 2, p. 946 and Robert L. Patten, *Charles Dickens and His Publishers* (Oxford: Clarendon Press, 1978), p. 242). *All the Year Round* was 'a phenomenal financial success': on 28 April 1859 '74,000 copies were already sold' and by mid May the sales had risen to 125,000 copies of No. 1. 'Sales of the next several numbers were steady at 100,000 or more and, over the years, sales of special issues, such as the extra Christmas numbers, reached as many as 300,000 copies' (Oppenlander, op. cit., p. 49).

28   See Oppenlander, op. cit., pp. 50–2.

29   On Wills, see Harry Stone (ed.), *The Uncollected Writings of Charles Dickens: Household Words 1850–1859* (London: Allen Lane, The Penguin Press, 1969), Vol. 2, pp. 659–60, and Lohrli, op. cit., pp. 461–70.

30   To Charles Welford, 20 May 1861, *All the Year Round* Letter-book, quoted by Oppenlander, op. cit., p. 52.

31   Nonesuch *Letters*, Vol. 3, p. 224, 7 June 1861, to Bulwer Lytton.

32   Rosenberg in his 'Preface' insists on the 'extraordinary degree of spontaneity with which Dickens seems to have conceived the book': 'necessity', he writes, 'was never more pressingly the mother of invention than in producing Pip and Magwitch and Joe: their incubation period seems to have been uniquely brief. If Dickens had any long-range premeditations about the novel, he kept them to

himself; but there is no evidence that he had. For no other novel from *Dorrit* to *Drood* is the record of the Notebook quite so tellingly silent' (op. cit., p. 308). The Notebook, to be sure, contains very little: only a few names among the entries for 1855, 'Mag, Magwitch, Provis, Clarriker, Compey, Pumblechook, Horlick, Doolge, Gannery-Gargery, Wopsell-Wopsle, Hubble, Skiffins', and an entry for 1858–60 about 'Toadies and Humbugs' which, Rosenberg notes, 'finds it way into chapter xi of the novel' (p. 307); see Fred Kaplan (ed.), *Charles Dickens' Book of Memoranda* (The New York Public Library, 1981). In a recent number of *The Dickensian* (vol. 82, Summer 1986, 'An Early Hint of *Great Expectations*', pp. 82–4), Dick Hoefnagel suggests that Dickens may have thought of the title and theme of his novel slightly earlier than is usually believed. He finds the evidence 'in a copy of the one-volume London Stereotype Edition of Samuel Johnson's *Dictionary of the English Language* (1825), which once belonged to Dickens and is now preserved in the Special Collections of the Dartmouth College Library. Written on the front fly-leaf in Dickens's handwriting, in blue ink, are his initials and "Tavistock House London. W.C. Christmas-Day 1856" followed by "Mordan Morden – Great Expectations. – Bagster (M.) – Magwitch – Menage – Mortimer" '. But these were mere words jotted down over the years, and it is unlikely that he gave life to these names or shaped his theme into a story until pressed by circumstances to write a new novel.

33   Nonesuch *Letters*, Vol. 3, p. 182, 4 October 1860.
34   Nonesuch *Letters*, Vol. 3, pp. 183–4, 6 October 1860. In reply to an inquiry of mine concerning the drops in the sales, Robert L. Patten writes: 'If Dickens says sales were declining in September 1860, he's likely to be right ... The small 1861 balances seem roughly consistent with the notion that sales were falling during Lever's serial run, because both the April and October figures show significant drops in net income.' But he also submits that, owing to a probable time-lag between 'the dates of the accounts' and 'the dates the books were closed', 'the 31 October 1860 balance probably included few of Lever's issues; and even if it does include all the issues the booksellers wouldn't immediately in August have reduced their orders, so the profits wouldn't shrink right away' (private letter, 23 July 1985).
35   See Forster, op. cit., Vol. 2, p. 281 (about *A Tale of Two Cities*).
36   Rosenberg, op. cit., p. 316.
37   See Oppenlander, op. cit., p. 52. Dickens's serial ran in *Harper's Weekly* from 24 November 1860 to 3 August 1861 (there was a one-week hiatus on 26 January): see George J. Worth, *Great Expectations: An Annotated Bibliography* (New York: Garland, 1986), p. 17, no. 39.
38   Rosenberg, op. cit., p. 317.
39   Nonesuch *Letters*, Vol. 3, p. 222, 24 May 1861.
40   Nonesuch *Letters*, Vol. 3, p. 224, 11 June 1861.
41   See Nonesuch *Letters*, Vol. 3, p. 225, 24 June 1861, to Bulwer.
42   Nonesuch *Letters*, Vol. 2, p. 543 [February 1854], to Forster.
43   See Forster, op. cit., Vol. 2, p. 281.
44   Nonesuch *Letters*, Vol. 3, pp. 216–17 [April] 1861, to Forster.
45   Nonesuch *Letters*, Vol. 3, p. 461, 20 February 1866, to Mrs Brookfield.
46   Ada Nisbet, 'The autobiographical matrix of *Great Expectations*', *Victorian Newsletter*, no. 15 (Spring 1959), p. 11.
47   See Rosenberg, op. cit., pp. 319–20.
48   See Forster, op. cit., Vol. 2, p. 208.
49   ibid., p. 200.
50   *Household Words*, vol. 17, p. 601. Reprinted in Stone, op. cit., Vol. 2, pp. 585–6. See also vol. 1, pp. 23–8.

51 See Patten, op. cit., pp. 261–2 and Arthur A. Adrian, *Mark Lemon, First Editor of Punch* (London: Oxford University Press, 1966), pp. 132–4.

52 Meanwhile, Dickens went on a reading tour; see Patten, op. cit., p. 263, and Oppenlander, op. cit., p. 6.

53 Dickens had first thought of 'Household Harmony' for a title, but Forster suggested that 'this might hardly be accepted as a happy comment on the occurrences out of which the supposed necessity had arisen of replacing the old by a new household friend', Forster, op. cit., Vol. 2, p. 227.

54 Reprinted in Stone, op. cit., Vol. 1, p. 26.

55 See Oppenlander, op. cit., p. 11.

56 'Smith, on behalf of Dickens, got *Household Words*, lock, stock, and copyright, for £3,550', Patten, op. cit., p. 269.

57 Annabel Endicott, 'Pip, Philip and Astrophil: Dickens's debt to Sidney?', *Dickensian*, vol. 63 (Autumn 1967), pp. 158–62. See also Sylvère Monod (trans.), *Les Grandes Espérances* (Paris: Garnier, 1959), p. i.

58 'Everybody who has written or thought about *Great Expectations*', writes Edgar Rosenberg, 'has seen it as one of Dickens' most deeply personal books ... but the novel bears traces, too, of Dickens' more immediately pressing concerns and anxieties', namely 'the prospects of his older sons', Walter running up debts in India, Charley's departure for Hongkong (op. cit., p. 319). See also K. J. Fielding, *Charles Dickens: A Critical Introduction* (London: Longmans, 1958), pp. 177–8.

59 The strain had adverse effects on his health and he suffered through most of the winter from neuralgic pains in the face; see his letter to Macready, Nonesuch *Letters*, Vol. 3, p. 224, 11 June 1861.

60 Anonymous, *Saturday Review*, 20 July 1861, reprinted in Norman Page (ed.), *Charles Dickens: Hard Times, Great Expectations and Our Mutual Friend*, Casebook Series (London: Macmillan, 1979), p. 97.

61 H. F. Chorley, *The Athenaeum*, 13 July 1861, reprinted in Page, op. cit., pp. 94, 96.

62 [E. S. Dallas], *The Times*, 17 October 1861, reprinted in Philip Collins (ed.), *Dickens: The Critical Heritage* (London: Routledge & Kegan Paul, 1971), p. 431.

63 'The enormous popularity of *Great Expectations* ... can be measured by the fact that it sustained a large readership in *All the Year Round* (perhaps 100,000 copies sold weekly), then circulated (as few others of Dickens's works seem to have done) through the lending libraries, and still was in demand for an exceptionally high price as Dickens's serials go', Patten, op. cit., p. 292.

64 Nonesuch *Letters*, Vol. 3, p. 196, 28 December 1860, to Mary Boyle.

CHAPTER 2

Manuscript and Memoranda

The manuscript of *Great Expectations* was presented by Dickens to his friend the Reverend Chauncy Hare Townshend[1] who bequeathed it to the town of Wisbech (Cambridgeshire), where it still lies in the Wisbech and Fenland Museum.

Neither Wisbech nor the manuscript are very easy of access and no decent reproduction of the document is available: it is too fragile to be xeroxed and the microfilm distributed by the Scolar Press (1977) is blurred and unreadable. Written in blue ink on blue paper, heavily corrected, Dickens's text is itself very difficult to decipher. For all these reasons, few scholars or editors of the novel have made use of it and most editions are based on the early book versions. To my knowledge, Edgar Rosenberg is the only textualist who has taken the trouble to examine attentively the many alterations, cancellations and insertions and to compare this version of the text with the galley proofs, the *All the Year Round* and *Harper's Weekly* instalments and the 1861 and 1868 editions in book form.[2] Some of his conclusions have been published in two excellent essays, 'A preface to *Great Expectations*: the pale usher dusts his lexicons' (1972) and 'Last words on *Great Expectations*: a textual brief on the six endings' (1981).[3] But the 'Preface' was a prelude to a Norton edition which has long been 'forthcoming' and has not yet appeared, and it is to be hoped that the 'last words' are his last words on the endings, not on the novel as a whole.

Although the novel was written to be published in weekly parts, Dickens, as K. J. Fielding remarks, 'still evidently had the monthly unit in mind as he wrote'[4] and the manuscript is divided into nine monthly portions, each corresponding to four weekly instalments and each of the three stages of Pip's expectations being divided into three monthly portions.[5]

The manuscript is also attended by memoranda, some of which were first discussed and published by John Butt in 1948 and 1949;[6] others were printed in T. W. Hill's 'Notes to *Great Expectations*' (1958 and 1960)[7] and in Rosenberg's 'Preface'. These notes read as follows:

Dates

Herbert Pocket speaks of Miss Havisham's matter having happened 'five and twenty years ago.' at that time, Pip is – say 18 or 19. Consequently it happened 6 or 7 years before Pip, and Estella – who is about his age – were born.

But say that the matter was a year or so in hand – which it would be – that would reduce it to 5 or 6 years before they were born.

Magwitch tells his story in the Temple, when Pip is 23. Magwitch is then about 60. Say Pip was about 7 at the opening of the story. Magwitch's escape would then be about 16 years ago. If Magwitch says he first knew Compey about 20 years ago, that would leave about 4 years for his knowledge of Compey and whole association with him up to the time of the escape. That would also make him about 40 when he knew Compey, and Compey was younger than he.

When Magwitch became known to Compey the end of Miss Havisham's matter would thus have taken place about 7 or 8 years before.

Estella, as Magwitch's child, must have been born about 3 years before he knew Compey.

The ages in the last stage of Pip's Expectations stand thus:

Pip	about	23
Estella	"	23
Herbert	"	23
Magwitch	"	60
Compey	"	52 or 53
Miss Havisham	"	56 (I judge her to have been the elder in the love time)
Biddy	"	24 or 25
Joe	"	45

Jaggers 55, Wemmick near 50, and so forth.

General Mems: 1
Miss Havisham and Pip, and the Money for Herbert. So
Herbert made a partner in clarriker's
Compeyson. How brought in?
Estella. Magwitch's daughter
Orlick – and Pip's entrapment – and escape
  – To the flight
                start
                Pursuit
                Struggle. Both on board[8]
                together. Compeyson drowned.
                Magwitch rescued by Pip and
                taken
Then: Magwitch tried, found guilty, & left for
                    DEATH
                Dies presently in Newgate
                Property confiscated to the Crown.
Herbert goes abroad:
  Pip perhaps to follow.
Pip arrested when too ill to be moved – lies in the chambers in
Fever. Ministering Angel JOE.
recovered again, Pip goes humbly down to the
old marsh Village, to propose to Biddy.
  Finds Biddy married to Joe.
General Mems: 2
So goes abroad to Herbert (happily married to Clara
Barley), and becomes his clerk.
  The one good thing he did in his prosperity,
the only thing that endures and bears good fruit

Tide
Down at   up
 9 AM   3 PM
 till   till
 3 PM   9 PM
Down 9 PM
till 3 morning

Down at 9 A.M., till 3 P.M Wednesday
Up at 3 PM – till 9.P.M. Wednesday
Down at 9 PM. till 3 A M Thursday morning

Up at 3 AM. till 9. A M Thursday morning
when the boat starts

These notes show us 'Dickens at work', mapping out his way through the last episodes of his novel, but it is unlikely that they were all written at the same time, even though they necessarily came rather close upon one another.

In the pages headed 'Dates', which precede the others, Miss Havisham's ex-lover goes by the name of 'Compey', as he does in the manuscript for chapters 42 and 45 (where the last three letters were added as an afterthought), whereas he was unhesitatingly renamed 'Compeyson' in chapter 47; from which we may infer that this section was written before Dickens wrote chapter 47 and before he corrected the name on the manuscript for chapter 45. On the other hand, the 'General Mems' must have been drawn up some time later, since Dickens had by then made up his mind that 'Compey' was 'Compeyson'.

Dickens in his first section tells himself more about the ages of his characters than he ever tells us in his novel, where only Pip's and Herbert's ages are specified. It is clear that the novelist wanted to check the consistency of his dates for his own guidance before writing chapters 48 and 50 in which Pip makes his inquiry into Estella's parentage and has to establish the chronology of long-past events to corroborate his conjectures. It is also obvious that he was then looking backward rather than forward: his quotation, 'five and twenty years ago', refers to chapter 22 (p. 204), when Herbert first related 'Miss Havisham's matter' to Pip. In the chapters to come, his phrasing will be different: Wemmick will inform Pip that Molly was tried for murder 'A score or so of years ago' (xlviii, 405) and Magwitch will use a similar expression 'a round score o' year ago' (1, 419) to date that 'dark wild part' of his life (1, 417) when telling it to Herbert.

The 'General Mems' cover most of the eighth and of the ninth monthly portions, but dating them and determining their respective functions is a rather tricky business and can only bring tentative answers. John Butt remarks:

It is only after Pip's entrapment by Orlick in chapter liii and his rescue that the events are forecast in detail. It would therefore appear that the sketch was written either immediately before or immediately after the completion of chapter liii, and that the first three entries are notes about matters still to be kept prominently in view.[9]

The only thing in fact that can be stated with any certainty is that from 'To the flight' onwards the notes were written by Dickens to help him in the composition of his last monthly number; and the fact that he did not strictly follow his own instructions in chapter 54 (Pip does not rescue Magwitch from drowning in the novel) shows that these chapter notes came before the chapter itself was composed. Besides, why write detailed notes on what is already done?

The first four entries are, to be sure, very sketchy and it is difficult to decide for some of them whether they merely served, as Butt suggests, to summarize chapters already completed or whether they were intended to outline chapters that Dickens was just about to write and for which he needed no detailed planning, knowing full well what he wanted to say.

The first entry refers to chapter 49, where Miss Havisham is persuaded by Pip to provide for Herbert, which paves the way for chapter 52 in which Herbert becomes a partner in Clarriker's. Since nothing is said either of Miss Havisham asking to be forgiven or of the accident that will cause her death, it would seem that the note was written after the chapter was completed and that Dickens retained only what would lead to the moral of the story, 'The one good thing he did in his prosperity, the only thing that endures and bears good fruit', and, possibly, to the not yet written chapter 52.

The third entry, about Estella being Magwitch's daughter, might well have been written before chapter 50, which ends with Pip declaring: 'And the man we have in hiding down the river, is Estella's Father', a statement which will be confirmed by Jaggers in the following chapter. That Estella was Magwitch's daughter must have been 'prominent' enough in Dickens's mind for him not to have to make a note of it as a mere reminder (the expression 'Estella, as Magwitch's child' which he uses in 'Dates' shows that the relationship between the two characters was for him a matter of course).

'Chapter 53', Butt writes, 'is sketched in the briefest possible way',[10] yet this sketch (fourth entry) may well have preceded the writing of a chapter that is more rhetorical and dramatic than eventful and therefore required little planning.

In short, these entries may have been written any time between the completion of chapter 49 and the beginning of chapter 54.

The second entry, 'Compeyson. How brought in?', is a puzzling question which comes at a rather odd place on the list between references to chapters 49/52 and 50/51. Compeyson, who has been 'actively shadowing Pip and Magwitch from the first chapter of the final stage'[11] and whose presence in London has been confirmed by Wemmick in chapter 45 (pp. 384–5), has been personally 'brought in' in chapter 47 where he made his ghost-like appearance during Wopsle's pantomime; and he will not reappear until chapter 54, for the pursuit. Put out by Dickens's question, Butt comes to the only possible, though not very satisfactory, conclusion that '"How brought in" must ... refer to Compeyson's part in the scene of Magwitch's capture'.[12] But still, why does it occur there?

It should also be noted that what now constitutes chapter 59 is entirely left out of Dickens's planning: nothing is said, and perhaps nothing was meant to be said, of what is to happen after Pip's departure for Cairo. Dickens may well have first intended to end his novel there and to finish it off on a moralizing note by celebrating 'the one good thing ... that endures', 'a far, far better thing' that the hero 'did in his prosperity' than he had ever done.

'Tide', the last section, is not a very thrilling one; but it shows how anxious Dickens was to create possible circumstances for his impossible story. The reason why he 'bothered to draw up two tables of tides' is probably, as Rosenberg suggests, that he first copied official information concerning the tide hours, then, having decided 'on the appropriate days for the venture' in his fiction, 'went back to the Mem., copying out once more the data already committed to paper and rounding out the information by adding his Wednesdays and Thursdays'.[13] A similar instance of his concern for plausibility is given by Forster, who relates how, on 22 May 1861, Dickens 'hired a steamer for the day from Blackwall to Southend' before writing the episode of the flight down the Thames 'To make himself sure of the actual course of a boat in such circumstances'.[14]

NOTES: CHAPTER 2

1 The Reverend Chauncy Hare Townshend (1798–1868), to whom the novel is 'affectionately inscribed', was bound to Dickens with long-standing friendship. Poet, antiquarian, amateur painter, collector, he was also greatly interested, like Dickens, in mesmerism and wrote a book on the subject, *Facts in Mesmerism*, in 1840. He was also an occasional *Household Words* contributor and the author of notes on religious matters, which Dickens edited after his death, although he had a poor opinion of them ('Religious Hiccoughs' he called them). He spent much of his life abroad and had travelled through New South Wales, where he said that nothing struck him more in the colony than 'the good behaviour of men who had been convicts' and 'was continually inclined to ask "Why have these men been transported?"' (Quoted in Samuel Sidney's *Emigrant Journal*, 1848–50: see Coral Lansbury, *Arcady in Australia*, Melbourne University Press, 1970, p. 64). For further information, see Madeline House and Graham Storey (eds), *The Pilgrim Edition of the Letters of Charles Dickens*, Vol. 2 (1840–1841) (Oxford, 1969), p. 110; Anne Lohrli (ed.) *Household Words: Table of Contents, List of Contributors and their Contributions* (Toronto University Press, 1973), pp. 449–50; and Fred Kaplan, *Dickens and Mesmerism* (Princeton University Press, 1975), *passim*.

2 For a detailed description of these documents, see George J. Worth, *Great Expectations: An Annotated Bibliography* (New York: Garland, 1986), pp. 17–19.

3 'A Preface to *Great Expectations*: the pale usher dusts his lexicons', *Dickens Studies Annual*, vol. 2 (1972), pp. 294–335 and 374–8; 'Last words on *Great Expectations*: a textual brief on the six endings', *Dickens Studies Annual*, vol. 9 (1981), pp. 87–115.

4 K. J. Fielding, 'The weekly serialization of Dickens's novels', *Dickensian*, vol. 54 (Autumn 1958), p. 139.

5 See Rosenberg, 'Preface', pp. 321–6, 'The monthly numbers'. See also the table, 'The Number Division', in Appendix 1, p. 276.

6 John Butt, 'Dickens at work', *Durham University Journal*, vol. 40, no. 3 (June 1948), pp. 65–77. There Butt suggested that the Mems had been drawn up at about the time Dickens wrote to Forster that the third stage should be read at a stretch (April 1861). But his views were challenged by Humphry House, 'G.B.S. on *Great Expectations*', *Dickensian*, vol. 44 (Autumn 1948), pp. 183–6, and he immediately reconsidered the matter and came to the new conclusion that 'It is more probable that the plan was made after Chapter 53 was written', 'Dickens's plan for the conclusion of *Great Expectations*', *Dickensian*, vol. 45 (Spring 1949), pp. 78–80. In *Dickens at Work* (John Butt and Kathleen Tillotson, London, 1957), Butt repeats his argument with a slight modification, 'either immediately before or immediately after the completion of chapter liii' (London: Methuen, 1968, p. 32).

7 T. W. Hill, 'Notes to *Great Expectations*', *Dickensian*, vol. 54 (Spring 1958), p. 125, 'Dates', and *Dickensian*, vol. 56 (Spring 1960), pp. 122–3, 'Tide'. Rosenberg is not, as he claims ('Preface', p. 326), the first publisher of these tables.

8 Rosenberg reads 'overboard' ('Preface', p. 327), which is more satisfactory because, as Butt and Tillotson remark, 'The course as planned was not strictly followed. Magwitch and Compeyson were not on board together' (*Dickens at Work*, p. 33). My own reading, from an enlarged photograph of the Scolar Press microfilm, is 'on board', but I wish it were not.

9 *Dickens at work*, op. cit., p. 32.

10 Butt, *Dickensian*, vol. 45 (Spring 1949), p. 78.
11 ibid., p. 79.
12 ibid.
13 Rosenberg, 'Preface', p. 330.
14 John Forster, *The Life of Charles Dickens* (London: Dent, 1966), Vol. 2, p. 287.

CHAPTER 3

The Public Reading Version

In April 1858, Dickens began a new career as a public reader. A born actor, often involved in private theatricals, he had also for some years given private readings of his stories to a chosen audience of friends and, for the past four years, he had given public readings of *A Christmas Carol* for charitable purposes and had been so successful that he had soon contemplated a platform career which he felt sure would bring him substantial profits,[1] besides the pleasure of facing large audiences of admirers. The purchase of Gad's Hill in 1856 and the break up of his marriage two years later hastened his decision to turn professional. He needed money: 'What do you think', he asked Forster in September 1857, 'of my paying for this place, by reviving that old idea of some readings from my books. I am strongly tempted. Think of it.'[2] He needed a change and craved for human warmth:

> I must do *something*, or I shall wear my heart away. I can see no better thing to do that is half so hopeful in itself, or half so well suited to my restless state,[3]

he wrote to Forster the following March. Forster objected, feeling that it was 'a substitution of lower for higher aims; a change to commonplace from more elevated pursuits' and that it had 'the character of a public exhibition for money'.[4] But Dickens had made up his mind, and on 29 April he gave his first recital in St Martin's Hall, in London. 'By mid-November', Philip Collins tells us in his detailed introduction to his edition of the prompt-copies, 'he had given a hundred performances.'[5] The financial returns were extremely gratifying compared with his earnings as a writer,[6] and the performances themselves, exhausting though they were, had the advantage of bringing him 'face to face with ... many multitudes'[7] and of strengthening 'that particular relation (personally affectionate and like no other man's)' which he felt existed 'between [him] and the public'.[8]

This reading career, which was to last for twelve years, had thus gone on for a two full years when he began *Great Expectations* (the writing of which was actually interrupted between 14 March and 18 April 1861 by six readings delivered in London at St James's Hall).

Both the dramatization of his texts and the emotional involvement it entailed must have affected his writing activity, and they probably account for the acutely personal theatricality of the two novels (*A Tale of Two Cities* and *Great Expectations*), which were written immediately after he embarked on this new occupation.[9] As a first-person narrative, *Great Expectations* offered challenging opportunities for public reading and Wopsle's one-man shows seem to have been, among other things,[10] mirrors held up in self-mockery to the 'author recitalist'.[11]

Great Expectations is the last of the eight novels from which Dickens devised a public reading. Collins submits that he prepared his reading copy during the Summer of 1861, when he thought of adding new items to his repertoire. But, like *The Bastille Prisoner* (devised at the same period from *A Tale of Two Cities*), the *Great Expectations* reading was never performed and the copy therefore did not undergo any revision. The text is reproduced in Philip Collins's *Charles Dickens: The Public Readings* from a privately printed copy.[12] In a brief presentation, Collins describes and analyses this dramatic version of the novel, and points in particular to the novelty of this adaptation in which Dickens

> departed from his usual practice when creating a Reading out of one of his novels, which had been either to take a single episode or short span of the narrative, or to centre the Reading on one prominent character (as in *Mrs. Gamp*). Instead, the *Great Expectations* Reading attempts to narrate the whole of one of the central plots, from ch. 1 to ch. 56.[13]

Actually, it might be more exact to speak of *the* central plot, since the narrative deals very strictly with Pip's expectations. Divided into three stages (which do not coincide with those of the novel), it relates: 1. 'Pip's Childhood', from the churchyard scene to Pip's first visit to Satis House; 2. 'Pip's Minority', including his return to the forge, his setting-off for London on being informed by Jaggers of his great expectations, and his life at Barnard's Inn; 3. 'Pip's Majority', including Magwitch's return, his abortive escape, his trial and his death. The unexampled theatricality of plot and theme in this novel permitted such a choice; but it also entailed drastic cuts and if, as Collins notes, the copy includes 'some of the incidental delights of the novel (such as Wemmick, the Aged P., and Miss Skiffins)', inevitably 'many other characters and episodes are omitted – Orlick, Trabb's boy, Drummle, the Barleys, and others',[14] some of whom could have been very effectively rendered from a reader's platform.

But, of course, the most spectacular omission (Collins calls it 'Dickens's most obvious economy')[15] is the love-story. Estella has been struck off the list of *dramatis personae*: there is no more place for her in the Reading version than at the end of the 'General Mems', and her absence means perhaps more than just 'economy'. Maybe Dickens felt he could do without her easily enough. Maybe he never considered that the love-story was a plot in itself.[16]

Magwitch, on the contrary, is the most prominent character of the third stage, which ends with Pip's prayer: 'O Lord, be merciful to him, a sinner!'. This much-discussed misquotation from Luke, xviii, 13 ('to him' instead of 'to me') is reproduced here from chapter 56 (p. 470) and Collins convincingly argues that it could not be Dickens's intention that this 'Reading should end on an ironical or ambivalent note',[17] as some commentators of the novel have suggested. Edgar Rosenberg expresses similar views: 'Dickens', he writes, 'would not have terminated the story with a calculated gesture of denigration.'[18] The distortion, in fact, was inevitable both in the novel and in the reading copy and may simply have meant that in Pip's eyes Magwitch, like all men (including himself), needed God's forgiving love.

Being somehow a summary of the novel, the public reading version brings out the salient points of the story, emphasizes the basic relationships between the hero and other characters and teaches us a lot about the novelist's intentions that we ought to remember when we return to the novel.

NOTES: CHAPTER 3

1 As early as September 1846, Dickens's private reading in Lausanne of the first Number of *Dombey and Son* prompted him to write: 'I was thinking the other day that in these days of lecturings and readings, a great deal of money might possibly be made (if it were not *infra dig*.) by one's having Readings of one's own books', Forster, *The Life of Charles Dickens* (London: Dent, 1966), Vol. 1, p. 421. After his Birmingham charity readings in 1853, W. H. Wills also felt convinced that 'If Dickens does turn Reader he will make another fortune', quoted in Philip Collins (ed.), *Charles Dickens: The Public Readings* (Oxford: Clarendon Press, 1975), p. xx. See also Forster, op. cit., Vol. 2, pp. 203–5.
2 Forster, op. cit., Vol. 2, p. 200.
3 ibid., p. 204.
4 ibid., p. 200.
5 Collins, op. cit., p. xxiii. For further information on the readings, see Collins, pp. xvii–lxix and Forster, Vol. 2, pp. 217–25, 236–60.
6 See Collins, op. cit., pp. xxviii-xxix.
7 ibid., p. xxii.
8 Forster, op. cit., Vol. 2, p. 205.
9 See below, ch. 13, 'Voices'.
10 See below, ch. 14, 'The other stage'.
11 Collins, op. cit., p. xlviii.
12 Collins, op. cit., pp. 307–63.
13 ibid., p. 305.
14 ibid.
15 ibid.
16 See below, ch. 12, 'The sense of two endings'.
17 Collins, op. cit., p. 306.
18 E. Rosenberg, 'A Preface to *Great Expectations*', *Dickens Studies Annual*, vol. 2 (1972), p. 312.

CHAPTER 4

A Chronology of *Great Expectations*

AN INNER CHRONOLOGY

In a late chapter of the novel, acting the detectives, Herbert and Pip investigate into the past of 'Uncle Provis' at the time when he lost his little child and they try to work out an exact chronology of some early events which are seminal to the plot:

> 'I want to know,' said I, 'and particularly, Herbert, whether he told you when this happened?'
> 'Particularly? Let me remember, then, what he said as to that. His expression was, "a round score o' year ago, and a'most directly after I took up wi' Compeyson." How old were you when you came upon him in the little churchyard?'
> 'I think in my seventh year.'
> 'Ay. It had happened some three or four years then, he said, and you brought into his mind the little girl so tragically lost, who would have been about your age.' (1, 419).

Suddenly alerted to the imperfection of our own information, we may feel at this stage desirous to establish a more consistent time-scheme and to retrace our steps right back to the beginning, looking for signposts we might have missed in the course of our reading. Dickens himself, at about this period, had felt it necessary to take his bearings, check upon what he had written so far, write the plan for the last episodes of the novel and sort out the ages of the different characters.[1]

His sorting out, however, is not perfectly congruent with the text, at least as regards Pip's age at the beginning of the book. 'Pip', Dickens writes in his memoranda, 'was about 7 at the opening of the story' and, even though his 'about' (repeated throughout when he lists the ages of the various characters) shows that he does not wish to commit himself too much, we take him to have meant that Pip was 'about' half-way between 6 and 8. Whereas, if Pip means what he says, 'I think in my seventh year', he is informing us that he was not yet 7 during the churchyard scene; and, considering that the scene takes place on Christmas Eve and that, as we shall learn later, his birthday is in November (xxxvi, 305), we may even deduce that he has just celebrated his sixth anniversary of his birth and is therefore closer to six than to seven, which would make him a year younger than he is usually considered to have been. 'At the beginning he is a child of seven',[2] writes Mary Edminson, the authority on chronology, not 'about' 7 or 'in his seventh year', just 'seven'. This is assuredly a minor point, but it raises the question whether, on such matters, we ought to trust Dickens the novelist or Dickens editing Dickens or critics editing Dickens's own edition of his text.

Another puzzler, which has preoccupied some annotators and critics, concerns the length of the term during which Pip pays his weekly visits to Satis House before going back to the forge to be apprenticed as a blacksmith. We know roughly when it begins, for Pip specifies just before relating the scene in which his sister informs him of the news: 'I think it must have been a full year after our hunt upon the marshes, for it was a long time after, and it was winter and a hard frost' (vii, 75). So that, depending on whom we have chosen to trust, Pip is seven or eight when he first goes 'up town' to play. But when he leaves for good is less easy to determine. In chapter 12 the narrator tells us: 'I am now going to sum up a period of at least eight or ten months' (p. 123), which makes Pip 'about' eight or nine at the end of the period. Two pages further, he writes: 'We went on in this way for a long time', but this 'long time', whatever that means, is compressed into one page, ending with Miss Havisham declaring: 'You are growing tall, Pip! . . . You had better be apprenticed at once' (xii, 125–6). T. W. Hill assumes that '"a long time" must have been at least five years' since 'The usual term of apprenticeship was seven years from the age of fourteen to twenty-one'.[3] This assumption is probably the right one: just before reporting Miss Havisham's remark on his growing tall, Pip took the trouble of informing us that he was 'fully old enough now, to be apprenticed to Joe' (xii, 125) and he certainly could never have been 'bound apprentice . . . in the Magisterial presence' (xiii, 132) if he had not by then reached the age required by the law. But, when he returns home after the ceremony of his indentures, Pip, pondering over his lack of interest in his future job, expresses himself in a way which seems to contradict Hill's arguments and conclusions:

> Finally, I remember that when I got into my little bedroom I was truly wretched, and had a strong conviction on me that I should never like Joe's trade. I had liked it once, but once was not now (xiii, 134).

> ... I had believed in the forge as the glowing road to manhood and independence. Within a single year, all this was changed (xiv, 134).

For Daniel P. Deneau 'This reference to a "single year," made after Pip's regular visits to Miss Havisham have ceased and after his apprenticeship has started, definitely seems to enforce the earlier reference to "eight or ten months"'.[4] Deneau's literal reading, however, is less satisfactory than Hill's interpretation, if only because it goes against Dickens's clearly expressed wish to have his hero properly apprenticed after the legislation in force at the time of his story. Trusting the teller so short-sightedly also compels us to distrust the tale: if Pip is no older than eight or nine when he begins to work with Joe, why, we wonder, should he be considered 'too big for Mr Wopsle's great-aunt's room' (xv, 136)? And if we accept that the fourth year of his apprenticeship to Joe, when he has to leave for London, is the year of his twelfth or thirteenth birthday, are we not left, in Deneau's own words, with 'many, many problems'?[5] Can we, in particular, reconcile his behaviour, interests and conversation with his alleged childish years?

Dickens, in his memoranda,[6] leaves no doubt as to what he wanted us to believe, which confirms the thesis put forward by Hill: 'at that time', he writes, 'Pip is – say 18 or 19'. This also tallies better with what we learn in chapter 22 of Miss Havisham's story. According to Herbert, 'this happened five-and-twenty years ago (before you and I were, Handel)' (p. 204). Judging by Dickens's reckoning in the notes appended to his manuscript, Miss Havisham is thirty-three years older than Pip (she is 'about' 56 when Pip is 'about' 23 and 'Compey' 'about' 52 or 53); if Pip is 18 when Herbert relates to him the Compeyson/Havisham story, it means that Miss Havisham, who is now 51, was jilted by her lover when she was 26 and he 22 or 23, which is plausible enough; if Pip is five or six years younger, we have to accept the idea of a young lady of 20 being forsaken on her wedding-day by a bridegroom of no more than 17 or 18, which is far less likely. It seems, therefore, reasonable to trust the tale and the editor rather than the teller, and to decide with Deneau that, in spite of textual evidence, 'it is convenient to accept Mr. Hill's glosses on Pip's age'.[7] We might actually reconsider the teller's words and take them less literally: 'Within a single year, all this was changed' might have meant simply that Pip's first year at Satis House was enough to make a new boy of him and that the following years merely confirmed the change. Yet, we cannot help regretting with Deneau that Dickens should have been 'a bit too indefinite about the growing-up years'[8] and that a number of odd years of Pip's life during the Satis House period should have been lost on his way from childhood to adolescence!

Things get worked out more neatly in the later episodes. Pip comes of age in chapter 36, eight months after his friend Herbert (pp. 304–5). At the beginning of chapter 39, when Magwitch reappears, he is 23: 'I was three-and-twenty years of age . . . and my twenty-third birthday was a week gone' (p. 330), he writes, from which we may infer that Magwitch returns in late November or early December. He pays his last visit to the old village in the following June and leaves England 'within a month', an indication that he is still in his twenty-fourth year. He returns in December eleven years later, 'probably shortly after his thirty-fifth birthday'.[9]

In its final version, therefore, the novel covers a time-span of about twenty-seven years: the sixteen years or so which constitute the main bulk of the story, followed by another batch of eleven years that Pip spends in the East between the penultimate chapter and the epilogue. (In the original version, the last meeting of hero and heroine in Piccadilly was postponed for another two years: 'It was two years more, before I saw herself' (Appendix A, p. 495).)

DATING PIP'S MANUSCRIPT

How long it took from that point for the hero to make up his mind to write his memoirs the text never says. His keen awareness as a narrator of the gap in years between 'then', when it all happened, and 'now, as I write' (xxxii, 281) does not prevent him from being

obstinately vague as to what 'then' and 'now' exactly correspond to.
He refers throughout, almost provocatively, to 'those days', 'that
time': 'Since that time, which is far enough away now' (ii, 46), as he
writes in the second chapter, is typical of his phrasing.

Comparisons between the vaguely distant past and the 'unspeci-
fied present'[10] are very numerous but of a general nature, and
merely serve to enhance the idea of change: Joe's house, for
instance, is described as 'a wooden house, as many of the dwellings
in our country were – most of them, at that time' (ii, 40); the road
between Hammersmith and London is 'not so pleasant a road as it
was then' (xxv, 226); London is no longer the same as it used to be:
'Alterations have been made in that part of the Temple since that
time' (xxxix, 331). The stress is clearly, as Edminson remarks, on
the 'changing scene'.[11]

In spite of such vagueness, it must have been assumed by
Dickens's first readers that the time of writing was more or less
simultaneous with the serialization of the story. Nowhere is there
any suggestion that it might be otherwise; no reason is ever put
forward why the manuscript should have been shelved for any
length of time and publication delayed. On the contrary, one or two
details point to an exact coincidence between the 'now' of the writer
and the 'now' of his first readers. As early as page one, the passing
remark about 'that universal struggle' (i, 35) must have been taken
by many as an allusion to Darwin's recently published *The Origin
of Species*, and the ideological debate of the book on true
gentlemanliness must have been redolent of that other best-seller,
Samuel Smiles's *Self-Help*, also published in 1859.[12]

An even more precise indication occurs in chapter 32, when the
narrator draws a comparison between the conditions of prisoners in
the past and in the present:

> At that time, jails were much neglected, and the period of exag-
> gerated reaction consequent on all public wrong-doing ... was
> still far off. So, felons were not lodged and fed better than soldiers
> (to say nothing of paupers), and seldom set fire to their prisons
> with the excusable object of improving the flavour of their soup
> (xxxii, 280),

he writes, commenting on his visit to Newgate. Not only do we
recognize here Dickens's voice ironizing on the question of 'Pet

Prisoners'[13] (one of his pet grievances), but it seems that the remark was prompted by the Chatham riots, which took place on 8 February 1861, just two months before the twentieth instalment (containing the remark) was published in *All the Year Round*.[14] The main grievance of the Chatham convicts had been a reduction in the prison diet and, as the event had been much in the news, few readers would have missed the topicality of the remark.

Such references to contemporary events are very few indeed, 'half a dozen or so', according to Rosenberg, 'most of them cast in a hurried phrase or metaphor',[15] and the detection of some of them must have required exceptional shrewdness, even in 1860 or 1861. Mary Edminson, for instance, detects a precise topical allusion in Pip's words when, in chapter 4, he declares, 'I moved the table, like a Medium of the present day' (iv, 60), a remark which, she submits, may have been suggested by 'the unmerciful "guying" of clairvoyance in *Punch* for July, August, and September of 1860'.[16] But not everybody would have perceived – or made – the connection and many must have merely interpreted it like Angus Calder as a 'jibe at the exploits of spiritualists who claimed, among many other things, to be able to invoke an unseen hand to move a table'[17] at a time when there was a craze for spiritualism.

Another clever guess is Rowland D. McMaster's identification of Lord John Russell as one of the 'many Johns' mentioned in chapter 54 when the narrator describes 'the figure-head of the John of Sunderland making a speech to the winds (as is done by many Johns)' (liv, 446): the parenthesis is interpreted as a reference not only to John the Baptist preaching in the wilderness but to the 'blatant speeches' that were 'given to the four winds' by the Foreign Secretary under Palmerston. Not obvious to all, the identification is none the less 'supported', says Rosenberg, 'by ... the circumstantial evidence of a verbal refrain in the correspondence'.[18]

More easily perceptible must have been the 'oblique reference to Louis Napoleon'[19] which occurs during the first part of the novel, when Mrs Gargery addresses Pip as 'Rantipole'. 'Rantipole' was a nickname given to Napoleon III in the 1850s and, since the Emperor of France was very unpopular when the novel was published, the association must have been automatic. But it was also misleading, for Mrs Joe cannot have intended to compare her little brother with the French Emperor unless she was gifted with prophetic vision or unless Dickens was guilty of anachronism. The nickname, however, had not been specially coined in honour of Louis Napoleon (The *Oxford English Dictionary* gives 1700 as the date of its earliest appearance), and it must have been applied to him for obvious reasons of homophony. Its meaning, 'A romp; a wild, ill-behaved or reckless person', literally 'a raving-head', must also have been considered fitting for a man whom Victoria, in more queenly English, called 'the *universal disturber* of the *world*';[20] but it had been thought a fit name for generations of men (or boys) before him and Mrs Gargery did not have to be either clairvoyant or anachronistic to call Pip a 'Rantipole'. The added reference to contemporary history would rather seem to have been a kind of private joke on the part of the narrator in which Mrs Joe had no share but which some readers might appreciate.

By creating the illusion of contemporaneity, topical allusions were clearly a means of strengthening the relationship between reader and narrator and of providing the right perspective (especially, as we shall see later, on matters of penal and social reform). As the story was set back in time, it was important that the standpoint should be that of a man who shared his readers' preoccupations and, it is hoped, their convictions and ideals. The message would be easier to perceive, coming from someone who might be a friend or a next-door neighbour than from some remote source of writing.

DATING THE STORY

Dating the story proper is certainly more delicate than dating the moment of writing: 'verification', says Edminson, 'demands close consideration of apparently trifling remarks scattered throughout the novel',[21] especially as Dickens was so very careful to make the date as vague as possible. Rosenberg even draws our attention to the fact that many slight changes in the manuscript obviously tended to make the text approximative and imprecise: 'a score of years ago' is changed to 'a score *or so* of years ago'; 'your age' becomes '*about* your age' (my emphasis): 'All these changes are slight enough,' writes the 'Pale Usher', 'but an altered phrase betrays an altered intention; and so we had better take notice of it. Clearly Dickens didn't want to commit himself overmuch: hence the cautious insertions of all these *abouts* and *might have beens*'.[22] Obviously, Dickens the serialist wanted to avoid inconsistencies, knowing that, should they occur, it would be too late for him to correct discrepancies, given his method of publication. But those critics who have annotated the text and placed it under cross-examination – T. W. Hill, M. Edminson, A. Calder, E. Rosenberg, to whom this chapter is heavily indebted – are all agreed that Dickens was exceptionally consistent in this novel and has succeeded, thanks to slight hints and period touches, in placing his story within a very precise time-frame ('1807–10 to 1823–26' in Edminson's estimation).[23]

The first time-indication in the novel occurs very early, when Pip refers to his parents' looks: 'I never saw my father or my mother,' he writes, 'and never saw any likeness of either of them (for their days were long before the days of photographs' (i, 35). This is vague enough, but it is a way of letting us know that Pip was born 'long before' 1839, when the first photographic print was made on paper by Fox Talbot, a year after Daguerre discovered the process.[24]

It soon appears very clearly that the whole novel is set in pre-Victorian days. The presence of the Hulks and the gibbet in the opening chapters is not in itself sufficient proof of an early date, for gibbets and hulks remained a familiar feature in the British landscape long after they were in disuse. But the last gibbeting occurred in 1832[25] and Pip's fear of meeting the fate of the pirate would have been less justified had the events related taken place long after that date (although we must make allowances for the fact that, even to this day, hanging and pirates belong to the lore of children). More significantly, the general acceptance by the Gargerys and the villagers of the convict-ship, and the gusto with which they join the hunt, seem to indicate that the novel begins before the system was condemned by a Parliamentary Committee in 1837, and very probably before it became objectionable.[26]

As early as chapter 5, we get confirmation of our guesses: the soldiers who interrupt the Christmas festivities at the Gargerys explain to the company that they are 'on a chase in the name of the king' (v, 61). There is no telling so far who that King is and it merely implies 'a date prior to 1837 (the accession of Queen Victoria)'.[27] Only later, after the cross-checking of other details, will the King appear to have been George III and the date prior to 1820.

It would be pointless to draw here the full list of the clues itemized by Hill and Edminson: a selection of three examples will suffice to illustrate Dickens's hint-dropping method. In chapter 2, for instance, Pip explains that he had to wait until 'the first faint dawn of morning' to rob his sister's pantry: 'There was no doing it in the night, for there was no getting a light by easy friction then' (ii, 47), he writes, indirectly informing us that the event took place before 1827, when lucifer matches were first introduced.[28] We come to a closer estimation a few chapters later when Mrs Joe is attacked and we are told that 'The Constables, and the Bow Street men from London – for, this happened in the days of the extinct red-waistcoated police – were about the house for a week or two' (xvi, 149), which is a means of telling us that this happened before 1829, when the Bow Street Runners were replaced by Robert Peel's Metropolitan Police Force. Much later in the novel, the circumstances attending Magwitch's return and trial point to even earlier dates: a date prior to 1834 for the last stage of Pip's adventures and to 1818 for the earliest, 1834 being the year when returning illegally from transportation was struck off the list of crimes punishable by death and when collective sentencing was abolished.[29]

But there are two indices (or series of indices) which do enable us to narrow the margin. The first is to be found in chapter 10 when, at the Three Jolly Bargemen, Pip is offered 'two fat sweltering one-pound notes' by a stranger (x, 107). The time-indication given by this remark has either passed unnoticed (Edminson does not mention it on her list) or been the source of inaccurate approximations. Hill takes it as a sign that 'The period of the story is therefore placed before 1826': 'Notes for £1 and 10/- are since 1914 current', he writes, 'but before that date and ever since 1826 no note of less value than £5 was used in England'.[30] And Calder reproduces the inaccuracy: 'One-pound notes were not current between 1826 and 1914'.[31] But Dickens was better informed: in a two-part article on 'Bank note forgeries' published in *Household Words* for 7 and 21 September 1850, he explains that forgeries had been so numerous after 1797, when one-pound notes were first put into circulation, that in 1819 a committee was appointed by the government to inquire into the best means of prevention and that 'the true expedient for at least lessening the crime was adopted in 1821' when the issue of small notes 'was wholly discontinued, and sovereigns were brought into circulation'.[32]

Confirmation of Dickens's dates is to be found in the Bank of England's publication, *The Bank of England Note: A Short History*:

... in 1797 a shortage of specie developed and the Bank obtained an Order of the Privy Council authorising them to stop paying notes in gold and silver; consequently notes for £1 and £2 were issued in payment ... In 1821 the Bank resumed the payment of their notes in gold and silver ... At the same time the Bank ceased to issue notes for less than £5 and this continued to be the rule until 1928, apart from an isolated issue of £1 notes in 1825–26 – an emergency measure at a time of financial crisis.[33]

Forgery was so widespread and so severely punished in the early years of the century that the measure adopted in 1821 could almost be described as a social reform: 'Social concern', writes Joe Cribb, 'centred on poor and uneducated people who could not distinguish genuine from forged notes, and who thus fell foul of the law themselves'.[34] In 1819 George Cruikshank, the cartoonist who was later to collaborate with Dickens, after seeing a woman hanged outside Newgate Prison 'for passing a forged note', sketched his famous 'Bank Restriction Note':

> His design is a horrific parody of a banknote, festooned with skulls and gibbets and ships for transportation. A ghastly Britannia gobbles infants, the pound sign is a noose and the note is signed by 'J. Ketch', the common nickname for a hangman. Along the left-hand edge of the note, Cruikshank printed sardonically 'Specimen of a Bank Note – not to be imitated'.[35]

Dickens was only nine when the restriction began, but it is quite probable that he heard of it even at the time: both the government motives in taking these measures and their consequences on practical life must have been discussed in his home and the connection with the world of criminals and counterfeiters cannot but have appealed to his childish imagination. Forty years later, it still appealed to his imagination as a novelist when he wrote *Great Expectations*, as the presence of Compeyson shows. And if Compeyson was to be transported for forgery and Magwitch for passing forged notes, the story of their conviction and transportation had to take place during the pre-restriction days. Knowing from his *Household Words* article on forgeries how conversant Dickens was with the facts concerning bank note circulation, we can also assert unhesitatingly that Pip was offered his 'two fat sweltering one-pound notes' before 1821: had the scene occurred later, Mrs Joe would never have hoarded them in the 'ornamental tea-pot on the top of a press in the state parlour' (x, 107).

Later in the novel, we find another reference to one-pound notes, which enables us to date the events with increased preciseness: travelling down from London to the marsh country by stage-coach, Pip overhears the conversation of convicts who are being carried to the dockyards; among them is the stranger who had, some years before, given him the money and whom he has just recognized:

> The very first words I heard them interchange as I became conscious were the words of my own thought, 'Two One Pound notes.'
> 'How did he get 'em?' said the convict I had never seen.
> 'How should I know?' returned the other. 'He had 'em stowed away somehows. Giv him by friends, I expect.'
> 'I wish,' said the other, with a bitter curse upon the cold, 'that I had 'em here.'
> 'Two one pound notes, or friends?'
> 'Two one pound notes. I'd sell all the friends I ever had, for one, and think it a blessed good bargain ...' (xxviii, 250–1).

It is clear that when this conversation takes place one-pound notes are still in circulation; otherwise, the convict would have no reason to express such lust for useless pieces of paper money. And since the scene takes place when Pip is eighteen, we infer that his eighteenth birthday cannot have occurred later than 1820, which pushes back the beginning of the novel to a period prior to 1809.

A third occurrence compels us to push the events even further back in time. When Magwitch returns, Pip alludes to the messenger who brought him the notes:

> 'He came faithfully, and he brought me the two one-pound notes. I was a poor boy then, as you know, and to a poor boy they were a little fortune. But, like you, I have done well since, and you must let me pay them back. You can put them to some other poor boy's use.' I took out my purse.
> He watched me as I laid my purse upon the table and opened it, and he watched me as I separated two one-pound notes from its contents. They were clean and new, and I spread them out and

handed them over to him. Still watching me, he laid them one upon the other, folded them long-wise, gave them a twist, set fire to them at the lamp, and dropped the ashes into the tray (xxxix, 335–6).

The scene takes place a week after Pip's twenty-third birthday and, since the notes are said to be 'clean and new' and liable to be of some use to some poor boy, we must deduce that it cannot be later than December 1820.

But then the margin has narrowed to the point of overlapping. For it has appeared from a previous conversation that Pip cannot have been twenty-one before 1819 at the very earliest. In chapter 36, when Pip comes of age, he meets Wemmick, whose advice he seeks concerning his friend Herbert whom he wants to help 'to a beginning':

'With money down?' said Wemmick, in a tone drier than any sawdust.

'With *some* money down,' I replied, '... and perhaps some anticipation of my expectations.'

'Mr Pip,' said Wemmick, 'I should like just to run over with you on my fingers, if you please, the names of the various bridges up as high as Chelsea Reach. Let's see; there's London, one; Southwark, two; Blackfriars, three; Waterloo, four; Westminster, five; Vauxhall, six.' He had checked off each bridge in its turn, with the handle of his safe-key on the palm of his hand. 'There's as many as six, you see, to choose from.'

'I don't understand you,' said I.

'Choose your bridge, Mr Pip,' returned Wemmick, 'and take a walk upon your bridge, and pitch your money into the Thames over the centre arch of your bridge, and you know the end of it. Serve a friend with it, and you may know the end of it too – but it's a less pleasant and profitable end' (xxxvi, 309–10).

Wemmick's far-fetched parable would seem again an almost undisguised means of helping us date the events: of the six bridges mentioned, three were built during the first quarter of the nineteenth century: Vauxhall, 1816, Waterloo, 1817, and Southwark, 1819; we are therefore told indirectly that the scene takes place after 1819.[36] Later in the novel, Pip, referring to London Bridge, will remark 'It was Old London Bridge in those days, and . . . I knew well enough how to "shoot" the bridge' (xlvi, 393). 'Shooting the bridge', Calder explains, 'involved choosing the exact moment when the current would sweep a small boat through one of the many narrow arches that were a feature of the Old London Bridge, which was pulled down in 1831'.[37] This enables us of course to realize that the action of this particular section is 'definitely not later than 1831', but also 'indeed possibly not later than 1824', the year when the first pile of New London Bridge was driven, since, as Edminson notes, 'Dickens nowhere mentions the building of a new bridge in his descriptions of the river scene'.[38]

The time-frame, therefore, is narrower than one would like it to be and Dickens's inconsistency (the almost inevitable consequence of his mode of publication) compels us, like him, to use some 'abouts' and 'might have beens'. All that can be asserted is that Pip must have been born with the century or slightly earlier and that he was Dickens's senior by 'about' ten years.

NOTES: CHAPTER 4

1 See above, ch. 2, 'Manuscript and memoranda'.
2 Mary Edminson, 'The date of the action in *Great Expectations*', *Nineteenth-Century Fiction*, vol. 13 (1958), p. 26.
3 T. W. Hill, 'Notes to *Great Expectations*', *Dickensian*, vol. 53 (Autumn 1957), p. 185.
4 Daniel P. Deneau, 'Pip's age and other notes on *Great Expectations*', *Dickensian*, vol. 60 (Winter 1964), p. 28.
5 ibid.
6 See above, 'Dates', p. 19.
7 Deneau, op. cit., p. 28.
8 ibid.
9 ibid.
10 Edminson, op. cit., p. 26.
11 ibid.
12 See below, ch. 8, 'The True gentleman'.
13 Dickens was always very much concerned with prison discipline and the treatment of prisoners (see Philip Collins, *Dickens and Crime*, London: Macmillan, 1962; 2nd edn 1965). In 1850 he contributed two major articles to *Household Words*, 'Perfect felicity', 6 April, vol. 1, pp. 36–8, and 'Pet prisoners', 27 April, vol. 1, pp. 97–103. On 25 March 1861 he asked Thomas Beard to write an essay for *All the Year Round* on the 'pet ways' of Jail-Chaplains (Nonesuch *Letters*, Vol. 3, p. 213): Beard's 'A dialogue concerning convicts', was published on 11 May 1861 (vol. 5, pp. 155–9).
14 13 April 1861. On the Chatham riots see Collins, op. cit., p. 20.
15 E. Rosenberg, 'A Preface to *Great Expectations*', *Dickens Studies Annual*, vol. 2 (1972), p. 318.
16 Edminson, op. cit., p. 25.

17   A. Calder (ed.), *Great Expectations* (Harmondsworth: Penguin, 1965), p. 500.
18   R. D. McMaster (ed.), *Great Expectations* (Toronto, 1965), p. 431 (quoted and commented upon by Rosenberg, op. cit., p. 377).
19   Rosenberg, op. cit., p. 318.
20   Quoted by Rosenberg, op. cit., p. 377.
21   Edminson, op. cit., p. 23.
22   Rosenberg, op. cit., p. 332.
23   Edminson, op. cit., p. 34.
24   Photography was actually discovered as early as 1820 by Nicéphore Niepce, but the first daguerreotype was made in 1838 and the craze for portraits began in 1840. It spread like wildfire.
25   See Collins, op. cit., p. 5.
26   The majority of the hulks were emptied of their criminal population soon after their condemnation, but the last closed as late as 1858 (see Collins, op. cit., p. 7).
27   Edminson, op. cit., p. 32.
28   ibid., pp. 28, 34.
29   See Keith Hollingsworth, *The Newgate Novel, 1830–1847* (Detroit: Wayne State University Press, 1963), pp. 232–3.
30   Hill, op. cit., p. 184.
31   Calder, op. cit., pp. 501–2.
32   'Two chapters on bank note forgeries', *Household Words*, vol. 1 p. 618.
33   Reprinted from the *Bank of England Quarterly Bulletin* (June 1969) pp. 212–13.
34   Joe Cribb (ed.), *Money From Cowrie Shells to Credit Cards* (London: British Museum Publications, 1986), p. 151.
35   ibid.
36   Dates of the bridges:
     Old London Bridge, 1176.
     Westminster, 1750 (rebuilt in 1862).
     Blackfriars, 1769.
     Vauxhall, 1816.
     Waterloo, 1817.
     Southwark, 1819.
37   Calder, op. cit., p. 510.
38   Edminson, op. cit., pp. 29–30.

CONVICTS AND GENTLEMEN

CHAPTER 5

'Convict' versus 'Gentleman'

Great Expectations is not, strictly speaking, a topical novel. It has none of the urgency of, say, *Bleak House, Hard Times* or *Little Dorrit*. It has no scandal to expose, no reform to advocate. It is, according to Edgar Rosenberg, 'the least topical of Dickens' novels'.[1] But it is also the most typical, the most representative of the novelist's concern with his age and society and, in particular, with that notion of class which so tormented him in personal life and which preoccupied so many of his contemporaries. To use one more superlative, it might even be described as the most Victorian of Dickens's novels, paradoxical though the statement may seem; for, although the events are set in pre-Victorian England, the book was written in the heyday of Victorianism and, as Humphry House remarks, its mood 'belongs not to the imaginary date of its plot, but to the time in which it was written'.[2] Thirty years before, when the country was far less secure socially and economically, the book would have been entirely different in focus and perspective; and even in 1860, had the story been told by some omniscient, anonymous, unconcerned narrator, it would have been read as a period novel on the bad old Regency days. But, as things are, it implicitly covers not sixteen but sixty years, and we read it as the story of a man who is still there, who is as old as the century, whose experience, though untold, has bridged the gap between those cruel and primitive times and the milder years of the Victorian era, who has matured and aged and improved during the 'Age of Improvement' like a true *enfant du siècle*, a perfect specimen of the newly educated, newly enriched, newly emancipated middle class.

The story itself is romantic and improbable, a 'sensational novel', as Mrs Oliphant called it, which 'occupies itself with incidents all but impossible'[3] and deals with a poor blacksmith's boy who, raised

overnight to the rank of gentleman through the mysterious workings of some unknown benefactor, eventually discovers that he
owes his rise in station to a criminal outcast. The many coincidences
and recurrences of the plot which, in Julian Moynahan's words
'violate all ordinary notions of probability',[4] have forced symbolic
readings and allegorizations on generations of critics. T. A. Jackson,
the Marxist, read it as an allegory of 'self-satisfied, mid-Victorian,
British society ... shocked to acknowledge indebtedness to the
labour of the depressed and exploited masses'.[5] Dorothy Van
Ghent, thinking on similar lines, also maintained that Pip 'carries
the convict inside him, as the negative potential of his "great
expectations" '.[6] Robin Gilmour, more convincingly, reads the
novel as a 'fable of emergence': Pip's predicament for him 'is
representative of a social class in the act of emergence; specifically,
of the Victorian middle class in its emergence from primitive origins'.[7] Interpretations may differ, but they all try to make sense of a
plot that crucially and disturbingly points to the interrelatedness of
crime and gentility and reverses the traditional relationship between
classes by giving an outcast the role of provider and of gentleman-
maker. In that respect, *Great Expectations* is a truly and literally
subversive novel and would deserve as much as *Little Dorrit* to be
described as a 'more seditious book than *Das Kapital*',[8] for it
challenges in an unprecedented way ideological and linguistic commonplaces.

Unmethodical, yet systematic, the reappraisal of accepted views
begins right at the beginning, centring on two key-words, 'convict'
and 'gentleman', two words which normally cover quite markedly
polarized ranges of meaning, but which in this novel at once strike
ironies off each other and will later give much pregnancy to the
book. It is remarkable how, in the opening chapters, through
accumulated details, slight touches, imperceptible side-information,
Dickens manages to convey simultaneously to hero and reader the
double-edgedness of those words, building meaning from almost
casual remarks, yet ensuring that we get a keen perception of the
hero's budding awareness of language and its complexities, and
thereby making sure that our own response to the narrative will be
attuned to his response to the events narrated.
    Significantly, Pip, although he lives in a prison-ship area, has been
kept for years in total ignorance of the existence of such next-door

realities as 'conwicts' (ii, 45) and 'Hulks'. He discovers the words
at the age of seven, on the occasion of the gun-firing that signals to
the neighbourhood that some prisoners have escaped: overhearing
a household conversation on the subject unexpectedly prompted
by the circumstances, he inquires from Joe 'What's a convict' and
then 'please, what's Hulks', a plain sign that neither word makes
any sense to him at this stage (ii, 45–6). But the word 'gentleman',
when it is uttered in his presence the day after, will arouse on his
part no request for information. To all appearances, Pip has been
taught so far only a carefully chosen selection of words and protected by his sister against the evil influence of even verbal knowledge of social wickedness and criminality. The ironic consequence
of this educational method is that he discovers the thing before the
word and befriends a convict without knowing it. The moral
advantage of it, probably unsought-for by Mrs Joe but well
thought out by the novelist, is that when the novel begins he is still
unprejudiced, so that in the churchyard scene the stranger who
jumps from among the graves is no outcast to him, but a man with
full rights, 'a fearful man' to be sure, yet one much to be pitied and
the sight of whom awakens in his youthful heart an outburst of
fellow-feeling.

When, on the evening of that memorable day, his worthy 'pursuit
of Knowledge under difficulties'[9] is at last requited by Mrs Joe 'who
always took explanations upon herself' (ii, 45), he is administered
the following definition which answers both questions at once:

> People are put in the Hulks because they murder, and because
> they rob, and forge, and do all sorts of bad; and they always begin
> by asking questions (ii, 46).

This unequivocal statement, with strong connotations of 'bad',
would certainly carry more conviction with the listener had it not
been imprudently advertised by the warning 'Ask no questions, and
you'll be told no lies'. Yet, its admonitory clause ambiguously
corroborates the unintentional invitation to self-identification that
Pip had previously gathered from Joe's inarticulate efforts at providing an explanation:

> I put my mouth into the forms of saying to Joe, 'What's a
> convict?' Joe put *his* mouth into the forms of returning such a

highly elaborate answer, that I could make out nothing of it but the single word 'Pip' (ii, 45).

In the latter instance, Pip the narrator urges the reader grossly to stretch the meaning of a mere apostrophe, an endearing form of address which is in fact one of the most recognizable speech mannerisms of Joe. But even if we are ready to follow the hint, we can by no means, considering the mild nature of the speaker, interpret his message as synonymous with his wife's explicit threat, and we can only take it as an implicit analogy between two categories of downtrodden creatures, the victims of social and of family oppression.

Thus, within a few paragraphs, the very same comparison is made to convey different and even diametrically opposite implications, a practice that is not likely to facilitate the moral and linguistic education of the child-hero and might even shatter a grown-up reader's deepest-rooted certitudes.

'Gentleman' is treated from the first with similar equivocation. On the day that follows this vocabulary lesson, Pip goes convict-hunting in the company of Joe, Mr Wopsle and a party of soldiers 'on his Majesty's service' (v, 62). 'Down banks and up banks, and over gates' (v, 66) they go, until they hear a voice calling out to them: 'Convicts! Runaways! Guard! This way for the runaway convicts!' (v, 66). They run to the spot and find themselves the dumbfounded witnesses of a hand-to-hand combat of the utmost brutality: at the bottom of a ditch, two men are fighting like 'two wild beasts' until, bruised and lamed, 'bleeding and panting and execrating and struggling' (v, 67), they are separated, handcuffed and tamed again. These men are no other than the two convicts whom Pip had met the day before and whom he now calls respectively 'my convict' and 'the other one'. '*I* took him', says Pip's convict whose voice it was that had called the attention of the hunters. '*I* give him up to you!' he explains, priding himself on his efficiency in helping recapture the other escapee and heedless of the fact that he has lost his liberty into the bargain:

I took him, and giv' him up; that's what I done. I not only prevented him getting off the marshes, but I dragged him here – dragged him this far on his way back. He's a gentleman, if you please, this villain. Now, the Hulks has got its gentleman again, through me (v, 67).

The remark gives rise to no narratorial comment, but we may assume that Pip is cute enough to catch its irony. He has every reason, besides, to perceive the exceptional character of the situation, knowing only too well that some genteel villains whom he might wish to see in the Hulks are not only at large, but free to bully him in complete impunity and given pride of place in his sister's parlour, that microcosm of polite society.

The scene remains just as mysterious as it is violent, raising questions that will go unanswered for over two-thirds of the novel. The convicts disappear into the Hulks and out of the book, or so it seems, and the curtain is dropped for another thirty-four chapters, another sixteen years of the hero's life. But our curiosity has been doubly aroused: we want to know, of course, 'what is going to happen next', but we are just as eager to improve our understanding of a puzzlingly controversial situation; for the conflict is clearly perceived to be thematic, not merely dramatic. This strange interplay of gentility and criminality, which is so memorably acted out on the marshes, will actually inform the novel as a whole.

When, after reappearing singly, the two men, years later, suddenly face each other again, Pip, who of course is attending, is again the helpless witness of a violent fight between them. The struggle, this time, takes place under water, beneath the mangling paddles of a steamer, right in the middle of the Thames estuary: 'fiercely locked in each other's arms', the deadly enemies fight their last fight: the villainous gentleman, now Compeyson, is drowned, Pip's convict, now Magwitch, is badly wounded and will die a few weeks later. He is meanwhile recaptured by the river-police and manacled once more 'at the wrists and ankles' (liv, 455), so that, in the long run, the battle is lost on both sides and the beginning of the end reproduces the same pattern as the end of the beginning. But we have in the meantime become personally acquainted with the fighters, we have learnt to judge them after their deeds, not after their condition, we have furthermore been educated into sharpened distrust of the laws of social and linguistic categorization, and we are in a position to decide who the moral winner is and to reassess the meaning of the earlier scene. The last narrative, therefore, is no mere duplicate of the first; we read it rather as an improved and conclusive version of the initial, puzzling brawl in the ditch, which it now highlights from a distance and from which it gains in return intensified dramatic efficiency. For *Great Expectations* is a novel that of necessity reads backwards as much as forwards. It is no accident, therefore, that the main bulk of the novel should be thus bracketed between these two scenes, two moments in Pip's life, besides, which remarkably epitomize his inner moral struggles, his conflicting aspirations and repulsions, and his wish to come to grips with a society within whose framework he is at pains to place himself.

Further proof is given of intentional structural unity in the fundamentally iterative nature of the narrative. It is particularly striking on three occasions when other fights fought by other actors are related to us with no other apparent purpose than to produce contrapuntal effects. As superfluous as if they were mere interpolated stories, these episodes obviously operate as thematic improvements on each other and anticipations of the final scuffle, each fulfilling the double function of prolepsis and analepsis or 'anachrony' as defined by Gérard Genette: 'An anachrony can reach into the past or the future ... Every anachrony constitutes, with respect to the narrative into which it is inserted – onto which it is grafted – a narrative that is temporally second, subordinate to the first in a sort of narrative syntax'.[10]

The first of these inserted narratives takes place at Satis House, in the backyard where the 'hired boy' has just been fed in 'dog-like manner' (xi, 118) before going back to the forge. As he is about to leave, Pip is invited to 'Come and fight' by a young stranger – 'a pale young gentleman', presumably belonging to the Havisham family circle – and he half-heartedly accepts the challenge. Against all expectations, for he is the smaller of the two and has no notion of the 'laws' of the game (and this is a game with 'Regular rules', xi, 119), it is the 'coarse common boy', once a convict's accomplice, who carries the day. But his victory leaves him with uneasy feelings:

> He seemed so brave and innocent, that although I had not proposed the contest I felt but a gloomy satisfaction in my victory. Indeed, I go so far as to hope that I regarded myself while dressing, as a species of savage young wolf, or other wild beast (xi, 120–1).

The last words literally echo those that had been used to describe the fighters on the marshes and act as an invitation to follow up the comparison and to read the new scene as a symbolic replay of the first. Pip, not being a gentleman, will necessarily appear to us as the impersonation of his ungenteel convict, an identification which probably does not reach the level of clear consciousness on his part as an actor but of which, as a narrator, he has implicit awareness as his self-quotation suggests. Ironically, although he has no reason to feel proud of himself for his brutal superiority over his adversary, Pip is rewarded for his feat with a kiss from Estella, the young 'lady' of the house for whose sake he so badly wishes to rise in society and get rid of his past degrading connections: 'The brief scene', comments Robin Gilmour, 'enacts the supreme paradox of Pip's life: Estella can only respond to him when he exhibits those qualities of physical force and animal aggression which, in order to win her, he is at pains to civilise out of himself'.[11] But the irony will be even intensified when we come to discover that this young 'lady' is no other than the daughter of Pip's own convict and when we realize that, while watching the tussle, she had somehow instinctively sided with Pip in proletarian sisterhood against his genteel aggressor and class-enemy. For, 'brave and innocent' though he may seem, the 'young gentleman' (not Herbert yet) is the representative of a social group which has power on its side. It is *he*, we must not forget, who provokes Pip into fighting, insisting that he knows the rules of the game, and acts 'in a manner at once light-hearted, businesslike, and bloodthirsty' (xi, 120). This fight undoubtedly suggests, as Gilmour writes, 'a schoolboy's imitation of the prize ring, then enjoying its golden age',[12] but are not the laws of the game themselves an 'imitation' of the laws of society, a society which, under the Bloody Code which was in force at the time of the story, was particularly aggressive, barbarous and 'bloodthirsty'? And when the fight is over, is it not the common boy aggressed by the genteel one who feels guilty and punishable:

My mind grew very uneasy on the subject of the pale young gentleman. The more I thought of the fight, and recalled the pale young gentleman on his back in various stages of puffy and incrimsoned countenance, the more certain it appeared that something would be done to me. I felt that the pale young gentleman's blood was on my head, and that the Law would avenge it. Without having any definite idea of the penalties I had incurred, it was clear to me that village boys could not go stalking about the country, ravaging the houses of gentlefolks and pitching into the studious youth of England, without laying themselves open to severe punishment (xii, 121).

The fact, besides, that the strange boy should remain anonymous throughout the episode, the fact that he should insistently be referred to as the pale young 'gentleman' – a word that has not been used once with marked social connotations since the fight on the marshes[13] – also seems to be a hint that the scene is a re-play and that Pip's adversary is acting the part of the 'young man' or villainous 'gentleman' of the early chapters. At this symbolic level, gentility is suspicious, be it ever so childish and inoffensive.

We get indirect confirmation of this in the next interpolated episode when, a year or so later, a fight is fought at the forge with a new cast of actors, Joe Gargery, the angelic blacksmith, and Dolge Orlick, his devilish journeyman. Before he fell out with his master, we had never heard of Orlick; but, like the 'pale young gentleman', he has just been introduced to us, as if for the purpose: '*Now*, Joe kept a journeyman' (xv, 139, my emphasis). This newcomer is described most depreciatingly as a man with an assumed name – 'He pretended that his christian name was Dolge – a clear impossibility –' (xv, 139) – and with a mysterious and even dubious past, a man from nowhere who is said to be 'always slouching . . . like Cain or the Wandering Jew' (xv, 140).[14] The comparison with Cain, which in itself is derogatory enough, will acquire new significance later in the book when Pip's convict reveals his identity, 'Magwitch, . . . christen'd Abel' (xl, 345), and when we realize that he was the *good* convict betrayed by his *bad* brother. These revelations will force, in retrospect, a comparison between Orlick and Compeyson, the true Cain of the story, and the analogy will be further strengthened when we learn they are associates, plotting against the returned convict and acting as informers for the criminal police, that is to say for the oppressive forces of the world of gentility.

The outcome of the fight is quite unpredictable as both fighters are men of exceptional strength: 'they went at one another, like two giants' (xv, 142), Pip reports; but Joe gets the upper hand of his opponent in no time and his easy victory is given quite unexpected formulation: 'Orlick, as if he had been of no more account than the pale young gentleman, was very soon among the coal-dust, and in no hurry to come out of it' (xv, 142). So, once more, and very explicitly, the text harks back to a previous one, as if each new description of a

fight was a new milestone, pointing to the cross-referential character
of the narrative, soliciting new comparisons. And the likening of
Orlick to the 'pale young gentleman', therefore indirectly to the
'young man' of chapter 1 (which aggravates the comparison both
ways), casts an even darker shadow on the Havisham–Pocket family
and on gentility at large.

Miss Havisham herself is one of the actors of the third inserted
contest – or rather what looks something like one – and, through the
network of identifications, she does not come out in a favourable
light either. The scene takes place late in the novel, when Pip is about
to smuggle Magwitch abroad. Pip has been requested by Miss Havisham to go to Satis House on a 'little matter of business' (xlviii, 401)
and takes his leave with a 'presentiment' that he will never be there
again. So, before going, he pays a parting visit to the ruined garden:

> I went all round it; round by the corner where Herbert and I had
> fought our battle; round by the paths where Estella and I had
> walked...
> ... I was going out at the opposite door ... when I turned my head
> to look back. A childish association revived with wonderful force
> in the moment of the slight action, and I fancied that I saw Miss
> Havisham hanging to the beam. So strong was the impression,
> that I stood under the beam shuddering from head to foot before I
> knew it was a fancy – though to be sure I was there in an instant
> (xlix, 413).

Then, passing into the front courtyard, as if seized with a strong pre-
monition of impending danger, he decides, quite unaccountably, to
go upstairs again 'and assure myself', he says, 'that Miss Havisham
was as safe and well as I had left her'. What follows reads almost like
a wish-fulfilment nightmare and needs quoting at some length:

> I looked into the room where I had left her, and I saw her seated in
> the ragged chair upon the hearth close to the fire, with her back
> towards me. In the moment when I was withdrawing my head to
> go quietly away, I saw a great flaming light spring up. In the same
> moment, I saw her running at me, shrieking, with a whirl of fire
> blazing all about her, and soaring at least as many feet above her
> head as she was high.
> I had a double-caped great-coat on, and over my arm another

thick coat. That I got them off, closed with her, threw her down, and got them over her; that I dragged the great cloth from the table for the same purpose, and with it dragged down the heap of rottenness in the midst, and all the ugly things that sheltered there; that we were on the ground struggling like desperate enemies, and that the closer I covered her, the more wildly she shrieked and tried to free herself; that this occurred I knew through the result, but not through anything I felt, or thought, or knew I did. I knew nothing until I knew that we were on the floor by the great table, and that patches of tinder yet alight were floating in the smoky air, which, a moment ago, had been her faded bridal dress.

Then, I looked round and saw the disturbed beetles and spiders running away over the floor, and the servants coming in with breathless cries at the door. I still held her forcibly down with all my strength, like a prisoner who might escape; and I doubt if I even knew who she was, or why we had struggled (xlix, 414).

'Who she was, or why we had struggled': Pip leaves these two questions unanswered, as if he was afraid to face the truth of his motivations and preferred to leave it to us to provide explanations. But further questions urge themselves on us as we obediently lead our own investigations: under what inner compulsions has he been acting? Why did he, even momentarily, rub out the name of his opponent from his consciousness? And, more puzzling still, why should he describe his attempt at saving this woman's life at the peril of his own in terms of aggression, why should an act of heroism and human solidarity be felt as a form of assault by the actor himself?

An answer to Pip's first question might give us a clue to all the others, and that answer seems obvious enough if we proceed as before and look for analogies. If this is one more repetition of the basic conflict of the book, as it well seems to be (the reference to the battle with Herbert implies such a connection), then we have no choice but to identify the 'prisoner' trying to wrench free from the grip of her antagonist with the villain of chapter 5: Miss Havisham in this scene is made to play the part of the genteel convict forcibly brought back to the Hulks by his sworn enemy.

From first meeting her, we had known this woman to be a prisoner, living in self-inflicted confinement behind the barred windows of a blind house, the inner landscape of which, with the 'wintry branches' of its candlesticks and the 'reluctant smoke' of its damp fires 'colder than the clearer air – like our own marsh mist' (xi, 112), had been redolent from the first of convict-country; disquieting connections had been established later between its cobwebs and those of Newgate (xxv, 230), while wickedness and crime had been repeatedly stamped on 'the Witch of the place' (xi, 113). Yet, the analogy implicitly drawn in this scene between her and the very man who had once broken her heart by deserting her on her wedding-day strikes us at first as grotesque and almost shockingly cruel. Only on second thoughts do we realize that it is in fact a well-deserved retribution: Miss Havisham is, after all, repaid in kind for behaving to others, and to Pip in particular, with revengefully misplaced cruelty. Impervious to any Christian message of humanity, unable to do to others as she would be done by, bent as she has been on 'beggaring' a poor innocent child, ruining his prospects and breaking his heart vicariously, she has succeeded in turning herself into a monstrous double of the man who once trespassed against her and whom she never forgave.

Forgiveness for 'what she has done' is precisely what she has been begging from Pip during their last conversation: 'If you can ever write under my name, "I forgive her," though ever so long after my broken heart is dust – pray do it!' she asked. And her prayer was heard favourably and answered at once:

'O Miss Havisham,' said I, 'I can do it now. There have been sore mistakes; and my life has been a blind and thankless one; and I want forgiveness and direction far too much, to be bitter with you' (xlix, 410).

But the scene that follows immediately arouses our suspicion about Pip's sincerity: is it not, we wonder, a repressed desire for revenge that finds its outlet in metaphorical language? Is it not the 'wild beast' still lurking in him that we see at work mauling the woman whom his better self is lending assistance to? Is it not even his own diabolical imagination that has kindled the fire when he unjustifiably decided to return upstairs, just as, a moment before, it had brought back the vision of the hanging figure in the brewery? At the end of his relation of the accident and of the subsequent simulacrum of a fight, he himself almost confirms our conjectures: 'Assistance was sent for and I held her until it came, as if I unreasonably fancied (I think I did) that if I let her go, the fire would break out again and consume her' (xlix, 414).

Pip's 'unreasonable' fancy that he is just as capable of extinguishing the flames as of letting them blaze up implies that he has a power of life and death over his prisoner. But obviously he has no wish to see her dead and never had: a close look at the text will easily convince us that his efforts from first to last have been to protect and save her and that the fight is over ('we *had* struggled') when *she* herself gives up struggling, which she does the moment there is nothing any longer to struggle for, that is to say when 'all the ugly things' dragged down by Pip with the heap of rottenness are burnt to ashes together with what 'had been her faded bridal dress'. Pip's, we then realize, was the violence of the exterminating angel, not of someone bent on mischief. Far from being driven by vindictiveness, he was called upon in this scene to purify the world of Satis House of its pestilence, 'set the clocks a going and the cold hearths a blazing, tear down the cobwebs, destroy the vermin – in short, do all the shining deeds of the young Knight of romance' (xxix, 253).[15]

In feeding the fire with all the attributes of vanity, 'the vanity of sorrow ... and other monstrous vanities' that are 'curses in this world' (xlix, 411), Pip is also acting in self-defence, fighting against his inner demons, breaking the infernal cycle of revenge, afraid as he has indeed every reason to be of catching the disease from the woman who has just recognized in him the image of her own younger broken self:

> 'Until you spoke to her the other day, and until I saw in you a looking-glass that showed me what I once felt myself, I did not know what I had done' (xlix, 411).

If, as a living mirror, Pip has had the power of calling up images of bygone days, the mirrored image in its turn must have operated on him as a prophetic or a threatening looking-glass, urging him to take prompt action against physical and moral decay. Years before, we remember, he had already had an 'alarming fancy' that he and Estella 'might presently begin to decay' (xi, 118), and he is now staving off further disaster by destroying the symbols of the decayed values attached to his now lost expectations and to the world from which he first caught his 'wretched hankerings after money and gentility' (xxix, 257). But what occurs now is no mere hallucination or gratifying 'fancy', for, as Moynahan rightly points out, 'Pip's destructive fantasy comes true in reality'.[16] And this is possible for the simple reason that the wish-fulfilment dream is first and foremost that of the writer himself.

Such gentility as Satis House represents – a mixture of decadence, idleness, cruelty and exclusiveness – is a social evil that Dickens obviously wishes to see eradicated; and, being a novelist, he can afford at will to make the dream come true, if not 'in reality', at least in the reality of his fiction. Surely, the achievement is least detrimental to verisimilitude if it occurs, as it does, in hallucinatory scenes or in scenes of highly conflictive intensity like those analysed above; but the recurrence of such scenes is a sign that the dream is sincere and compulsive. Like repetitions in classical or pulpit rhetoric, iteration in narrative syntax partakes of the art of persuasion and, for that matter, of self-persuasion. It is as if, writing this novel, Dickens was defeating the villains of society by instalments, rehearsing for his own and our pleasure anticipatory versions of some ultimate real-life victory of the weak over the strong, of the innocent over the crooked, of the gentle over the genteel, of Abel over Cain.[17]

NOTES: CHAPTER 5

1 E. Rosenberg, 'A Preface to *Great Expectations*', *Dickens Studies Annual*, vol. 2 (1972), p. 318.
2 H. House, *The Dickens World* (London, 1941; 2nd edn 1942, Oxford Paperback, 1960), p. 159.
3 Reprinted in P. Collins (ed.), *Dickens: The Critical Heritage* (London: Routledge & Kegan Paul, 1971), p. 439.
4 Julian Moynahan, 'The hero's guilt: the case of *Great Expectations*', *Essays in Criticism*, vol. 10 (January 1960), p. 62.
5 T. A. Jackson, *Charles Dickens: The Progress of a Radical* (London: Lawrence & Wishart, 1937), p. 197.
6 Dorothy Van Ghent, *The English Novel: Form and Function* [1953] (New York: Harper Torchbooks, 1961), p. 133.
7 Robin Gilmour, *The Idea of the Gentleman in the Victorian Novel* (London: Allen & Unwin, 1981), p. 137.
8 George Bernard Shaw, Foreword to *Great Expectations*, The Novel Library (London: Hamish Hamilton, 1947), p. xii.
9 'The pursuit of Knowledge under difficulties' is the running headline to chapter 2, p. 7, in the Charles Dickens Edition (1868). See Appendix 2, p. 280 and Gilmour, op. cit., p. 120.
10 Gérard Genette, *Narrative Discourse*, translated by Jane E. Lewin (Oxford: Blackwell, 1980), p. 48.
11 Gilmour, op. cit., p. 139.
12 ibid., p. 129.

13 In chapter 11, the word is merely used as a polite way of introducing Cousin Raymond and Mr Jaggers (pp. 109, 111).
14 cf., Carlyle, *Sartor Resartus*, II, 6: 'Thus must he [Teufelsdröckh], in the temper of ancient Cain, or of the modern Wandering Jew,... wend to and fro with aimless speed' (London: Dent, 1973), p. 120. There might also be some relationship between Orlick and the fiery Orc of Blake's *The Book of Urizen*.
15 This is clearly the role David Lean gives him in his film (1946).
16 Moynahan, op. cit., p. 76.
17 cf. *Our Mutual Friend*, IV, vii, 'Better to be Abel than Cain'.

CHAPTER 6

Perspectives

The world depicted in *Great Expectations* is one where violence from above eventually breeds violence from below, rather than the other way round. It is a world where the underprivileged by birth are shown to be constantly victimized, antagonized, beggared by their social betters and further crushed by an unfairly repressive legislation. The iniquity of the criminal law, made for their own benefit by the privileged few, is nowhere more dramatically illustrated than when Magwitch tells Pip and Herbert how he, the underdog, and Compeyson, the gentleman, were tried together as accomplices but sentenced separately, each according to his manners, looks, accomplishments, and circle of acquaintances:

'When we was put in the dock, I noticed first of all what a gentleman Compeyson looked, wi' his curly hair and his black clothes and his white pocket-handkercher, and what a common sort of a wretch I looked. When the prosecution opened and the evidence was put short, aforehand, I noticed how heavy it all bore on me, and how light on him. When the evidence was giv in the box, I noticed how it was always me that had come for'ard, and could be swore to, how it was always me that the money had been paid to, how it was always me that had seemed to work the thing and get the profit. But, when the defence come on, then I see the plan plainer; for, says the counsellor for Compeyson, "My lord and gentlemen, here you has afore you, side by side, two persons as your eyes can separate wide; one, the younger, well brought up, who will be spoke to as such; one, the elder, ill brought up, who will be spoke to as such; one, the younger, seldom if ever seen in these here transactions, and only suspected; t'other, the elder, always seen in 'em and always wi' his guilt brought home. Can you doubt, if there is but one in it, which is the one, and, if there is two in it, which is much the worst one?" And such-like.

And when it come to character, warn't it Compeyson as had been to the school, and warn't it his schoolfellows as was in this position and in that, and warn't it him as had been know'd by witnesses in such clubs and societies, and nowt to his disadvantage? And warn't it me as had been tried afore, and as had been know'd up hill and down dale in Bridewells and Lock-ups? And when it come to speech-making, warn't it Compeyson as could speak to 'em wi' his face dropping every now and then into his white pocket-handkercher – ah! and wi' verses in his speech, too – and warn't it me as could only say, "Gentlemen, this man at my side is a most precious rascal"? And when the verdict come, warn't it Compeyson as was recommended to mercy on account of good character and bad company, and giving up all the information he could agen me, and warn't it me as got never a word but Guilty? And when I says to Compeyson, "Once out of this court, I'll smash that face of yourn!" ain't it Compeyson as prays the Judge to be protected, and gets two turnkeys stood betwixt us? And when we're sentenced, ain't it him as gets seven year, and me fourteen, and ain't it him as the Judge is sorry for, because he might a done so well, and ain't it me as the Judge perceives to be a old offender of wiolent passion, likely to come to worse?' (xlii, 364–5).

This text might almost have earned *Great Expectations* the right to be classed as a Newgate novel. Reading it, we are reminded, as many Victorians must have been, of the famous trial scene in *Paul Clifford* in which the hero, speaking in self-defence before his judges, reverses the roles and puts society in the dock:

I hesitate not to tell you, my lord judge – to proclaim to you, gentlemen of the jury, that the laws which I have broken through my life I despise in death! Your laws are but of two classes; the one makes criminals, the other punishes them. I have suffered by the one – I am about to perish by the other.

My lord, it was the turn of a straw which made me what I am. Seven years ago I was sent to the House of Correction for an offence which I did not commit; I went thither, a boy who had never infringed a single law – I came forth, in a few weeks, a man who was prepared to break all laws!... The laws themselves caused me to break the laws ... your legislation made me what I am! and it now *destroys me, as it has destroyed thousands, for being what it made me!*... Let those whom the law protects consider it a protector; when did it ever protect *me*? When did it ever protect the poor man? The government of a state, the institutions of law, profess to provide for all those who 'obey.' Mark! a man hungers – do you feed him? He is naked – do you clothe him? If not, you break your covenant, you drive him back to the first law of nature, and you hang him, not because he is guilty, but because you have *left* him naked and starving![1]

But, barring the use of rhetorical questions, Paul's style is very different from Magwitch's, less in character, more urgently polemical. His speech sounds more like an educated man's indictment of the system than a poor man's plea for mercy. Writing in 1830, at the dawn of the age of legal and penal reform, Edward Bulwer Lytton was less concerned with the probability of his hero's rhetoric than with the desire to mobilize public opinion and urge his readers into humanitarian action. The tone is that of a pamphlet written for the present times.

Writing in 1860, Dickens, by setting his story back in the first quarter of the century, was providing a different perspective. Transportation to New South Wales had been discontinued for ten years already; the last of the hulks had closed two years before; the treatment of criminals, prison discipline and sanitation had been much improved; many offences had been struck off the list of crimes punishable by death (among which was returning illegally from transportation). 'When Dickens died, in 1870,' Philip Collins writes, 'the system for dealing with criminals was recognisably the one we have inherited; the system that obtained in his boyhood belongs to another world, at least as much akin to the sixteenth century as to the twentieth'.[2] 'It is this sense of belonging to "another world" that *Great Expectations* so powerfully conveys', Robin Gilmour comments. 'There must have been many contemporary readers of *Great Expectations*', he adds, 'for whom this sense of division was a felt reality, who shared the social and historical perspective which Dickens was exploiting'.[3] Not unreasonably stressing Victorian awareness of improvements in social and penal matters, Gilmour defines 'perspective' as follows:

by reminding his readers of the brutal way in which a primitive society treated its criminals, Dickens is able to show the complex

origins of the Victorian preoccupation with refinement and gentility – how the desire to become a gentleman was not just a
snobbish aspiration out of one's class, but was also a desire to be
a gentle man, to have a more civilised and decent life than a
violent society allowed for most of its members.[4]

Gilmour is certainly quite right in putting the stress on the attitude of
the gentleman towards the criminal rather than on the criminal
himself. Magwitch, as opposed to Paul Clifford, is not the main
character of the book in which he appears, and he has no reason to
be. When the real hero decides to put pen to paper, he has been dead
and buried for over forty years. He and the likes of him clearly
belong to the past and Newgate novels are no longer fashionable.
Looking back to the days when gibbets and hulks were part and
parcel of the scenery, when convicts were chained and ironed and
flogged and treated 'as if they were lower animals' (xxviii, 249),
when gaols were filthy and overcrowded and when criminals
received their sentence in herds on the last day of a Sessions, like
cattle condemned to the slaughter-house, many must have been
Dickens's contemporaries who, used to milder practices and possibly encouraged into self-righteous complacency by the comparison,
must have formed a very poor opinion of the 'genteel' people who
then enforced the law and who could 'live smooth' only because
others 'lived rough' (xxxix, 337). And it is certainly no accident that
Drummle, the most high-born character in the novel, 'the next heir
but one to a baronetcy' (xxiii, 215), should be so brutal and coarse
and cruel; Gilmour defines him as 'an upper-class equivalent of the
journeyman Orlick',[5] a comparison that is well-deserved and
becomes particularly appropriate towards the end of the novel
when the two men associate against the hero and his benefactor.
But, significantly, Mrs Pocket, with her regard for blue blood and
red books, is blind to his viciousness and holds him in high esteem.
Seen from a distance, Regency gentility must have been perceived by
fastidious Victorians as something very crude and closer indeed to
criminality than it seemed to dear Belinda.

But the story is not simply seen from a distance by Dickens's
genteel – and hopefully gentle – Victorian readers. Nor is it simply
told by the discriminating Victorian gentleman we assume Pip to
have become. Dickens's narrator, on the contrary, makes a point of
recapturing the past as he apprehended it when it was the present, at

a time, that is to say, when he had no means of telling whether he himself was a gentleman in the making or some potential gaol-bird, and when, being like England itself on the wrong side of improvement, he had none of his future readers' criteria by which to judge his country's institutions or to appreciate the moral tenets of his age. The novel we read is very much the book of a green hero and young observer; a book, besides, in which focus and perspective can never be dissociated. It is through Pip that we can see Magwitch, and it is between the lines of his own life-story that we can read the social history of his age. The emphasis, therefore, is on complexity: because of his youth and inexperience, because of the precariousness of his social position, because of his acute sensibility, because of the discrepancy between his prejudices and his sympathies, his aspirations and his attainments, Pip always appears to us as someone who is ill at ease and out of place. Wherever he happens to find himself, he seems to belong to 'another world', though what this world may be is anybody's guess: he is too genteel for the forge, too common for Satis House, too much of a scholar for Joe, too much of a blacksmith's boy for Estella and Miss Havisham, too refined for the company of convicts, too unpolished for that of true-born gentlemen, and, in any case, too deeply involved to be entirely reliable and consistent.

Pip's early entanglement with criminals, quite paradoxically, shows him both at his most decent and at his most vulnerable; and his association with an outcast can at no stage be mistaken for some 'freemasonry' of fellow-ruffians: he commits his theft out of pity for a poor wretch and also because he has pledged himself to do so under the threat of being 'torn and ate', but he remains prim and proper, and almost gentlemanly, throughout the episode and carries his guilty conscience across the fields and into the pantry, getting all the remorse and none of the pleasure of robbing Mrs Joe of her Christmas pork pie, behaving in fact as if he had some intimate knowledge that guilt is the only means for him of repudiating the disgraceful connection. He certainly identifies himself with the criminal, as has often been pointed out, but his identification is quite plainly the expression of his fear of meeting a similar fate: 'I felt fearfully sensible', he writes, 'of the great convenience that the Hulks were handy for me. I was clearly on my way there' (ii, 46); and, during the night before he does the deed, he has a horrible dream in which he imagines himself 'drifting down the river on a strong spring-tide, to the Hulks' while 'a ghostly pirate' calls out to him through a speaking-trumpet that he 'had better come ashore and be hanged there at once, and not put it off' (ii, 47).

Pip's fears are not so fantastic or wide of the mark as might appear to a modern reader: children of six or seven are reported to have been placed in the hulks for minor offences at the time of the story,[6] and Dickens must have known that in 1825, about the time when he himself 'lounged about the streets, insufficiently and unsatisfactorily fed' and when, 'but for the mercy of God', he 'might easily have been, for any care that was taken of [him], a little robber or a little vagabond',[7] special hulks for young villains had been stationed at Chatham[8] of all places. The comic exaggeration of his hero's nightmarish vision – the revenge of art on life – is typical of his talent for turning fact into fiction. Here is brilliantly rendered the agony of soul of a whole class and generation of men born into a pitiless world at a period of intense social instability. Dickens's own 'descent into [a] poor little drudge'[9] when he was no older than ten, his first-hand knowledge of struggling poverty so poignantly recorded in the fragment of autobiography that Forster published on his death, had early made him acutely aware of the guilt and misery bred by insecurity.

Of his traumatic experience Pip breathes no word to anyone, not even to Joe, showing himself as reticent about his shameful descent into the world of crime as Dickens had been about his social disgrace and his father's imprisonment in the Marshalsea until the confidence was wrenched from him by Forster. As soon as the convicts disappear into the Hulks he drops the curtain and brings his energies to bear on self-betterment, strongly determined as he is to help himself out of his condition, and again reminding us of little Charles and of his 'early hopes of growing up to be a learned and distinguished man':[10] 'What a scholar you are', Joe says to him admiringly in the following chapter. 'I should like to be', he replies (vii, 75).

In his pioneering inroad into the psychoanalysis of Dickens's fiction, Edmund Wilson writes: 'For the man of spirit whose childhood has been crushed by the cruelty of organized society, one of two attitudes is natural: that of the criminal or that of the rebel. Charles Dickens, in imagination, was to play the rôles of both'.[11] Dickens's readiness, blatantly instanced in this scene, to project himself into his self-helping heroes, seems to come under neither of these attitudes and to invalidate the last term of the statement; but Joe Gargery who, short of reading Wilson, has listened to his wife, invites us to reconsider the matter: 'she an't over partial to having scholars on the premises', he says of Mrs Joe, 'and in partickler would not be over partial to my being a scholar, for fear as I might rise. Like a sort of rebel, don't you see?' (vii, 79) Dickens must have 'seen'. The poor drudge who, thanks to his talent and obstinacy, had risen to fame and recognition must have known that self-promotion was a form of rebellion and it is obvious, with Joe and Biddy approving, that his hero is quite welcome in his turn to rise self-helpingly, be it ever so rebelliously.

But when, under the influence of Satis House, his rightful ambitions are altered into the desire to become a 'gentleman', Pip loses the support of his author's mouthpieces. On receiving his confidence, Biddy reacts disapprovingly: 'I wouldn't, if I was you', she says. 'I don't think it would answer' (xvii, 154).

It certainly won't. Turning a deaf ear to the admonitions of his moral advisers, Pip will go on dreaming until the dream comes true and he suddenly gets patronized into gentility and into further and lasting uneasiness. At no stage, not even before he discovers the origins of his fortune, will he succeed in attaining the happiness, serenity of mind and wholeness of being that he had naively and expectantly associated with the rank of gentleman.

The irony of his plight, however, is not just a form of moral retribution. Neither is it merely the sign that he is henceforth disowned by his creator self-righteously aware that in his own case there was never anyone but himself to thank for his achievements and worldly success. Pip's predicament is the typically ambivalent situation of an individual who has long been seeking some secure social position, yet finds himself unconsciously unwilling to accept it when he does get it. It is the predicament of one doomed, and indeed self-doomed, like so many Dickens characters and like Dickens himself, to be a social wanderer. Paradoxically, it is when the novelist seems to dissociate himself most from his hero that he is closest to him. To his personal experience and inner contradictions we must therefore turn once more as a major source for the understanding of his hero's ambiguities.

Dickens is a notoriously difficult man to place socially and ideologically. Presumably rebellious at heart, he never was openly, least of all triumphantly so. But, on the other hand, this 'honourable man' never properly 'gentlefolked'. It has been said of him that he was not a gentleman, that he could not depict a gentleman,[12] that he could not write like a gentleman, and it is true that his ornate, Micawber-ish prose could no more be mistaken for a genteel form of writing than his red waistcoats for a genteel form of dressing. Perhaps he felt that he owed to the past this tribute of *un*gentility and of singularity. For, even at the apex of success, 'famous and caressed and happy', he remained an exile in bourgeois society and would often 'wander desolately back to that time of [his] life'[13] when, paradoxically, he had been in exile in working-class surroundings. It may be a commonplace to say so – but commonplaces sometimes have to be rehearsed – the Warren's Blacking episode made him an outcast for life.

'Outcast' is actually a mild word compared to the one Dickens himself uses in the 'fragment' to describe the state of utter rejection that he went through at the time: 'I (small Cain that I was, except that I had never done harm to anyone)',[14] he writes, inflicting upon himself a comparison that he knows to be undeserved, behaving in fact as if being sinned against had somehow turned him into a sinner.

The self-directed cruelty which is so typical of this autobiographi-cal document is equally characteristic of his fictional writings of the confessional type. Pip's masochistic dream of the pirate and, even more strikingly, his later nightmarish identification with Cain-like Orlick in the sluice-house scene disturbingly echo the self-indict-ments of the autobiographer: 'You done it; now you pays for it' (liii, 437), says the slanderous voice of the subconscious.

The cruelty with which Dickens's imagination conjured up visions of the painful past was matched only by the ungratefulness of his memory when involved in the act of creating fiction, a phenomenon strikingly exemplified by the literary fate of poor Bob Fagin, one of the most innocuous workmates of the 'small Cain'. Bob Fagin, it will be remembered, is the boy who, on the day of Charles's arrival in the Strand, had shown him the tricks of his work and helped him in various ways. He had also nursed him one day when he was unwell and had even offered to see him safely home after work. But 'home' then was the Marshalsea prison and Charles, too proud to let his companion discover the truth of his condition, had shaken hands with him 'on the steps of a house near Southwark Bridge' under the pretence that this was where he lived. 'As a finishing piece of reality in case of his looking back, I knocked at the door, I recollect, and asked, when the woman opened it, if that was Mr. Robert Fagin's house.'[15] 'Bob Fagin', he writes, 'was very good to me'. But the poor lad was ill repaid for his goodness: 'I took the liberty of using his name, long afterwards, in *Oliver Twist*', adds the novelist perfunctorily.[16] 'So casual and off-hand a revelation of what must by nature be a highly charged fact is itself evidence of the high charge',[17] comments Steven Marcus. The ways of creators are unfathomable and many alternative readings of this strange metamorphosis are possible. Drawing our attention to the mixture of fascination and dread – 'the attraction of repulsion' – that the dubiously 'respectable old gentleman' inspires in Oliver, Marcus argues that it is because it was at once 'needed and intolerable' that Bob's protectiveness was transformed into Fagin's 'treacherous maternal care'.[18] The interpretation that will be submitted here is that, in 'using' Fagin's name for the second time, Dickens was repeating, and probably improving, the scene of his youth when by a bold act of the imagination, which was also an act of self-preservation, he had already turned his companion into someone else, the impossible dweller in the Southwark Bridge house, and thus alienated him.

The early metamorphosis had been a mild form of alienation; the second one was no less than a form of ostracism: the undesirable witness of his shame, whose solicitude had been a threat and a nuisance, the fellow-worker and, as such, the *alter ego* who had initiated him into a type of work for which he had no taste and to which he felt unsuited was now removed into another sphere, cast away, turned into a dangerous criminal, eventually sentenced to death. Bob Fagin was somehow immortalized as the Cain that the novelist had long been at pains to exorcize out of himself. But the ambiguous personality of Orlick, a strange combination of 'Cain' and of 'the Wandering Jew', and his even more ambiguous relationship with Pip, his workmate at the forge, would seem to indicate that the exorcism was not entirely or lastingly successful.

One of the reasons, probably, why critics of the novels constantly revert to Dickens's unfinished biographical record, sketchy as it is, is precisely that fiction and confessions interact so closely within the text, highlighting each other, suggesting a relationship of mutual inheritance. Both the Cain image, which must have been the writer's rather than the child's, and the explicit reference to *Oliver Twist* are examples of literary feedback on real-life experience; inversely, the obsessional recurrence in the novels of a particular breed of 'baddest'[19] men of the Cain/Fagin type is a sign that *Oliver Twist* did not have on its author the lasting cathartic effect he must have expected from it, and that the shame and guilt associated with the Warren's Blacking episode were to be inexhaustible, if long hidden, springs of the novelist's fiction. For the work of Dickens is clearly the work of a man who never forgot, a man who remained to the end a prisoner of the hated past and who, novel after novel, like Dorrit in dotage, welcomed his readers to the Marshalsea.

Pip is just as ill-fated as his creator and, like him, haunted in adult life by the shadows of his childhood. Significantly, when, after long years of expectations, he is given his chance of rising in society, circumstances cruelly compel him to walk through genteel life as he had walked across the fields one Christmas morning, as if his convict's iron was riveted to his leg. On arriving in Little Britain, one of the first objects on which he happens to set his eyes is the pair of awful casts in Jaggers's office, and the first building he sees in London is the prison of Newgate; while looking about him, he is even invited by some half-drunk minister of justice 'to step in and hear a trial or so'. He declines the proposal, but is none the less offered a glimpse of the courtyard:

> ... he was so good as to take me into a yard and show me where the gallows was kept, and also where people were publicly whipped, and then he showed me the Debtors' Door, out of which culprits came to be hanged: heightening the interest of that dreadful portal by giving me to understand that 'four on 'em' would come out at that door the day after to-morrow at eight in the morning, to be killed in a row. This was horrible, and gave me a sickening idea of London' (xx, 189–90).

What reader would fail to associate this scene with the meeting on the marshes and perceive the irony of this untimely intrusion of the past, at the very moment when the hero is in 'for London and greatness'? Whether the hero himself perceives the association the text does not say, leaving us free to choose what interpretation we like best. But Pip very explicitly establishes a connection between Newgate and the marshes on the occasion of his second visit to the prison where Wemmick shows him around; back in the street where

he waits for Estella, he lets his thoughts linger on the strangeness of
his fate:

> I consumed the whole time in thinking how strange it was that I
> should be encompassed by all this taint of prison and crime; that,
> in my childhood out on our lonely marshes on a winter evening I
> should have first encountered it; that, it should have reappeared
> on two occasions, starting out like a stain that was faded but not
> gone; that, it should in this new way pervade my fortune and
> advancement. While my mind was thus engaged, I thought of the
> beautiful young Estella, proud and refined, coming towards me,
> and I thought with absolute abhorrence of the contrast between
> the jail and her. I wished that Wemmick had not met me, or that I
> had not yielded to him and gone with him, so that, of all days in
> the year on this day, I might not have had Newgate in my breath
> and on my clothes. I beat the prison dust off my feet as I sauntered
> to and fro, and I shook it out of my dress, and I exhaled its air
> from my lungs. So contaminated did I feel, remembering who was
> coming (xxxii, 284).

His commentary is both prophetic and analeptic, pointing, as critics
have often remarked, to his ultimate recognition of the inter-
relationship between the two worlds of gentility and of criminality
that he had so badly tried to ignore before discovering the origins of
his wealth and of Estella.

Quite understandably, this paragraph has attracted more critical
attention than the pages that lead to it. The visit to Newgate is as a
rule only quoted (if at all) for its topical interest.[20] But Dickens in
this scene is not merely comparing the state of prisons at thirty
years' distance. He also invites us to look at the visitors and
compare their reactions in front of the same sight. Wemmick, not
Pip, is at the centre of the scene: jocular, talkative, he goes about the
place totally unruffled by its wretchedness and that of its inmates,
happy in his dual role of guide and fees-raiser, playfully acting
Pancks for the benefit of Jaggers and cynically securing 'portable
property' for himself from a prisoner whose execution he knows to
be imminent. Obviously, Wemmick is not encumbered here with his
Walworth sentiments; but Pip, whose self is not so comfortably split
and who carries his feelings with him wherever he goes, is revolted
at this sight: a 'frouzy, ugly, disorderly, depressing scene' (xxxii,

280) he finds it. His sympathies are not enlisted with the prisoners (he is much too biased against criminals for that), but he is unable to share his companion's light-heartedness and to take Newgate for granted. If violence and repression are the price genteel society has to pay for its security and for its prosperity, Pip, who by now is a gentleman and wishes to remain one, has no choice but to accept it, but he must take the 'soiling consciousness' into the bargain, and the soiling consciousness harks back to the past and to the soiled conscience. His idea of gentility is henceforth tainted and contaminated: as Biddy had predicted, it does not 'answer'. Contamination is no doubt a clue to Pip's uneasiness and inability to enjoy his new condition as a London gentleman. The following chapter, which is devoted to his life in '*gai* London', extravagance and dissipation, shows him full of misgivings and pathetically apologetic.

But if they spoil his progress in life, his qualms do not turn him into a reformist; and not a minor (though probably unintentional) irony of the Newgate scene is that it should give us the opportunity of discovering that the sensitive young man who cannot overcome his revulsion at the sight of neglected prisoners is destined to become the priggish narrator who makes derisive comments on the pampered state of modern felons. The remark is usually read as Dickens's, not his hero's, and it is difficult indeed not to recognize here the voice of the novelist and detect in it traces of this ' "I've always kept myself respectable" habit of mind' which, in Orwell's terms, Dickens shows 'As soon as he comes up against crime or the worst depths of poverty'.[21] But, even if this is an illustration of the dangers of writing in the first person, the laws of fiction compel us to believe that Pip expresses his own views on a matter that has for many years disturbed and preoccupied him. Concern with crime and punishment, after all, is by no means Dickens's prerogative and if he himself had 'strong and conflicting feelings about criminals',[22] as Philip Collins tells us, there is no reason why his hero should be denied the right to be, like him, divided between leniency towards the criminal that he might have been and contempt for the criminal that he never was.

'The complexity of Dickens appears ... in his opinions on public issues', Collins writes. 'Sometimes there is a development over the years, sometimes a simple inconsistency; anyway, it is rarely safe to take a single statement or dramatisation as fully representing his views on a matter which engaged his attention more than momentarily ... One must read and accept the lot, taking and trying to explain the developments or inconsistencies as they come'.[23] We may substitute Pip's name for that of his creator and follow Collins's advice: 'accept the lot'.

One of the greatest merits of the book is precisely that there should be in it so much to accept. Pip is, and by far, Dickens's most complex hero, 'restlessly aspiring' (xiv, 135), yet uncertain as to what he wants, torn between conflicting demands, tossed between antinomic worlds, waging with himself, at each new stage of his life, the paradigmatic battle once fought out on the marshes; he is also, and by far, his most complex and subtle narrator, offering us the double perspective of the once blacksmith's boy and of the gentleman to be.

NOTES: CHAPTER 6

1 Edward Bulwer Lytton, *Paul Clifford* [1830] (London: Routledge, 1854), pp. 309–10.
2 Philip Collins, *Dickens and Crime* (London: Macmillan, 1965), p. 3.
3 Robin Gilmour, *The Idea of the Gentleman in the Victorian Novel* (London: Allen & Unwin, 1981), p. 136.
4 ibid., p. 129.
5 ibid., p. 139.
6 'In 1810 a shop-boy, Samuel Oliver, was convicted at the Old Bailey of the theft of two shillings from his master', and 'to the hulks went that incorrigible villain', writes W. Branch-Johnson, *The English Prison Hulks* (London: Christopher Johnson, 1957), p. 146.
7 See Forster, *The Life of Charles Dickens* (London: Dent, 1966), Vol. 1, p. 25.
8 The Hulk was called 'The Euryalus': see Branch-Johnson, op. cit., p. 123.
9 See Foster, op. cit., Vol. 1, p. 21.
10 ibid., p. 22.
11 Edmund Wilson, 'Dickens: the two Scrooges', *The Wound and the Bow* [1941] (London: W. H. Allen, 1952), p. 13.
12 Discussed by G. K. Chesterton, *Appreciations and Criticisms of the Works of Charles Dickens* (London: Dent, 1911), pp. 124–6; George Bernard Shaw, Foreword to *Great Expectations*, The Novel Library (London: Hamish Hamilton, 1947), p. ix; Gilmour, op. cit., pp. 105 ff.
13 Quoted by Forster, op. cit., p. 23.
14 ibid.
15 ibid., p. 27.
16 ibid., p. 22.
17 Steven Marcus, *Dickens from Pickwick to Dombey* (London: Chatto & Windus, 1965), p. 364.
18 ibid., p. 367.
19 cf., *Little Dorrit*, ed. Harvey Peter Sucksmith, Clarendon Dickens (Oxford, 1979), II, xiii, 561.
20 See above, ch. 4, 'Chronology', p. 34.
21 George Orwell, 'Charles Dickens' [1940], *Critical Essays* (London: Secker & Warburg, 1954), p. 27.
22 Collins, op. cit., p. 1.
23 ibid., p. 25.

CHAPTER 7

The Australian Convict

'Victorian preoccupation with refinement and gentility'[1] is also perceptible if we consider the way England treated its convicts in the penal colonies and the complex interaction of transportation and emigration at mid-century.

When Dickens wrote *Great Expectations*, the days of transportation were virtually over and convicts had already gone down in legend and history. New South Wales, which for more than fifty years had been the most important dumping ground for the unwanted population of Great Britain, was no longer a penal colony; transportation there had been abolished as early as 1840 by an order-in-council ineffectively revoked eight years later by Earl Grey: when, in 1849, two vessels loaded with convicts reached Melbourne, they were refused permission to disembark their passengers. Anti-transportation petitions were signed to prevent further attempts at re-establishing the odious system and in October 1850 the New South Wales Council resolved that 'no more prisoners should be received under any conditions'.[2] In April 1851, Earl Grey's revocation of the order-in-council was rescinded and New South Wales was henceforth and for good a land of free citizens. For another two years, prisoners were still sporadically shipped off from England to Van Diemen's Land (Tasmania) and, although the first Penal Servitude Act was passed in 1855 substituting imprisonment with hard labour at home for long sentences of transportation, it was not until 1868 that Western Australia discontinued the practice of receiving convicts; but here there was only a small settlement where less than 10,000 male prisoners in all were ever sent, a low figure in comparison with the 84,000 or so (including 11,500 women) who were landed at Port Jackson or in Botany Bay between 1788 and 1840 and with the 67,000 who reached Van Diemen's Land (or Van Demon's, as it was called derisively)[3] during the years that transportation lasted there (1803–53).

Australia itself was no longer the same country in the 1860s as it had been at the turn of the century, in the early days of transportation: viewed from the mother country, it was by then a land of settlers and of gold prospectors, not the distant gaol that it used to be when Botany Bay was no better than 'Convicts' Bay'.[4]

In order to try and understand the attitude of mind which must have been that of Dickens's readers when the book came out and to compare it with the mentality of young Pip's contemporaries, it is necessary here briefly to go over the eventful period that spans the last quarter of the eighteenth century and the first half of the nineteenth.

'1775 and all that ...' might be the title of this chapter of history. It had all begun with the War of Independence which had 'interrupted', as it was thought at first, but actually 'ended' transportation to the American colonies. This had raised difficulties, as England no longer knew what to do with its surplus criminal population: prisons at home were not numerous enough to accommodate all those who were convicted of crime. But, because it was believed that, after the war, transportation to America would be resumed, it was decided that, in the meantime, the prisoners would be housed in floating gaols and 'kept to hard labour in the raising of sand, soil and gravel, and cleansing the river Thames'. Thus began the era of 'Thames-side convicts'.[5] 'Convicts at work', writes W. Branch-Johnson, became one of the familiar 'sights of the capital': they were occupied at converting banks into docks, quays and yards, 'chained two and two' even when at work, loaded with heavy fetters when crimes had been 'enormous', and watched by guards 'with drawn cutlasses to prevent their escape and likewise to prevent idleness'.[6] Moored on the shores of the river, the hulks after a time became part of the landscape: authorized for two years in 1776, they were to last eighty-two. The hulks were dank and dark, badly ventilated, fever-ridden, unhealthy places, offering the one advantage of being 'cheaper than the erection of new prisons ashore'.[7] And even when the building of penitentiaries was considered, there were 'disputes about sites'[8] and delays owing to the costs.

The hulks were never popular. People were afraid at the thought of 'so much villainy lodged so casually on their doorsteps'[9] and, in the early days, when the police were not over-efficient, many prisoners escaped inland, hiding in farm-buildings, threatening the population. In March 1786, Londoners petitioned against the dangers of the hulks. The same year, a mutiny at Portsmouth was violently repressed: eight convicts were shot dead on that occasion. Transportation seemed the only answer. A new place had to be found and in August 1786 the government 'fixed on New South Wales'.[10]

'Government motives for the establishment of Botany Bay', writes A. G. L. Shaw, 'are not easy to determine. Neither Cook nor Banks had spoken well of New South Wales in their *Journals*. It seemed so much out of the world and track of commerce that it could never answer'.[11] Joseph Banks said that, seen from a distance, the island continent looked like 'the back of a lean Cow'[12] and Samuel Sidney, writing in 1850, reported that a voyager first reaching Port Jackson found it 'an iron-bound coast, dark, desolate, barren ... an uninhabitable land, the dwelling-place of demons'.[13] A fit place for creatures of damnation it must have seemed in the eyes of those whose sole wish was to get rid of the undesirable: 'good riddance to bad rubbish expressed in legal terms',[14] as Coral Lansbury puts it. It was above all a faraway place from which those who went were unlikely to return; the voyage took a full year ('I've been sea-tossed and sea-washed months and months', Magwitch says, xxxix, 339), and even though, contrary to expectations, 'ex-convicts reappeared in London',[15] the majority never set foot on British soil again. Many were lost track of, many were given up for dead, and the convict became a legendary figure; the returned convict was often pictured as a ghost, whose image haunted the imagination of the people and inspired that of poets and novelists.

Bentham at once exposed the system as a sign of governmental irresponsibility:

I sentence you, but to what I know not; perhaps to storm and shipwreck, perhaps to infectious disorders, perhaps to famine, perhaps to be massacred by savages, perhaps to be devoured by wild beasts. Away – take your chance; perish or prosper, suffer or enjoy; I rid myself of the sight of you.[16]

It goes without saying that Bentham was prophetic. Many died on the voyage out or on arriving at the colony, owing to the rough living conditions, bad food, ill-treatment, flogging, pillorying, accidents, fevers, lack of medical attendance. But some were given a chance of starting afresh: the well-behaved were, after a time, assigned to private service and became shepherds or cowherds and some did not do too badly. Besides, since there were few free settlers in this inhospitable country, and since there was much land to clear for cultivation, the British government, as early as 1790, instructed the governors to grant land to expirees in order to encourage emancipist farming and prevent too many returns. The practice went on well into the next century and began to decrease after 1817 because of the growing scarcity of 'disposable'[17] land. After 1821, land was sold and grants ended.

Shaw insists that 'we should not underestimate the difficulties' emancipist farmers had to face: the convicts were mostly Londoners and 'few' therefore 'were farmers by training'; they had furthermore to 'compete against officer-farmers who had received land grants in 1793 and who were more efficient, better equipped and more adept at obtaining convict service'.[18] But, by the turn of the century, the emancipist settlers were doing better and some succeeded in accumulating capital. So much so that, hearing the stories, often exaggerated, of their successful fellows in the Antipodes, some of those who had stayed in the hulks (before 1818, 'less than a third were actually sent away')[19] behaved badly to get dispatched to the colony. Hearing similar stories, righteous citizens were shocked that huge fortunes were made in the Bush and began to fear that, instead of acting as a deterrent, transportation would soon become a means of getting on in life and should therefore encourage crime: 'the ancient avocation of picking pockets will certainly not become more discredited from the knowledge that it may eventually lead to the possession of a farm of a thousand acres on the River Hawkesbury',[20] wrote Sydney Smith in 1798. Smith is also reported to have declared to the Home Secretary that, 'translated into commonsense', a sentence to transportation to Botany Bay meant this:

> Because you have committed this offence, the sentence of the court is that you shall no longer be burdened with the support of your wife and family. You shall be immediately removed from a very bad climate and a country overburdened with people to one of the finest regions of the earth where demand for human labour is every hour increasing and where it is highly probable you may ultimately regain your character and improve your future.[21]

Smith's figures were grossly inflated, since each expiree was granted only 30 acres (plus 20 for his wife and 10 for each living child), not 1,000. Not very many, anyway, could benefit by such privileges during the first years of the century. During the Napoleonic wars, convict labour was needed at home and few prisoners, and in any case only lifers, left the country: the hulks overflowed with men. But, with increasing post-war criminality and also because workers objected to convicts as competitors on the labour market when wages were low and employment scarce, transportation was resumed at a growing rate from 1811 onwards, peaking in the 1820s.

This period corresponds roughly to Magwitch's transportation. There is, as has been shown, a margin of uncertainty concerning the dating of Dickens's story: '1807–10 to 1823–26' according to Mary Edminson's reckoning, 1804–1807 to 1820–1823 according to mine;[22] if we consider December 1807 as a likely date for the first scene on the marshes, Magwitch could not have reached Botany Bay before the end of 1809 at the very earliest: we must allow enough time for him to have been 'tried again for prison breaking, and got made a Lifer' (xxviii, 251) and then for being transported to the colony. It could not have taken place much later either if he was to get his sentence remitted and to make his fortune before Pip was eighteen: there is only a lapse of eleven years between chapter 5, when Magwitch is recaptured, and Jagger's visit to the forge in chapter 18.

Had he been a man of flesh and blood, and not *un être de papier*, Magwitch would have been placed in penal servitude when Governor Macquarie was in office, or just before his arrival, and much of their time in New South Wales would have overlapped since Macquarie was in charge of the colony between 1810 and 1820. The new governor had come to replace Governor Bligh, against whom convicts had rebelled. Unlike his predecessor, he was an enlightened man, eager to improve and rehabilitate those 'creatures of neglect'[23] placed under his care and, in his own words, to see them restored 'to the rank in Society which [they] had forfeited'.[24] By granting them land, but also by granting them pardons and indulgences, by trusting them and not inquiring into their past, he hoped he would help them make a fresh start. Historians are not agreed as to whether he was successful or not. Shaw reports that, 'according to Macquarie, many convicts were "reclaimed" by transportation' and he further specifies that between 1810 and 1820 'only 389 convicts left New South Wales',[25] that is, only 10 per cent of those who were free to go. Christopher Hibbert, on the contrary, considers the enterprise to have been a complete failure:

> He hoped that grants of land to convicts when their years of enforced labour had expired would make them good and ambitious citizens; but he was to be disappointed. The convicts preferred to sell their newly-acquired land and go back to the towns they had helped to build so that they could spend their money on women and drink, or to go home to England. His hope that if convicts were given posts of responsibility when they were freed, they would become reliable, was also to be unrealized. Few convicts, after the treatment they had received, proved worthy of the opportunities granted them.[26]

Governor Macquarie may well have met disappointment, but his was an interesting pioneering experiment in penal methods. Much ahead of his time, often criticized for his leniency, even by the English Government which had deputed him overseas, he acted as a 'gentle man', bent on civilizing violence out of the poor wretches who were entrusted to his care, treating them like men so that they should behave like men, which was not often the case with minor offenders who had remained in the English gaols and hulks.

It is nowhere suggested in Dickens's novel that Magwitch benefited by any grant of land, whereas it is made clear that, although a 'Lifer', he was emancipated. After telling Pip about his experience as a 'hired-out shepherd in a solitary hut', which seems to have lasted long enough for him to have 'half forgot wot men's and women's faces wos like' (xxxix, 337), he goes on to say: 'From that there hut and that there hiring-out, I got money left me by my master (which died, and had been the same as me), and got my liberty and went for myself' (xxxix, 338–9). It is noteworthy that Dickens makes him the beneficiary of an emancipist farmer who himself might have been granted land by the authorities in the days when there was plenty, so that his fortune – before it is passed on to Pip, and then, ironically, to the Crown – appears as one of the links of a great chain of human solidarity.

England, in the meantime, was still in the dark ages of repression and, even as late as the 1820s, which is the period of Magwitch's return, prejudices were equally strong against the hulks' population and Australian outcasts. But, in the second quarter of the century, heralded by the Prison Act of 1823, a new era was to begin, leading to the Act of Penal Servitude of 1855, with, in between, the Reform Bill of 1832, the Prison Acts of 1835 and 1839, and the condemnation of the hulks in 1837, as major landmarks of progress in penal and civil reform. England was entering an age of greater leniency, greater democracy and greater tolerance. And it was only when charity began at home that the whole issue of transportation and emigration could be envisaged dispassionately.

Unemployment was a crucial problem throughout the century and, with Australia, a new country to exploit, emigration was an obvious answer to the problem. Prevention being better than cure, it gradually asserted itself as a solution much preferable to the transportation of rick-burners, machine-breakers, Chartist rioters or men driven to theft or murder by starvation. It was better for the mother country to send emigrants than criminals to its distant colony. But this required education and propaganda as well as financial help for the poorest who did not 'travel at His' or, as it came to be, Her 'Majesty's Expense'.[27] In 1826, the Emigration Committee was founded to encourage and help the departure of free citizens willing to try their luck, and the most adventurous began to trickle out of England. But it was not until the colonies objected to being mere receptacles for the undesirable and stopped receiving their annual shiploads of prisoners that the great exodus began.

By mid-century, vigorous campaigning was carried out in the press, and Dickens's own *Household Words* played no minor part in promoting emigration projects, especially for working-class settlers. Before launching his journal, Dickens had mentioned to Miss Burdett-Coutts his intention of 'doing something useful, in the Periodical, on the subject of emigration',[28] and in the first number (30 March 1850) he personally contributed an article, 'A bundle of emigrants' letters', in which he gave publicity to Caroline Chisholm's newly founded 'Family Colonization Loan Society' and explained its purpose and advantages. In the article, he quoted, with her permission, six letters addressed to Mrs Chisholm by poor people who had emigrated to Australia and wrote to the effect that emigration meant no less for them than 'the end of starvation'.[29]

Samuel Sidney was the most influential and regular *Household Words* contributor on Australian matters. He had never been to

Australia himself, but his brother John, who lived there, supplied him with material and personal observations. Together, the bushman and the writer had published the very popular *Sidney's Australian Handbook* (1848) and, in 1847, Samuel had lent his pen to John for the publication of *A Voice from the Far Interior of Australia. By a Bushman.*[30]

Some of Sidney's *Household Words* articles were documentary items, offering information on such matters as life in the bush, the Australian climate, the gold mines or the history of the colony, and providing practical advice to those who wanted to go, such as 'What to take to Australia' or what to expect from the Family Colonization Loan Society. Others, which were later incorporated into *Gallops and Gossips in the Bush of Australia* (1854) and dedicated to Dickens, were homiletic tales of successful emigrants and reclaimed convicts. Clearly, their author was desirous to fight off deep-rooted prejudices which might hold back the fearful or the righteous, by presenting convicts in a new light: they were made to appear as the helpless victims of oppression and brutalization, 'wretched of the earth', 'pris'ners of starvation'.[31]

'An Australian ploughman's story', which was the first of the series (6 April 1850), is considered by Coral Lansbury to have had for its hero 'the origin of the "romantic convict" in English literature – not the Botany Bay pickpocket – but an honest man driven by hunger to crime'.[32] It tells the story of one Jem Carden, a poor country labourer who, in hard times, gets transported for rioting and machine-breaking; once in the settlement, he has to face new difficulties, but is ultimately helped out of despair and corruption by an agent working for some emigration society, who succeeds in bringing his family to Australia at long last; he thereafter becomes again the honest and industrious man he had been in earlier life and, when his benefactor last sees him, he is a prosperous farmer, anxious to have his never-too-late-to-mend message delivered to those who have stayed at home or were not fortunate enough to be transported: 'tell the wretched and the starving', he says, 'how honest, *sober* labour is sure of a full reward here. Tell them that here poverty may be turned to competence, crime to repentance and happiness'.[33]

'Crime' and 'poverty' were insistently shown by Sidney to be social rather than personal evils, and convicts and emigrants were made to appear as one brotherhood of social outcasts. 'Christmas

Day in the Bush' (21 December 1850) ends on its central character, Mr Paige, an emigrant, declaring to young visitors: 'Eight years ago, I left Devon a beggar and an outcast. But now, thanks be to the Lord, I know all was for the best'.[34]

But even more characteristic is 'Two scenes in the life of John Bodger' (15 February 1851). Bodger, a former freeholder, has been ruined by Joseph Lobbit, 'farmer, miller, and chairman of the vestry of the rich rural parish of Duxmoor', and has ended up in the workhouse where he stays until he decides to emigrate to Australia, where he prospers. Ten years later, Lobbit's own son, a good-for-nothing who has jeopardized his father's property, leaves England for the colony; but he drinks himself to death during the crossing, while his wife dies on arriving; and good John Bodger, who happens to be there, rescues their orphan baby girl: 'In my mind's eye', concludes the narrator, 'there are sometimes two pictures. John Bodger in the workhouse, thinking of murder and fire-raising in the presence of his prosperous enemy; and John Bodger, in his happy bush home, nursing little Nancy Lobbit'.[35] The dual image of Bodger shows the deserving emigrant pauper as a criminal-who-might-have-been. He has emigrated; he might have been transported. In any case, he was, or would have been, a victim of society, and his predicament had to be blamed on the system.

But whereas England had only Newgate, the gallows and the hulks to offer to her criminals and 'Poor-Law Bastilles' to her starving paupers, Australia gave a new and an equal chance to the self-banished and the cast away and helped all those who helped themselves. In *The Caxtons* (1849), a novel partly written under the influence of Sidney's *Handbook* to which it often refers, Edward Bulwer Lytton, in one of his typical outbursts of lyricism, apostrophizes Australia as 'Canaan of the exiles, and Ararat to many a shattered Ark!':[36] Dickens must have agreed that the Arks which sailed to the new country were the bearers of more blissful prospects and expectations than the 'wicked Noah's Ark[s]' hopelessly 'Cribbed and barred and moored by massive rusty chains' (v, 71) to the British shores. Those whom he sent there (Martha and little Emily, in 1850) fared better than those whom he left in the English gaols. Magwitch himself, had he not decided to return to England, would have ended his days in prosperity.

Sidney's stories of redemption and promotion all tended to illustrate the unprejudiced, egalitarian hospitality of a country which, like Governor Macquarie, was less concerned with the past of its settlers than with their future and where suffering and industry acted as both moral and social levellers: thus, the convict plough-man,·no matter what he had done, was said, once redeemed, to be 'growing rich, as *all* such industrious people do in Australia'.[37]

Life in the bush also abolished social distinctions: 'Now, living in the Bush', Sidney writes in 'An Australian ploughman's story', 'and especially while travelling, there is not the same distance between a master and a well-behaved man, although a prisoner, as in towns'.[38] Birth no longer made the man or the gentleman: the stress was on the self-help values of the new colonial period, when a minority of rich aristocratic squatters no longer lorded it over their herds of hired, contemptible slaves. Under the circumstances, the notion of 'gentility' had to be reconsidered and, as a matter of fact, 'gentleman', 'gentlemanly', 'genteel' were often used with deroga-tory connotations: 'he became really rich; but instead of turning "*gentleman*", after the vulgar colonial fashion ... he had pursued his plain Yeoman style of life',[39] wrote the narrator of 'Father Gabriel', whose hero also congratulated himself on having remained a simple country labourer: 'The Lord be thanked, my father never made a gentleman of me; I took my turn at all farming work, from driving to ploughing, from cutting and plashing hedges to building a wheat-stack'.[40] And in the Christmas number of *Household Words* for 1851, Charles Barnard, another of Sidney's emigrant heroes, returning home after years in Australia, explained how in the colony he had been cured of his genteel ideals: 'the leading principles I had imbibed, were to the effect, that work of any kind was low, and that debts were gentlemanly ... I began to perceive that work was the only means of getting on in a colony ... My fashionable affectations died away; my life became a *reality*, dependent on my own exertions.'[41]

Ironically, the long-despised penal colony had a lesson in democ-racy and true gentlemanliness to give to the mother country; trans-lated into Bulwer Lytton's hyperbolic language, it went: '*De-fine-gentlemanise* yourself from the crown of your head to the sole of your foot, and become the greater aristocrat for so doing.'[42] But England lagged behind in the process of 'de-fine-gentlemanisation' and, a decade after young Pisistratus Caxton had heard this advice, it was still possible for another fictitious young man to dream of emigrating to Australia as to an ideal country with a classless society: 'I will make my own way in the world, somehow. I will go to Australia; yes, sir, that will be best. I and Mary will both go. Nobody will care about her birth there', says Frank Gresham in Trollope's *Doctor Thorne* (1858).[43]

Thus, Sidney's *Handbook* and *Household Words* pieces much contributed to publicizing the democratic character of the colony and, indirectly, to awakening the political consciousness of his English readers. Written in plain English, presented as real-life anecdotes about ordinary men, these stories were to give credibility to works of fiction which they inspired or for which they paved the way. The most outstanding of Sidney's epigones after Bulwer Lytton was Charles Reade, whose *It is Never too Late to Mend* told 'in long and tedious strains'[44] how a young thief 'turned into a fiend by cruelty'[45] in the English gaols could be turned back into a man by transportation to the penal colony. After serving his time, Tom Robinson, the hero, returns to England, but finds his mother country rather inhospitable and decides to emigrate back to Australia where he becomes successful, 'respected... sober, industrious, pushing, and punctilious in business'.[46] But the crowning anecdote is when, towards the end of the novel, he becomes the employer of his former Sydney master, a spendthrift, dissolute man who, having now 'risen to be [Tom's] servant', proves a worthy 'gentleman', at once 'civil and respectful'.[47]

Paradoxically, 'the idea of the gentleman' in the nineteenth century was intimately linked to 'the idea of the convict'. The promotion of the latter helped the betterment of the former. The Australian gentleman was an improvement on the English gentleman, just as the Australian convict was an improvement on the Newgate prisoner; and in those days, when novels were turning into edifying stories, the 'romantic convict' was rapidly superseding the genteel-looking 'aristocrat of crime' of the Newgate novels so fashionable in the 1840s. It is in fact of some significance that the author of *Paul Clifford* and *Eugene Aram* now wrote *The Caxtons*. Gay's *The Beggar's Opera* (1728) ended with the Beggar's speech to the audience, by way of epilogue:

'Through the whole piece you may observe such a similitude of manners in high and low life, that it is difficult to determine whether (in the fashionable vices) the fine gentlemen imitate the gentlemen of the road, or the gentlemen of the road the fine gentlemen.'[48]

Now, some novelists bent on moralizing and Christianizing the idea of the gentleman and the idea of the convict were writing novels to the effect that, 'in the fashionable virtues', it was difficult to determine whether the de-fine-gentlemanised men imitated the redeemed convicts or the redeemed convicts the de-fine-gentlemanised men!

Thus publicized by works of fiction, Australia, when Dickens wrote *Great Expectations*, had entered popular mythology as a place where Magwitches could rub shoulders with Peggottys and Micawbers. But it does not follow, as Coral Lansbury seems to suggest, that Pip should have contemplated emigrating there if he had not been such a snob: '*Great Expectations* is Dickens's vanity fair of social aspirations and status', she writes. 'Pip does not, even in his despair, consider going to Australia.'[49] But how could he? Had Dickens sent him to build his fortune afresh in the very land where Magwitch had slaved away inefficiently for him, the outcome of his fable would have been more cynical than truly edifying. The novel, besides, is set at a period when going East was more probable and when Australia was still the place where to send a Charley Bates or an Alice Marwood. Another time, another plot. *Great Expectations* was published ten years after *David Copperfield*, but the historical perspective chosen did not allow the same plot opportunities and Dickens's contemporary readers would be all the more able to appreciate the novelist's intentions for having read the earlier novel.

NOTES: CHAPTER 7

1   Robin Gilmour, *The Idea of the Gentleman in the Victorian Novel* (London: Allen & Unwin, 1981), p. 129; see above, ch. 6, 'Perspectives', p. 64.
2   Charles Bateson, *The Convict Ships* (Glasgow: Brown, Son & Ferguson, 1959), p. 7.
3   See Coral Lansbury, *Arcady in Australia* (Melbourne University Press, 1970), p. 28: 'In *George Cruikshank's Omnibus*, Van Diemen's Land became *Van Demon's Land*'.
4   Lansbury, op. cit., p. 10.
5   W. Branch-Johnson, *The English Prison Hulks* (London: Christopher Johnson, 1957), p. 2.
6   ibid., pp. 3–4.
7   ibid., p. 27.
8   A. G. L. Shaw, *Convicts and the Colonies* (London: Faber & Faber, 1971), p. 44.
9   Lansbury, op. cit., p. 8.
10 Shaw, op. cit., p. 48.
11 ibid., p. 53.
12 Quoted by Lansbury, op. cit., p. 4.

13 Samuel Sidney, 'Land Ho! – Port Jackson', *Household Words*, 14 December 1850, vol. 2, p. 276.

14 Lansbury, op. cit., p. 10.

15 L. L. Robson, *The Convict Settlers of Australia* (Melbourne University Press, 1965), p. 111.

16 Bentham, *Penal Law*, bk v, ch. 2 (1791), quoted by Shaw, op. cit., p. 57.

17 Shaw, op. cit., p. 96.

18 ibid., p. 65–7.

19 ibid., p. 150.

20 Sydney Smith, quoted by Shaw, op. cit., p. 77.

21 Sydney Smith, quoted by Christopher Hibbert, *The Roots of Evil* (London: Weidenfeld & Nicolson, 1963), p. 145.

22 See above, ch. 4, 'Chronology', pp. 37, 38–42.

23 'A visit to Newgate', *Sketches by Boz*, The New Oxford Illustrated Dickens (London: Oxford University Press, 1963), p. 207.

24 See Shaw, op. cit., p. 85.

25 ibid., p. 103.

26 Hibbert, op. cit., p. 143.

27 See Edgar Rosenberg, 'A Preface to *Great Expectations*', *Dickens Studies Annual*, vol. 2 (1972), p. 296: 'transported convicts ... are popularly said to "travel at His Majesty's Expense"'.

28 Edgar Johnson (ed.), *Letters from Charles Dickens to Angella Burdett-Coutts, 1841–1865* (London: Jonathan Cape, 1955), 4 February 1850, p. 164.

29 *Household Words*, vol. 1, pp. 19–24. On C. Chisholm, see Anne Lohrli (comp.), *Household Words: Table of Contents, List of Contributors and their Contributions* (Toronto University Press, 1973), pp. 226–8.

30 On John and Samuel Sidney, see Lohrli, op. cit., p. 428–32.

31 The original version of *L'Internationale* by Eugène Pottier (1871) runs: 'Debout les damnés de la terre/Debout les forçats de la faim'; 'forçats' is more apt since it means 'transported convicts'.

32 Lansbury, op. cit., p. 70.

33 *Household Words*, vol. 1, p. 43.

34 ibid., vol. 2, p. 310.

35 ibid., vol. 2, pp. 484–91.

36 Edward Bulwer-Lytton, *The Caxtons* [1849] (London: Routledge, 1874), part XVIII, ch. 1, p. 475.

37 *Household Words*, vol. 1, p. 43 (my emphasis).

38 ibid., p. 39.

39 ibid., 12 October 1850, vol. 2, p. 67.

40 ibid., 19 October 1850, vol. 2, p. 87.

41 ibid., vol. 4, Christmas number, 'What Christmas is after a long absence', p. 17.

42 Bulwer, *The Caxtons*, op. cit., part XII, ch. 6, p. 328.

43 Anthony Trollope, *Doctor Thorne* [1858] (London: The Zodiac Press, 1950), p. 419.

44 Charles Reade, *It is Never too Late to Mend* [1853] (London and Newcastle: The Walter Scott Publishing Co., undated), ch. 77, p. 467.

45 ibid., ch. 43, p. 297.

46 ibid., ch. 85, p. 508.

47 ibid., pp. 509, 508.

48 John Gay *The Beggar's Opera* [1728] (London: Dent, 1984), III, xvi, p. 158.

49 Lansbury, op. cit., p. 148.

CHAPTER 8

The True Gentleman

When Magwitch reappears in London after long years of exile, England is much the same as when he left it, blindly intolerant, brutally repressive. Back on his native shores, the redeemed Australian convict is again no better than a British outcast once 'expatriated for the term of his natural life' (xl, 351), unlikely to get a pardon for his 'act of felony', liable, on the contrary, 'to the extreme penalty of the law': 'Death by the rope, in the open street' (xl, 348). He will henceforth get hunted down and ultimately receive the sentence he had expected. The savagery of Newgate, the overburdening atmosphere of Little Britain, the uncompromising malignancy of the legal and penal world, have amply prepared us for this unchristian reception of the stray sheep into the fold.

Pip's reaction at the sight of the ghostly sea-voyager is in true conformity with the spirit of the age. To be sure, it never occurs to him to hand the criminal over to the legal authorities and he will do his utmost to prevent the man's arrest, but the 'pitying young fancy' (v, 64) which had drawn him to his old 'fugitive friend' on the marshes has long since dried up and he now recoils from him as he would from a snake (xxxix, 338); he is repelled by his coarse ways of 'sitting and standing, and eating and drinking' and he loads him 'with all the crimes in the Calendar' (xl, 353) and makes useless attempts at disguising him to obliterate the image of the returned convict:

> The more I dressed him and the better I dressed him, the more he looked like the slouching fugitive on the marshes ... I believe too that he dragged one of his legs as if there were still a weight of iron on it, and that from head to foot there was Convict in the very grain of the man.
>
> The influences of his solitary hut-life were upon him besides, and gave him a savage air that no dress could tame ... In all his ways ... and a thousand other small nameless instances arising

every minute in the day, there was Prisoner, Felon, Bondsman, plain as plain could be (xl, 352–3).

Unable to recognize the man behind the outcast, Pip merely sees a stereotype, as the capitalized words, 'Convict, Prisoner, Felon, Bondsman', clearly show. But his revulsion, which is so often blamed on his snobbery and on his inability to face 'the truth of [his] position' (xxxix, 336), is in fact typical of the period in which the events are supposed to take place and of the class to which he has been raised. Social exclusiveness is neither the prerogative of a young snob nor, for that matter, of 'choleric' gentlemen like the one who, travelling on a coach where convicts had been placed, 'flew into a most violent passion, and said that it was a breach of contract to mix him up with such villainous company, and that it was poisonous and pernicious and infamous and shameful!' (xxviii, 249). Their prejudices are widely shared, as Dickens is careful to show: even gentle Herbert Pocket finds the sight of convicts a 'degraded and vile' one (xxviii, 248) and is radically put off by Pip's strange visitor: 'I saw my own feelings reflected in Herbert's face', Pip says, 'and, not least among them, my repugnance towards the man who had done so much for me' (xli, 355).

Driving past Newgate, Estella had once expressed in one word this universal contempt and aversion: 'Wretches!' she had said (xxxiii, 289). A terrible word, as unknowingly and ironically cruel as Cosette's candid question in Hugo's *Les Misérables*: 'est-ce que ce sont encore des hommes?' Cosette asks Jean Valjean, little suspecting that her adoptive father is a returned convict. 'Quelquefois'[1] is Jean Valjean's laconic answer, an answer that has moved to tears generations of readers. The discovery that 'sometimes' convicts are still men, and even better men than some 'gentlemen', is as much Dickens's message as Hugo's. It is clearly one of the lessons that Pip has to learn during the third part of the book. It is a lesson that late Victorians had already learnt. And many are those in 1861 who, hearing Magwitch go over 'the book of his remembrance' (xlii, 364), must have recognized at once the familiar figure of the 'romantic convict' made popular ten years before by Sidney's and others' tales. Chapter 42 reads like one of those exemplary stories:

'I've been done everything to, pretty well – except hanged. I've been locked up, as much as a silver tea-kettle. I've been carted here and carted there, and put out of this town and put out of that town, and stuck in the stocks, and whipped and worried and drove ... I first become aware of myself, down in Essex, a thieving turnips for my living. Summun had run away from me – a man – a tinker – and he'd took the fire with him, and left me wery cold.

'I know'd my name to be Magwitch, chrisen'd Abel' (xlii, 360).

Everything, including the use of the passive voice, and, of course, the Christian name, proclaims Magwitch a victim, the victim of neglect, poverty and repression, 'driven by hunger to crime',[2] forsaken from childhood, and ever since relentlessly persecuted and prosecuted.

As he goes on with his narrative, Magwitch shifts from the first to the third person pronoun and, through this process of alienation, compels his listeners (or readers) to imagine 'young Abel Magwitch', the little neglected child, how with other treatment, might have turned into another man:

'So fur as I could find, there warn't a soul that see young Abel Magwitch, with as little on him as in him, but wot caught fright at him, and either drove him off, or took him up' (xlii, 361).

Then, back to the first person, he lapses into self-pity but checks himself at once, giving up self-contemplation as an impossibility, a right which his condition has from the start denied him, and, swinging from 'I' to 'he' and further alienating himself into '*this* boy' or '*a* hardened *one*' by quoting what 'they' said of '*him*' (my emphasis), he works up our feelings to a climax of commiseration and indignation:

'I was took up, took up, took up, to that extent that I reg'larly grow'd up took up.

'This is the way it was, that when I was a ragged little creetur as much to be pitied as ever I see (not that I looked in the glass, for there warn't many insides of furnished houses known to me), I got the name of being hardened. "This is a terrible hardened one," they says to prison wisitors, picking out me. "May be said to live in jails, this boy." Then they looked at me, and I looked at them, and they measured my head, some on 'em – they had better a measured my stomach – and others on 'em giv me tracts what I

couldn't read, and made me speeches what I couldn't unnerstand'
(xlii, 361).

The oblique indictment of phrenologists, prison visitors, evangeli-
cals, and 'gabblers of many little dog's-eared creeds',[3] the plea for
social solidarity and responsibility, the appeal to sympathy and
understanding, which might bring a blush to the cheeks of many
'Right Reverends and Wrong Reverends'[4] and a tear in the eyes of
some Dickens readers in recollection of Jo and other ill-used children always told to 'get a move on', are equally unsuccessful in
awakening Pip's sense of social injustice or in getting the better of
his aversion: 'He regarded me with a look of affection that made
him almost abhorrent to me again, though I had felt great pity for
him', he says (xlii, 366). His ingrained prejudices are more powerful
than the subtle rhetoric of pathos whose effects do not outlast the
act of enunciation, stronger even than his natural inclinations. The
words labelled on his visitor stick to him mercilessly, 'Convict,
Prisoner, Felon, Bondsman'.

But the mistake is humiliatingly, though unwillingly, reciprocated:
'and this is the gentleman what I made', Magwitch exclaims
triumphantly, sticking his own label like a trade-mark on the
packed product, 'The real genuine One!' (xl, 346). In the expression of his admiration and of his self-satisfaction as gentleman-
maker, there are two words too many and the 'real genuineness' of
Pip's gentility is shattered even as it is asserted. For the second time in
the novel, and through the same voice, the idea that 'gentility' (or
'gentlemanliness'?) might be unauthentic is explicitly stated, dramatically, urgently raising the question that had always been there,
surreptitiously underlying the whole book, yet always brushed
aside, ignored or circumvented: 'What is a gentleman?'
      The puzzled reader in this extremity may turn to his dictionary
and will get something like this by way of an answer:

1   A man of gentle birth (entitled to bear arms).
2   A man of gentle birth attached to the household of a sovereign,
    1463.
3   A man of chivalrous instincts and fine feelings (Middle English).
4   A man of superior position in society: often, a man of money and
    leisure.

In recent use: a courteous synonym for a man, 1583.
In plural, a polite term of address without reference to rank, 1579.
In legal documents, a person who has no occupation, 1862.

'Now, you know what a gentleman is', Mr Gradgrind would say.
But who else would dare?

Broadly speaking, the history of the word follows the chronology
of the *Oxford English Dictionary* and some specific meanings –
'entitled to bear arms', 'attached to the household of a sovereign',
'chivalrous' – neatly fell into disuse over the centuries, but none of its
fundamental attributes was ever definitely superseded by new ones.
The evolution of the word is a process of accretion, of grafting rather
than pruning. Even the original sense, 'a man of gentle birth', was
never eradicated by the modern 'polite term of address without reference to rank'; if it had been, the word itself would have become obso-
lete as did the French *gentilhomme* from which it was originally
derived and which, Tocqueville reminds us, 'dropped out of common
use' after the Revolution. But the perenniality of the English term
'gentleman', the history of which, says Tocqueville, is 'the history of
democracy itself',[5] rests on much compromise and is the source of
many ambiguities and ironies. Satellite terms gravitating round it,
'genteel, gentlemanly gentility, gentleness, gentlemanliness', sometimes prevent misunderstandings. In their absence the word to this
day remains polysemous, requiring constant revaluations.

Numerous attempts were made during the Victorian period to
redefine and modernize the concept. In the middle of the century,
'from roughly 1840 to around 1880' according to Robin Gilmour,
'the nature of gentlemanliness was more anxiously debated and
more variously defined than at any time before or since'.[6]

Predominant among the voices heard (Ruskin's, Trollope's, Mere-
dith's, Dr Arnold's), was that of Samuel Smiles, whose popular
Self-Help came out just a year before *Great Expectations* began to
be serialized. The main bulk of the book actually did little more
than propagandize in plain English the Gospel of Work and the
meritocratic philosophy of society that Carlyle had expounded thirteen years earlier in *Past and Present*. 'The duty of work is written
on the thews and muscles of the limbs, the mechanism of the hand,
the nerves and lobes of the brain – the sum of whose healthy action
is satisfaction and enjoyment', Smiles wrote, insisting that 'pains-
taking labour' and 'steady application to work'[7] were the surest

way to success and respectability, surer even, he argued, than either wealth or rank or exceptional gifts that remained uncultivated.

The book was conceived as a practical guide to success and Smiles illustrated his message with exemplary biographies: aristocrats of talent, famous inventors, captains of industry, men of many callings who owed their rise in society solely to their personal merit and unflinching industry were briefly introduced and portrayed, offering a huge range of models to go by. Whoever wished to succeed in life had only to take example from one of them: it was a mere matter of will-power, resolution and 'untiring perseverance'.[8]

Had it ended with chapter 12, however, the book, though quite representative of mid-Victorian beliefs and aspirations, could hardly be quoted for its relevance to the idea of the gentleman in the nineteenth century. Admirable as they are said to be, Smiles's illustrious models are nowhere referred to as 'gentlemen'. They are all 'great men', 'great names', 'great inventors', 'great leaders of industry' and when the word 'gentleman' occurs in the text, it is used indifferently and, one would think, almost inadvertently. Only in the last chapter does it make its real and, to be sure, spectacular entrance: given pride of place in the title, 'Character: The True Gentleman', it becomes the key-word of the concluding pages.

Those pages, it should be noted, are slightly different in mood and purport from the preceding chapters, less utilitarian, less meritocratic. The stress is no longer primarily on success and achievements or on acquired rank, wealth or celebrity, and the concept of gentlemanliness clearly supersedes that of gentility. The 'true gentleman' is depicted as someone who is respected, recognized and admired by all, regardless of his station: 'It is a grand old name, that of Gentleman, and has been recognized as a rank and power in all stages of society.'[9]

Courageous, self-sacrificing, generous, noble-minded, the gentleman described in these pages is not necessarily cut out to become a leader of men or a moneyed businessman and may well be, and remain for life, a poor and obscure citizen: 'Riches and rank have no necessary connexion with genuine gentlemanly qualities. The poor man may be a true gentleman – in spirit and in daily life. He may be honest, truthful, upright, polite, temperate, courageous, self-respecting, and self-helping – that is, be a true gentleman.'[10] Moral excellence rather than social or pragmatic accomplishments is the criterion by which to recognize the true gentleman, to tell 'the genuine article' from the 'many counterfeits',[11] and 'Gentleness', Smiles concludes, 'is indeed the best test of gentlemanliness'.[12] Thus redefined, the 'grand old name of Gentleman' may be applied with equal propriety to a Joe Gargery, a Robert Peel, a Josiah Wedgwood or a Professor Owen.

Smiles's formula was not in itself revolutionary. Gentleness throughout the centuries had been one of the constituents of gentlemanliness, especially during the Christian medieval ages, when the concept was highly moralized. And even during the not particularly chivalrous days of Lord Chesterfield, qualities of the heart were often listed as the necessary attributes of 'The Complete Gentleman': 'When I think of the Heart of a Gentleman', Steele declared in *The Guardian*, 'I imagine it firm and intrepid, void of all inordinate Passions, and full of Tenderness, Compassion and Benevolence'.[13] But Steele, like his contemporaries, had not 'de-fine-gentlemanized' his ideal gentleman: 'by a Fine Gentleman I mean a Man compleatly qualified as well for the Service and Good, as for the Ornament and Delight of Society', he wrote in the same essay; whereas, for Smiles, the moralization of the concept went in step with its democratization.

Smiles's concern was not so much the individual as the group, or rather the group as a sum of individuals, and his ultimate aim was to energize the industrial society of his age and promote the common people in spite of itself, for its own good and for the good of the nation. With its twofold message, his book was doubly gratifying and alluring as a double incentive to industry and dynamism: it assured the poor man on the one hand that virtue was its own reward, and on the other that success was within his reach. The plebeian image of the gentleman that it advertised as a possible version of a universal concept had an immediate appeal for the common man, though the success stories that it related remained its greatest attraction. Not surprisingly, the book rapidly became the creed of a class: selling no less than 25,000 copies in the first year, it went through countless reprintings during its author's lifetime. 'There are few books in history', notes Asa Briggs, 'which have reflected the spirit of their age more faithfully and successfully than Smiles's *Self-Help*'.[14]

But the spirit of an age is never entirely free from the spirit of previous ages: prejudices linger, old and new concepts overlap and intermingle, new ambiguities arise, causing new misunderstandings and new perplexities. In an age when so much emphasis was put on industry and self-reliance, work, the newly promoted value, and birth, the newly discarded one, were the two most crucial issues.

'The very social forces which were bringing new groups knocking on the door of gentility', explains Gilmour, 'were rendering problematic the qualifications on which they could be admitted' and, for many social and professional groups, 'the rank of gentleman, though theoretically open, was put effectively out of reach by the abiding separation of work and income on which the social exclusiveness of the traditional gentleman was based'.[15] What trades or professions were compatible with a genteel station was a very puzzling dilemma throughout the Victorian period, and subtle discriminations were made between the occupations you could pursue without demeaning yourself and those you could not for a moment consider entering upon. The question is humorously expounded in *Great Expectations* by Herbert Pocket when, although supposedly speaking in the 1820s, he expresses truths that still held forty years later and hold to this very day:

> 'Her father was a country gentleman down in your part of the world, and was a brewer. I don't know why it should be a crack thing to be a brewer; but it is indisputable that while you cannot possibly be genteel and bake, you may be as genteel as never was and brew. You see it every day.'
>
> 'Yet a gentleman may not keep a public-house; may he?' said I.
>
> 'Not on any account,' returned Herbert; 'but a public-house may keep a gentleman' (xxii, 203).

Dickens's fable goes even further in demonstrating that, 'indisputably', while you cannot possibly be genteel and forge if you are a blacksmith, you may be as genteel as never was and forge if you are a counterfeiter. The Hulks may have its gentleman, but the Forge may not, even though the ungenteel 'forger' may be required in the name of the law to hammer manacles for the genteel one.

In *Great Expectations*, gentlemanliness and gentility remain hopelessly at variance and Joe's noble figure is the perfect illustration of this discordance. Upright, truthful, generous, industrious, 'proud' (remembering, of course, that 'there are many kinds of pride', xix, 175), gentle, 'in his combination of strength with gentleness' (xviii, 168), Joe, although not 'genteelly brought up' (viii, 92), is of all the characters in the novel the one who best qualifies for the name of 'true gentleman' after the Smilesian and Dickensian ideal. Often the word 'gentleman' is used in close proximity to eulogistic remarks on his worthiness, but applied to someone else and strongly suggestive of misapplication: 'I hope', Biddy writes to Pip, 'and do not doubt it will be agreeable to see him even though a gentleman, for you had ever a good heart, and he is a worthy worthy man' (xxvii, 240). Readers understand that if someone deserves the name, Joe is that man, but they also realize that he may be called a 'gentleman' only metaphorically, between inverted commas, and Dickens, in his awareness of the fact, cleverly chooses never to call him that in order to avoid ambiguities and improprieties. But he pays him much greater homage by splitting the word in two and retaining only the ethical implications of its components or, in Gilmour's words, separating the word 'gentleman' 'into its classless elements'[16] to express the gentleness and the manliness of the 'Man' (xxxv, 301) Joe is: 'O God bless him! O God bless this gentle Christian man!' (lvii, 472), says Pip in truly Dickensian admiration.

The prestige of birth, which in pre-industrial England had been a token, possibly a factor, of social stability, strangely outlived the economic and social upheavals that took place in the late eighteenth and early nineteenth centuries. The parvenu, so dear to Samuel Smiles, did not as a rule like to be reminded of his humble origins and rarely boasted of his hard beginnings, though he might have looked back on them with legitimate pride. As things were, the Veneerings far outnumbered the Bounderbys: family crests were unearthed, 'crusading ancestors' found out, and forests of family trees sprang up on the social map. It was difficult, besides, for the second-generation businessman or mill-owner who was already a gentleman's son, whatever that meant, to resist 'the lure of social ideals older than capitalism';[17] but 'the attractions of a graceful and effortless country gentlemen's society'[18] threatened to foster idleness in the workshop of the world. The preachers of the new Gospel were alarmed at the danger. Carlyle raved at 'Do-Nothingism' and entreated his 'brethren of the Idle Dilettantism'[19] to reform their ways before it was too late. Smiles warned his readers against the deceptive and nostalgic fascination of rank:

Many barons of proud names and titles have perished, like the sloth, upon their family tree, after eating up all the leaves; while others have been overtaken by adversities which they have been unable to retrieve, and sunk at last into poverty and obscurity. Such are the mutabilities of rank and fortune.[20]

Snobbery, however, was stronger than self-help wisdom: 'In the battle between the self-made man and the gentleman,' writes Asa Briggs, 'the self-made man won in England only if he became a gentleman himself, or tried to turn his son into one'.[21]

Dickens's stand in this debate is less consistent than he would have us believe and, presumably, than he himself believed it to be. Indeed, if we considered only his explicit declarations, we would have no difficulty whatsoever in placing him. He never had, to say the least, much sympathy for gentlemen 'of considerable birth'[22] like the Chesterfieldian Chester of his *Barnaby Rudge* and might even be suspected of having harboured class prejudices against them. His fictional aristocrats as a matter of fact are not very numerous and those few who are allowed into his books clearly belong to the past, half paralysed and mummified as they all are in an anticipation of death, ready like Sir Leicester Dedlock (the name itself is significant) to join their ancestors on the walls of the family portrait galleries and leave there 'coloured shadow[s]'[23] of themselves destined to be 'confusedly identified' by future visitors with 'a glory that was departed',[24] as are the 'renowned Venetians' that so fascinate Frederick Dorrit on his daily visits to the museums. The inaccessible and parasitical Lord Barnacle, 'altogether splendid, massive, over-powering, and impracticable', is himself little more than a *tableau vivant*: 'He seemed to have been sitting for his portrait to Sir Thomas Lawrence all the days of his life',[25] says the narrator of *Little Dorrit*, thus freezing him into his own effigy. And Lord Snigsworth, though still alive, never appears in flesh and blood, but is represented by his portrait showing him 'snorting at a Corinthian column' and 'as somehow in the act of saving his country',[26] a museum-piece already.

'Dandiacal' snobs like Turveydrop (himself the copy of an engraving representing the late Prince Regent),[27] upstarts of the Podsnap or Veneering type (mere reflections in a looking-glass, mere wall-flowers on the Dickens stage) are not treated with much considerateness either. Dickens has no more patience with toadies to the great than with 'bran-new' imitators of gentlemen born and bred, and his pen never spares the worshippers of outdated idols and ideals.

His own 'true gentlemen' on the contrary – David Copperfield, George Rouncewell, Daniel Doyce, Charles Darnay, Allan Woodcourt, to list only the names that first come to mind –, involved as they are in the economic, social and artistic life of their time, are all men who represent the dynamic forces of the new society and whose biographies, success stories all of them, might be anthologized into a new, albeit fictitious, version of *Self-Help*. None of them is left on the fringes of the plots or sent to the museum as are the genteel, inefficient, 'living fossils',[28] and, though they are not necessarily given the leading parts to play, they are all real actors, more active sometimes than the heroes themselves, as is Daniel Doyce in *Little Dorrit*, to whom Arthur Clennam owes his success and salvation and, to some extent, his heroic status.

There is no question but that Dickens's leanings are on the side of meritocracy and that his overt pronouncements are consistently favourable to a modern, dynamic view of society, turned towards the future, not towards the past; and it would be pointless to press the matter further if some latent implications of his stories did not betray some archaic thought-pattern and did not therefore insidiously contradict the manifest discourse of his writings. But, unmistakably, a thread of nostalgia runs through the novels, a wistful longing for some coincidence between birth and merit, an ill-suppressed desire to bring forth the true marriage of essence and existence; and one is tempted, of course, to trace this back to the Dickens of prelapsarian days, the Dickens who 'stopped growing'[29] when his other self embarked on the battle of life.

The biographical approach is, however, as baffling as it is necessary. Anyone acquainted with 'the personal history' of Charles Dickens is bound to read it as a watermark left on the novels and to seek in Dickens the man the ambivalence of Dickens the novelist; but there are no means, in the absence of documents other than the novels themselves, of clearly discriminating between the two. The critic, therefore, is placed in the paradoxical situation of someone who reads the fiction in the light of a reality itself immersed in this very fiction. It is to this difficulty that George Bernard Shaw already pointed in his famous 'Foreword to *Great Expectations*':

For Dickens, in spite of his exuberance, was a deeply reserved
man: the exuberance was imagination and acting ...; and we
shall never know whether in that immensely broadened outlook
and knowledge of the world which began with *Hard Times* and
Little Dorrit, and left all his earlier works behind, he may not
have come to see that making his living by sticking labels on
blacking bottles and rubbing shoulders with boys who were not
gentlemen, was as little shameful as being the genteel apprentice
in the office of Mr. Spenlow ...[30]

We shall never know. On the tiny, and none the less contradictory,
evidence of what he said about himself and what he withheld, we
may even decide with little risk of being wrong, that *he* never knew;
and we may safely endorse the accepted view that, in Gilmour's
words, he was to the last 'divided between the claims of inherited
and acquired status, between the part of himself which wanted to
believe that he was a gentleman's son and the part which took pride
in having overcome Bulwer Lytton's "twin jailers of the daring
heart – Low birth and iron fortune" '.[31]

There is no doubt that the author of *David Copperfield* was
proud of being self-made. Otherwise he would not have felt so much
admiration for a hero whose career imitates his own so closely. But
his pride was his secret, since none of his readers was supposed to
know or was meant ever to be informed that he had put so much of
himself in the book. The now tediously familiar story of the
Warren's Blacking episode did not come out until after his death,
when Forster published his biography in 1872, and no one until
then (Forster excepted) had any suspicion that the successful novelist had started life as a 'labouring hind'.[32] He never 'in any burst of
confidence with any one, [his] own wife not excepted', disclosed
anything about that part of his childhood, as he himself explains at
the end of the fragment.[33]

This pathological reticence (partly prompted, it should be noted,
by the attitude of his parents who themselves were 'stricken
dumb'[34] on leaving the Marshalsea) would seem to indicate that he
was more class-conscious than he might have wished to be. So
would his discretion concerning the fact that his grandparents had
been in domestic service. So would, even more significantly, this
letter written a year before his death, in which, forgetting that he
was the author of the hilarious page on Veneering's 'camel of all

trades', he described his father's crest: 'I beg to inform you that I have never used any other armorial bearings than my father's crest: a lion couchant, bearing in his dexter paw a Maltese cross. I have never adopted any motto, being quite indifferent to such ceremonies.'[35] Critics and biographers have not failed to pick out this document as an instance of his self-division concerning the question of birth: '(The movement of thought here, from the modest assertion of inherited gentility – "my father's crest" – to the protested indifference to "such ceremonies", is of course characteristically ambivalent, simultaneously claiming the status and dissociating himself from those who take it too seriously)', comments Robin Gilmour in a brilliant parenthesis.[36]

Another text on which biographers inevitably pounce is that passage in the fragment where Dickens explains how at Warren's he was treated 'on a different footing' from the other employees: 'Though perfectly familiar with them', he says of the boys, 'my conduct and manners were different enough from theirs to place a space between us. They, and the men, always spoke of me as "the young gentleman" '.[37]

The word 'gentleman' in this context actually sounds rather ambiguous, something half-way between a nickname and a title, though Charles seems to have favoured the second interpretation and accepted this form of address as his due: 'Poll Green uprose once, and rebelled against the "young-gentleman" usage; but Bob Fagin settled him speedily',[38] he relates, clearly approving of Bob's intervention.

The son of a clerk, the grandson of a steward, although he did not belong to the lower orders, Dickens was no gentleman by birth and knew very well that he had no right to the name; but he clung to it none the less, even after twenty years. He had to, of course, if he wished to report verbatim on the events and to place himself with some accuracy on the social scale in relation to his workmates. But there also emerges from the fragment a sense of superiority that has nothing to do with class distinctions, a claim for what might be termed 'natural gentility', a form of Rousseauism implying the right to be 'recognized' on purely personal grounds, singled out from the common herd for his personal merit. This 'natural gentility', unfortunately, had passed unnoticed in the family circle. Of his being prematurely snatched away from school and sent to work he writes:

It is wonderful to me how I could have been so easily cast away at such an age. It is wonderful to me that, even after my descent into the poor little drudge I had been since we came to London, no one had compassion enough on me – a child of singular abilities: quick, eager, delicate, and soon hurt, bodily or mentally – to suggest that something might have been spared, as certainly it might have been, to place me at any common school. Our friends, I take it, were tired out. No one made any sign. My father and mother were quite satisfied. They could hardly have been more so, if I had been twenty years of age, distinguished at a grammar-school, and going to Cambridge.[39]

Discussing his social comedown, Steven Marcus compares him to a 'young prince' who 'suddenly discovers that he may be the swineherd's son':[40] is he not rather the banished Prince whose legitimacy is at last recognized by the swineherds when they dub him 'gentleman'?

But the child who had early dreamed of being learned and famous could not be so easily satisfied, and nothing short of universal recognition could reinstate him in his primeval 'princely' condition. Significantly, it is not as the son of John Dickens but as Boz the Inimitable that Charles emerged out of anonymity and undeserved obscurity.

Literary success, however, even though it soon encouraged Charles to doff his pen-name and assert himself under his true patronymic, failed to restore real confidence and lasting peace of mind to the man whose sense of identity had been so severely shattered in early life. As much as the ever-renewed conquest of his 'dear' reading-public, novel-writing, judging by the subject-matter of the books, seems to have been for him a form of self-therapy, a means of coming to terms with a past whose shadow was 'dark upon himself',[41] each new novel offering him fresh opportunities to probe 'the substance of the shadow' and vicariously piece his broken self together. Beginning with Oliver Twist's ontological wanderings and ending with John Harmon's, Dickens's novels are all, in Lawrence Frank's terms, stories of 'reconstruction', 'pilgrimages of being'.[42] Over and over again, they relate the same journey from dispersal to unity, from namelessness (or pseudonymity) to regained identity, from homelessness to stability, from accidental or intentional obscurity to recovered gentility, from moral, social, ontological, even bodily[43] fragmentation to integrity.

But *Great Expectations* is different from the other books. It is a construction, not a re-construction novel, in which gentility, which was not there in the first place, cannot be recovered or even expected to be.

Writing this novel, his most in-depth study in personal ambition, probing in a first-person narrative the legitimacy of genteel aspirations in an ungenteel hero, must have been for Dickens an exceptionally maturing experience. The enterprise was courageous, entailing the discomfort of self-reappraisal and the questioning of things established. To aggravate the subversion of this investigation, it is, as we have seen, a convict, and not a gentleman, who raises the question of true gentility. Of course, when he greets him as 'real' and 'genuine', Magwitch has no intention of throwing doubt on the authenticity of his own 'London brought up gentleman', but, like a ventriloquist, he produces two voice-sounds, one, admiring, sincere, self-complacent, his own, the other, cruelly ironic and recognizably the author's, a voice that by now is familiar to the reader as it has made itself heard before through other mouthpieces.

Being two-thirds into the novel, we have in fact acquired a fairly accurate idea of what a true gentleman should be by authorial standards; we might imagine him as some crossbreed between Joe Gargery and Matthew Pocket, 'worthy', 'good faithful tender' (xviii, 168), 'natural' and 'unaffected' (xxiii, 212), 'not time-serving' (xxii, 205) and, above all, 'gentle'.

We have an even clearer notion of what a gentleman worthy of the name should *not* be like on any account, thanks to Herbert's memorable declaration:

'I have heard my father mention that he was a showy-man, and the kind of man for the purpose. But that he was not to be, without ignorance or prejudice, mistaken for a gentleman, my father most strongly asseverates; because it is a principle of his that no man who was not a true gentleman at heart, ever was, since the world began, a true gentleman in manner. He says, no varnish can hide the grain of the wood; and that the more varnish you put on, the more the grain will express itself' (xxii, 204).

The 'showy-man' in question is no other than Compeyson. But Herbert's message is obviously uttered for the benefit of Pip, his interlocutor, who is just embarking on his London apprenticeship as a gentleman when the conversation takes place. And the question we ask ourselves immediately, and which will linger at the back of our minds during the whole novel, is whether Pip will eventually succeed in becoming a 'gentleman at heart'. We are indeed entitled to worry on that issue, for his beginnings as a gentleman have not been very promising and, even before leaving the Forge, he has shown himself far more concerned with manners and social prestige than with matters of the heart. The 'virtuous and superior tone' in which he spoke of 'improving dear Joe' in order to remove him some day 'into a higher sphere', his patronizing attitude, his contempt for his friend's lack of learning and manners, aroused at once Biddy's (and our) suspicion: 'Yet a gentleman should not be unjust neither', she said to him before he went (xix, 175–6). These, significantly, though they are not supposed to have been her parting words, are the last words repeated to us, a warning both for the protagonist and for the reader, who will henceforth be on the look-out for some moral improvement.

Unfortunately, by the time Pip's benefactor returns, we have seen no sign of any such improvement and, if his London training has made him a paradigm of gentility, he is certainly not at this stage a paragon of gentlemanliness: he is not faithful enough, he is not unselfish enough, he is not considerate enough to meet the authorial requirements and qualify so far for a 'real genuine gentleman'.

In his admiration Magwitch, however, is the victim of no delusion. The gentleman he contemplates with the pride of ownership in the Garden-court chambers is every inch the one he had dreamt of in the loneliness of his Australian hut: made to measure by Jaggers according to his instructions, his protégé answers every single one of his expectations. He has manners, power, money, which he can spend '*like* a gentleman' (xl, 347). He has, above all, sartorial elegance and bookish education:

'Look'ee here!' he went on, taking my watch out of my pocket, and turning towards him a ring on my finger, while I recoiled from his touch as if he had been a snake, 'a gold'un and a beauty: *that's* a gentleman's, I hope! A diamond all set round with rubies; *that's* a gentleman's, I hope! Look at your linen; fine and beautiful! Look at your clothes; better ain't to be got! And your books too,' turning his eyes round the room, 'mounting up, on their shelves, by hundreds! And you read 'em; don't you? I see you'd been a reading of 'em when I come in. Ha, ha, ha! You shall read 'em to me, dear boy! And if they're in foreign languages wot I don't understand, I shall be just as proud as if I did' (xxxix, 338).

As gentleman-maker, Magwitch had looked forward to no less and no more than this. Smart clothes and scholarship were given at the outset as the two prerequisites for Pip's genteel promotion: 'It is considered that you must be better educated, in accordance with your altered position, and that you will be alive to the importance and necessity of at once entering on that advantage', Jaggers told Pip immediately after imparting to him the news of his good fortune, and Pip answered that he 'had always longed for it' (xviii, 166). 'First', Jaggers went on explaining, 'you should have some new clothes to come in, and they should not be working clothes (xviii, 167). And Pip had obediently gone on his memorable visit to Trabb's shop whence he had come out 'measured and calculated' (xix, 178) and soon to be dandified and tailor-made, 'resartus' in his genteel clothes.

A man of mode, a man of means, a man of learning, designed for no profession and 'well enough educated' to ' "hold [his] own" with the average of young men in prosperous circumstances' (xxiv, 220), Pip corresponds literally to one of the several and none the less orthodox definitions of the term 'gentleman' itemized in the dictionary: 'A man of superior position in society; often a man of money and leisure'.

But these standards, which Magwitch takes for granted, simply do not happen to tally with those of the novelist. Magwitch, we must remember, is about half a century older than his creator (Dickens gives him to be sixty when he comes back from the penal colony in the 1820s) and it is quite natural that his idea of the gentleman should be old-fashioned, closer to the worldly eighteenth-century or Regency models, which were all he had to go by when he left the old country, than to the ideals of a reforming age the advent of which was still too far ahead to be foreseeable. His protégé is, quite naturally, a typical young dandy after the style of the day, with nothing except his low birth to differentiate him from other young men of fashion like the foppish Finches of the Grove.

'For Magwitch is a snob',[44] Humphry House rightly says. But it is also very pathetic to consider that, in his desire for revenge, the convict should have had no other aim than to reproduce a human type that he ought to abominate and add a new specimen to a race of men who from childhood persecuted him, famished him, imprisoned him, eventually cast him away. This might even backfire on him and it is actually a matter of a hair's breadth if, on first recognizing him, Pip does not send him back to where he has just come from.

Another inevitable and ironic consequence of his revengeful strategy is that what he most admires in his 'dear boy' when he sees him – good looks, good breeding, articulateness – is what he has always most detested in his long-standing enemy whose would-be gentlemanliness is his constant butt:

> 'He set up fur a gentleman, this Compeyson, and he'd been to a public boarding-school and had learning. He was a smooth one to talk, and was a dab at the ways of gentlefolks. He was good-looking too' (xlii, 361)
> '... what a gentleman Compeyson looked, wi' his curly hair and his black clothes and his white pocket-handkercher' (xlii, 364–5).

The moral suspense – What sort of a gentleman will Pip turn out to be? – is henceforth a crucial issue, and all the more so as Magwitch's notion of genuineness hinges precisely on the line he draws, quite arbitrarily, between the gentleman he brought back to the Hulks and the gentleman 'what [he] made' (xl, 346). Whether or not Magwitch will prove to have been his own dupe (and if so, the dupe of society) is for Dickens now to decide.

Not too surprisingly, considering the gentlemanly and often self-critical tone of this first-person narrative, which from the start made the mystery an open secret, Dickens decides in favour of the hero's change of heart. But, far from being attributable to some rose-water sentimentalism, this decision is a bold and deeply subversive one. For it is the convict's affectionate presence, his loving trust, his loyalty, his uncomplaining endurance, his generosity, and not some artificially worked-out miracle, that will gradually bring about the change. Magwitch's example, a convict's, will succeed where even Joe's and Matthew Pocket's have failed. Pip somehow acknowledges his debt when, back in the galley with his wounded and defeated friend after the abortive escape, he ponders on the turn their relationship has taken:

For now, my repugnance to him had all melted away, and in the hunted wounded shackled creature who held my hand in his, I only saw a man who had meant to be my benefactor, and who had felt affectionately, gratefully, and generously, towards me with great constancy through a series of years. I only saw in him a much better man than I had been to Joe (liv, 456–7).

'Dear boy,' Magwitch then says to him, knowing that death is not far ahead, 'I've seen my boy, and he can be a gentleman without me' (liv, 457). Here again, we can hear two voice-sounds, Magwitch's and the writer's. What Magwitch has in mind is his protégé's financial inheritance and social promotion; but what he does not realize, and cannot suspect, is that if his 'dear boy' had never seen him, he would never have become a true gentleman at heart, after the wish of the author, and this is a meaning that we feel invited to read into his prophetic words since it is in fact the message of the book.

Magwitch has thus been given a double role to play as gentleman-maker. First, as a distant, unknown provider, he has made Pip a gentleman, but a gentleman of the archaic type. Then, as a man with his human warmth and manly worthiness, he has made Pip a gentleman, and a gentleman of the modern type. The outcast, with his money earned at the sweat of his brow, had only been a factor of enrichment and material progress. The returned convict, thanks to his presence, however illegal, has been a factor of moral improvement.

Dickens pushes the subversion even further in having him condemned by his judges to 'the extreme penalty of the law', the better to rescue him from a shameful death. Anticipating on the time-table of the London Court of Justice, he makes him die of his wounds and kills him with kindness. Of all the people who die in this novel, Magwitch, the romantic convict, is quite noticeably the only one who has the honour of a death-bed scene. He dies 'gently' (lvi, 470), the happy father of a 'lady' and the happy maker of a 'gentleman'.

Had Dickens lived to write more than one and a half novel, *Great Expectations* would be easier to place in his literary production, and it would probably appear, like *Dombey and Son*, as a major landmark. As things are, no theory can be advanced concerning the

lasting effects of this audacious book on 'the Dickens novel'. But
one thing is certain: his experience enabled him, when he next set
out to write a novel, to present himself with a new challenge, revert
to the long-discarded plot-pattern which had been his favourite one
from *Oliver Twist* to *David Copperfield*, the filial pilgrimage of a
gentleman's son. *Our Mutual Friend* is certainly no pious revival of
the genre, but a latter-day, enlightened sequel, a song of experience
echoing from the distance the early songs of innocence.

It is of some interest that *Oliver Twist*, Dickens's most innocent
song and first reconstruction story, should have been written in the
tradition of the picaresque novel. *Humphry Clinker*, *Peregrine
Pickle*, *Tom Jones*, *Roderick Random*, had been young Charles's
favourite companions during the happy Chatham days, and he had
read them over and over again before they were sold to the Hamp-
stead Road bookseller when the family could no longer make ends
meet: 'I have been Tom Jones ... for a week together. I have
sustained my own idea of Roderick Random for a month at a
stretch, I verily believe',[45] writes David Copperfield in a notable
autobiographical passage. Through those identifications, the highly
imaginative child must have constructed his first conception of
himself and of the world. 'Nature, not art', writes Barbara Hardy,
'makes us all story-tellers';[46] but what story-teller was not first a
listener, or for that matter a reader? We cannot dream without
words and the very first words we use are already quotations, the
first stories we tell already imitations. When little Charles in real life
found himself in a predicament which was not unlike the lapses
from grace that his favourite heroes had gone through, his day-
dreams of a happy end could not but be inspired by the archaic
wish-fulfilment stories that had fostered his youthful imagination,
with some good Squire Allworthy acknowledging at last 'his Merit'
and 'his Birth';[47] and when the adult wrote his impossible story of
the deserving parish-boy who ends up in the shoes of a gentleman's
son, when he entrusted good Mr Brownlow with the task of recovering the boy's parentage and inheritance which would justify that
'something'[48] in his face that had from the first bespoken his birth
and his innocence, what else did he do but recreate the dream in a
gratifying, albeit pathetic, attempt to recover the blissful state of
childhood?

Dickens never wrote such another fairy-tale. The self-help stories
that came next, written in a more realistic mode, featured probable

heroes who were no longer presented as 'the principle of Good',[49] but had their shortcomings and human weaknesses and proved in fact more deserving in 'adverse circumstance' than perfection incarnate. Yet, the novelist no more faced the problem of class than he had done in the earlier story. His deserving young men, Nicholas Nickleby, son of Nicholas Nickleby, Martin Chuzzlewit, grandson of Martin Chuzzlewit, David Copperfield the Younger, son of David Copperfield the Elder, were all of middle-class stock (whether wealthy or shabby-genteel) and in the course of their moral and geographical peregrinations none of them covered any social distance really worth mentioning. Merit and birth still went hand in hand and those *Bildungsromane* were still by-products of the wish-fulfilment story.

Great Expectations broke the spell, and *Our Mutual Friend* is another story. For, in spite of appearances, John Harmon's filial pilgrimage is a far cry from Oliver's. The usual peregrinations do bring him back to square one, the genteel son of his father, but they do so with a difference. Someone has stepped in now (irreversibly, one would think) between the father and the son: *Our Mutual Friend* is a novel in which Magwitch has made Boffin necessary . . . and Brownlow outdated.

John Harmon is assuredly reinstated at the end of the book into his father's money and into his father's name. But he gets nothing in direct succession from his old sire: everything comes to him through the hands of Boffin, Boffin the servant, the ungenteel, the illiterate man who, like Magwitch, has to be read to, Boffin who, in the course of the novel, plays in turn the part of son to his old 'governor'[50] and of spiritual father to his governor's son.

It is Boffin, we must remember, who, in strict obedience to old Harmon's last will, is the lawful heir to the property. It is Boffin who, by divesting himself of his inheritance, makes it possible for Harmon's son to inherit. It is Boffin, the 'Golden Dustman', who turns the dust of Harmon's fortune into gold. It is Boffin, the moral alchemist, who turns Bella into 'golden gold'. It is Boffin's role that makes John's story much closer to Pip's than might at first meet the eye: formidable as he had seemed, the ghost of old Harmon, which presided over the novel and haunted John's memory, turns out to have been no more than his son's Miss Havisham, a tyrant who had been thought to have forced on his son his money and the girl that went with it, but whose power proves after all to have been quite deceptive. Boffin's mediation is, after Magwitch's, the greatest ideological revolution in the Dickens plot.

Dickens in *Our Mutual Friend* harvests what he has sown in *Great Expectations*. It is, therefore, no accident that we should find there what is somehow Dickens's testament on the main subject of that book, true gentility, or true gentlemanliness. Significantly, it is a ruined aristocrat who is entrusted by the novelist with the subversive message:

'I say', resumes Twemlow, 'if such feelings on the part of this gentleman induced this gentleman to marry this lady, I think he is the greater gentleman for the action, and makes her the greater lady. I beg to say that when I use the word gentleman, I use it in the sense in which the degree may be attained by any man.'[51]

NOTES: CHAPTER 8

1 Victor Hugo, *Les Misérables* [1862], Oeuvres Complètes (ed. Jean Massin), Le Club Français du Livre (Paris, 1969), Vol. XI, p. 652 (IV, iii, 8).

2 See above, ch. 7, 'The Australian convict', p. 81.

3 *Hard Times*, eds George Ford and Sylvère Monod (New York: Norton, 1966), II, vi, 125.

4 *Bleak House*, eds George Ford and Sylvère Monod (New York: Norton, 1977), xlvii, 572.

5 Alexis Tocqueville, *L'Ancien Régime et la Révolution* [1856], Oeuvres (Paris: Gallimard, 1952), Tome II, Vol. 1, pp. 148–9: 'suivez à travers le temps et l'espace la destinée de ce mot de *gentleman*, dont notre mot de gentilhomme était le père. Vous verrez sa signification s'étendre en Angleterre à mesure que les conditions se rapprochent et se mêlent. A chaque siècle on l'applique à des hommes placés un peu plus bas dans l'échelle sociale. Il passe enfin en Amérique avec les Anglais. Là on s'en sert pour désigner indistinctement tous les citoyens. Son histoire est celle même de la démocratie.

'En France, le mot de gentilhomme est toujours resté étroitement resserré dans son sens primitif; depuis la Révolution, il est à peu près sorti de l'usage, mais il ne s'est jamais altéré.'

It is worth noting that no French word today, including 'gentleman', which has been borrowed back into the French language, is capable of covering the huge semantic field of the English term and of rendering its complexities. In his introduction to *Les Grandes Espérances*, his French translation of *Great Expectations*, Sylvère Monod remarks: 'il nous est arrivé de le traduire par "un monsieur" (ce sera le cas le plus fréquent ici), "un gentilhomme", "un homme du monde", "un honnête homme", "un homme de bien" et parfois, en désespoir de cause, ... "un gentleman" ' (Paris: Garnier, 1959, p. xlv).

6 Robin Gilmour, *The Idea of the Gentleman in the Victorian Novel* (London: Allen & Unwin, 1981), p. 2.

7 Samuel Smiles, *Self-Help* [1859] (London: Sphere Books, 1968), pp. 27 and 106.

8 ibid., p. 69.

9 ibid., p. 254.
10 ibid., p. 256.
11 ibid., p. 248.
12 ibid., p. 260.
13 Richard Steele, *The Guardian*, ed. John Kalhoun Stephens (The University Press of Kentucky, 1982), no. 34, 20 April 1713, p. 143.
14 Asa Briggs, Preface to the Centenary Edition of *Self-Help* (London: John Murray, 1958), p. 7.
15 Gilmour, op. cit., pp. 6, 7.
16 ibid., p. 143. For Q. D. Leavis, the expression 'seems to represent an uneasy gesture of the novelist's towards making a special status for Joe', in F. R. and Q. D. Leavis, *Dickens the Novelist* (Harmondsworth: Pelican 1972), p. 422.
17 Asa Briggs, *Victorian People* (Harmondsworth: Pelican, 1965), p. 142.
18 ibid.
19 Thomas Carlyle, *Past and Present* [1843] (London: Dent, 1947), p. 178.
20 Smiles, op. cit., p. 137.
21 Briggs, *Victorian People*, op. cit., p. 142.
22 See Lord Chesterfield, *Letters to His Son and Others* (London: Dent, 1984), p. 70.
23 *Bleak House*, op. cit., xvi, 196.
24 *Little Dorrit*, ed. Harvey Peter Sucksmith, Clarendon Dickens (Oxford, 1979), II, v, 466.
25 ibid., I, x, 106.
26 *Our Mutual Friend*, The New Oxford Illustrated Dickens (London: Oxford University Press, 1963), III, xvii, 620.
27 See Michael Steig, *Dickens and Phiz* (Bloomington: Indiana University Press, 1978), p. 138; Anny Sadrin, 'Présence et Fonction de l'Art et de l'Artiste dans *Bleak House*', *Annales Littéraires de l'Université de Besançon* (Paris: Les Belles Lettres, 1985), pp. 131–50.
28 cf. Charles Darwin, *The Origin of Species* (Harmondsworth: Penguin, 1984), p. 151.
29 cf. Dickens, 'Where we stopped growing', *Household Words*, 1 January 1853, vol. 6, pp. 361–3.
30 George Bernard Shaw, Foreword to *Great Expectations*, The Novel Library (London: Hamish Hamilton, 1947), p. v.
31 Gilmour, op. cit., p. 113.
32 John Forster, *The Life of Charles Dickens* (London: Dent, 1966), Vol. 1, p. 20.
33 ibid., p. 33.
34 ibid.
35 Nonesuch *Letters*, ed. Walter Dexter (London, 1938), Vol. 3, p. 717, 5 April 1869, to James Orr Marples. It should be specified that this was written 'In reply to [a] letter of enquiry'.
36 Gilmour, op. cit., p. 108.
37 See Forster, op. cit., Vol. 1, pp. 25–6.
38 ibid., p. 26.
39 ibid., p. 21.
40 Steven Marcus, *Dickens from Pickwick to Dombey* (London: Chatto & Windus, 1965), p. 362.
41 *A Tale of Two Cities*, The New Oxford Illustrated Dickens (London: Oxford University Press, 1962), III, iii, 255.
42 Lawrence Frank, *Charles Dickens and the Romantic Self* (Lincoln, Nebr.: University of Nebraska Press, 1984), pp. 3–30.
43 Thus, Silas Wegg's anxious reclaim of his amputated leg, Dickens's most

graphic and ironic illustration of this compelling process of 're-collection', is the necessary condition to his access to the rank of gentleman, as he explains to Mr Venus, the taxidermist: 'I have a prospect of getting on in life and elevating myself ... and I shouldn't like – I tell you openly I should *not* like – under such circumstances, to be what I may call dispersed, a part of me here, and a part of me there, but should wish to collect myself like a genteel person', *Our Mutual Friend*, op. cit., I, vii, 82. On Wegg as self-parody, see Anny Sadrin, *L'Etre et l'Avoir dans les Romans de Charles Dickens* (Lille-Paris: Didier Erudition, 1985), 'Weggery, Portrait d'une thématique', pp. 661–76.

44 Humphry House, 'G. B. S. on *Great Expectations*', *Dickensian*, vol. 44 (Spring 1948), p. 68.
45 *David Copperfield*, ed. Nina Burgis, Clarendon Dickens (Oxford, 1981), iv, 48.
46 Barbara Hardy, *Tellers and Listeners* (London: The Athlone Press, 1975), p. vii.
47 Henry Fielding, *Tom Jones*, eds Martin C. Battestin and Fredson Bowers (Oxford: Clarendon Press, 1974), Vol. 2, Bk XVIII, ch. ix, p. 954.
48 *Oliver Twist*, ed. Kathleen Tillotson, Clarendon Dickens (Oxford, 1966), xi, 61.
49 Dickens's Preface to the third edition of *Oliver Twist* (1841), op. cit., p. lxii.
50 'Governor', a colloquial or slang word for 'employer' (1802), was often 'applied by sons to their fathers' (1827) in the nineteenth century (*Shorter Oxford Dictionary*).
51 *Our Mutual Friend*, op. cit., IV, xvii, 819–20.

A NOVEL WITH
A HERO?

CHAPTER 9

In the Name of the Father and of the Son

> My father's family name being Pirrip, and my christian name Philip, my infant tongue could make of both names nothing longer or more explicit than Pip. So I called myself Pip, and came to be called Pip (i, 35).

The inaugural paragraph of *Great Expectations* does more than acquaint the reader with the name of its hero. For all the light-hearted, matter-of-fact and somewhat childish simplicity of its style, it establishes at the outset a complex relationship between a son and his father, it encapsulates within two short sentences the ontological drama of one whose identity should not be mistaken for identification and it alerts, in so doing, our critical attention.

Pip's self-christening, in the surname of the father and in the first name of the son, is at once an act of bondage and a gesture of autonomy. Without denying the contingencies of his birth – his ritual visits to his parents' graves even show a keen sense of rootedness and allegiance –, the child, thanks to his lingual, therefore linguistic, awkwardness, early frees himself from the dictates of family onomastics: 'it's a kind of a family name what he gave himself when a infant, and is called by' (x, 105), Joe will say later, echoing Pip's first statement, 'I called myself Pip, and came to be called Pip'.

Severance, to be sure, does not entirely preclude reverence. But in calling himself 'Pip', therefore adopting for a name the smallest common denominator between his genitor's patronymic and his own Christian name (acknowledged as personal, though also inherited at first hand from Philip Pirrip the Elder), the young orphan is paying, in a literal sense, lip-service to the narcissism of his dead and buried father. 'Dead and buried' indeed is the 'Philip Pirrip, late of this parish' whose name is no more than a few signs inscribed on a tombstone, a name never to be passed on to the son, as it should legitimately be. Pip is Pip from the start and will remain so right up to the end.

The circuitous phrase 'my father's family name' shows lasting impertinence on the part of the narrator – no longer the blundering, inarticulate infant whose tongue slipped inadvertently, but an elderly, polite gentleman – and plainly expresses a lasting ambivalent claim to kinship and alienation. No legitimate son in his right mind would ever choose, unless in jest, to introduce himself so deviously when a plain statement, 'my family name', would do just as nicely. The incongruous interpolation of the genitive creates a grammatical and sentimental disruption in the sentence and distorts the relationship between possessor and possessed: the name belongs to the father, the father belongs to the son, and the son belongs nowhere. And if, undeniably, the formulation gives pride of place to the child's sire as life-giver, it also most cheekily dismisses him as name-transmitter.

Before we proceed beyond the first page, our attention is drawn again to the importance of naming. Self-awareness, Pip tells us, is simultaneous and, it would seem, synonymous with linguistic awareness:

> My first most vivid and broad impression of the identity of things, seems to me to have been gained on a memorable raw afternoon towards evening. At such a time I found out for certain, that this bleak place overgrown with nettles was the churchyard; and that Philip Pirrip, late of this parish, and also Georgiana wife of the above, were dead and buried; and that Alexander, Bartholomew, Abraham, Tobias, and Roger, infant children of the aforesaid, were also dead and buried; and that the dark flat wilderness beyond the churchyard, intersected with dykes and mounds and gates, with scattered cattle feeding on it, was the marshes; and that the low leaden line beyond, was the river; and that the distant savage lair from which the wind was rushing, was the sea; and that the small bundle of shivers growing afraid of it all and beginning to cry, was Pip (i, 35–36).

In thus rehearsing the 'identity of things', Pip puts himself *in medias res* and begins his life-story like a *Book of Genesis*, where creation and naming are not to be dissociated. Then, the master of words, he signs his name at the bottom of his list as any artist would do at the bottom of a picture or any poet at the bottom of a sonnet. As we read these lines, we soon realize that we are attending nothing less than the birth of a writer: self-authored in the midst of the world that he has just conjured up and himself the word made flesh, Pip is not brought to life in a traditional manner like any of his famous predecessors. No Mrs Thingummy, no Dr Chillip, no Doctor Parker Peps is called to the rescue as they were to help forth Oliver, David or Paul. His is an oral delivery, a kind of posthumous birth among the graves of distant, almost imaginary parents:

> As I never saw my father or my mother, and never saw any likeness of either of them (for their days were long before the days of photographs), my first fancies regarding what they were like, were unreasonably derived from their tombstones. The shape of the letters on my father's, gave me an odd idea that he was a square, stout, dark man, with curly black hair. From the character and turn of the inscription, '*Also Georgiana Wife of the Above*,' I drew a childish conclusion that my mother was freckled and sickly (i, 35).

A beautiful tribute is paid here to the poetic powers of the written word. Like all writers, it is as a reader that Pip begins his career. Like all budding autobiographers, it is the book of his origins that he is first given to read. And, of course, he rewrites it. There is little else he could do. Those parents are so far away that he has in fact no choice but to recreate them before he recreates himself. But behind the fiction of the freckled mother and of the dark, curly-haired father, the reality of the 'real' Georgiana and of the 'real' Philip is clearly perceptible and the information scattered over the page about this couple whose only daughter 'married the blacksmith' and whose five eldest boys 'gave up trying to get a living, exceedingly early in that universal struggle' tells us a great deal about the predicament of their youngest surviving son. Within a single page, we have learnt enough about the young tomb-reader to know 'for certain' that he is more to be pitied for his wretched condition than admired for his talent. So does indeed the 'small bundle of shivers growing afraid of it all and beginning to cry', an exhausted and pathetic demiurge abandoned to himself in the wilderness, a king without a kingdom, as helpless as Lear on the heath, as vulnerable as little Oedipus exposed on the mountain.

For, in proclaiming his singularity, Pip in fact proclaims his utter solitude. Undeniably the most proletarian and the most desperately orphaned of all Dickens's heroes, he embarks upon life without any of the romantic assets that in many novels can ensure success to even the most destitute. He has not the advantage of illegitimacy or of mysterious origins, which were so promising in 'the Parish Boy's Progress'; nor can there be in his case any whisperings of some secret legacy: the Pirrips do not belong to the class of testators in which as a rule Dickens places his heroes. Philip Pirrip the Elder was even so ignorant of conventions that he has mistakenly christened his last born child after himself, when any bourgeois would have known that this is the prerogative of the eldest son and rightful heir to the property.[1] But what does it matter to one born so low whether he be called Philip, Alexander or Bartholomew? 'Pip' in fact expresses this helplessness 'with a vengeance' and brings the orphan child down to the level of the poorest, the Dicks, the Johnnies and the Joes who cannot afford a family name, do not even know that most people do, 'Never heerd of sich a think'. Unlike the crossing sweeper, the son of Philip Pirrip knows very well, of course, that 'everybody has two names' and that Pip 'is short for a longer name', but he none the less 'Thinks it long enough for *him*',[2] long enough for a boy who has no one but himself to rely on, no birthright, no prospects of inheritance, no expectations whatever and whose only chance, with such a nickname of a name, would be to belong to a fairy-tale!

Should we therefore already begin to doubt the promises of the title? We should and we do. But only up to a point. For what novel-reader worthy of the name would be prepared to renounce the pleasure of subscribing to the illusion of the text and of letting himself be mystified by a story whose main attraction, as he can perceive on reading the first lines, is its equivocation?

Great Expectations is indeed a fundamentally ambiguous novel: it has, as we shall see, the narrative ambiguity of a story that hesitates between verisimilitude and implausibility, the ideological ambiguity of a message that hesitates between utopia and resignation, the psychological ambiguity of a hero who hesitates between two heroic callings, the formal ambiguity of a text that hesitates between several literary genres, the functional ambiguity of a method that hesitates between irony and objectivity.

The reader's participation in this enterprise is amply solicited: he is invited to play the double game of credulity (through his identification with the hero) and of alienation (through his identification with the narrator), to suspend at will 'his disbelief and (what is harder) his belief'.[3] Gullible and cautious, the dupe of the narrator and his confidant, he is expected to cope with two simultaneous, contradictory readings, to listen at once to the sirens' song and to Pumblechookian premonitory outbursts: 'Take warning, boy, take warning!' (xv, 145) the text says to him at each page. But should he opt for critical insight and dry-as-dustness, should he happen to be impervious to the charm of romance and romanticism and deprived, to boot, of common humanity, he would be entitled, when the novel comes to a close, to exclaim triumphantly: 'But what else could be expected! What else could be expected!' (lviii, 483).

NOTES: CHAPTER 9

1 Dickens actually changed his mind about the father's first name. George J. Worth notes in his *Annotated Bibliography* (New York: Garland, 1986, p. 17, no. 39) that in the *Harper's Weekly* text, which Dickens had not corrected 'thoroughly or at all', 'Pip's late father is still named Tobias rather than Philip'. Tobias is the name of one of the 'five little brothers' to whose memory the five little stone lozenges in the churchyard are sacred (and not the eldest, one would think, since his name comes fourth on the list). The novelist presumably decided on second thoughts to emphasize the sonhood of the surviving son and make his hero symbolically closer to the father than any of the dead children.

2 *Bleak House*, eds George Ford and Sylvère Monod (New York: Norton, 1977), xi, 134.

3 cf. C. S. Lewis, *An Experiment in Criticism* (Cambridge University Press, 1961), p. 68.

CHAPTER 10

Oedipus and Telemachus

As the least perspicacious reader will come to realize at the end of
the book, the narrator of *Great Expectations*, in choosing such a
title for his autobiography, has chosen to express himself in the
ironic mode. Having now reached maturer years and given up
impossible dreams, he can afford to recollect emotions in tran-
quillity, look at his younger self with amused and sympathetic
superiority and take pleasure in misleading all the other fools who
are ready to follow in his steps. His readers' delusions are now those
that once were his: is it not the prerogative of all ironists to write in
bad faith?

But the method entails critical difficulties; as it consists mainly in
concealing, at best half-concealing, the truth, postponing revelations, expressing feelings that cannot always be attributed with
authority to the 'visionary boy' (xliv, 377) or to the wise chronicler,
it is at times next to impossible to draw the line between deception
and sincerity. 'What to believe, in the course of [our] reading' is our
'chief literary difficulty indeed'; and if, like Boffin, we decide 'to
compound with half', the question still remains, 'which half'?[1]
How, in particular, are we to account for the many outbursts of
self-pity that punctuate the book from beginning to end? When he
speaks of 'wretched me' (xxxix, 340), of his 'ecstacy of unhappiness' (xliv, 378), of 'that poor dream ... all gone by' (lix, 490),
must we impute the emotion to the narrator's legitimate desire to
recreate the passionate atmosphere of the past or should we understand it as the expression of lasting regrets and undying nostalgia?
When he grows lyrical and resorts to personal apostrophes to the
reader, 'Pause you who read this' (ix, 101), must we dismiss them as
pure rhetoric and turn a deaf ear to the pathos of such passages?
Sometimes, to be sure, the emotion is cautiously dated as definitely
belonging to the past, as in the following instance: 'When I woke up
in the night ... I used to think, with a weariness on my spirits, that I

should have been happier and better if I had never seen Miss Havisham's face' (xxxiv, 291); but what are we to make of a remark like this one: 'I washed the weather and the journey from my face and hands, and went out to the memorable old house that it would have been so much the better for me never to have entered, never to have seen' (xliii, 372)? The pathetic accents of passages like this one ring truer and more heart-felt than the sedate tone adopted at the last minute when, in less than a page, the narrator sums up eleven years of 'happy' industry and frugality:

> Many a year went round, before I was a partner in the House; but, I lived happily with Herbert and his wife, and lived frugally, and paid my debts ... I must not leave it to be supposed that we were ever a great House, or that we made mints of money. We were not in a grand way of business, but we had a good name, and worked for our profits, and did very well (lviii, 489).

We would like to take his word for it that he has given up for good 'those wretched hankerings after money and gentility' (xxix, 257) that had so disturbed his boyhood and that the Victorian gospel of work, wisdom and contentment is all he goes by now. But should we not rather read this declaration as one more instance of his self-swindling?

The question remains all the more perplexing as we know so little of the man's present life. Some critics, on the strength of the very last words of the revised ending, take it for granted that he has married Estella and lived happy ever after.[2] But this is to stretch unduly the meaning of a purposely evasive sentence and, as far as we can tell, there is no 'dear presence' attending on him as, 'far into the night',[3] he writes his recollections, no dear little heads to confirm such assumptions, no homely scene as in the closing chapter of *David Copperfield*. Other commentators assume that the act of narration is accomplished by one Mr Pirrip;[4] but for all we know, the narrator is still Pip, or more appropriately maybe, Mr Pip, or 'Philip Pip, Esquire', to use Wemmick's form of address (xliv, 379), though even this is purely conjectural. It would be fairer in fact to describe him as someone who used to go by the name of Pip and has, in the course of years, dissolved into anonymity and into non-entity, someone who has no present life, just a past to relate and re-live and whose recollections read almost like 'memories from beyond the grave'.

Such reticence is most frustrating. It deprives us of the necessary perspective and referential standpoint from which to make final pronouncements on the hero's progress and the meaning of his life, so that any attempt at aligning him with other Dickens heroes is bound to bring tentative answers.

It is difficult in particular to decide whether this story is, in the long run, a Victorian success story after the *David Copperfield* pattern or Dickens's 'Tale of Lost Illusions' as it has been called;[5] and it is therefore difficult to appreciate the hero's modernity fairly. If we consider with Marthe Robert that modernity in fiction-writing must be understood as 'the self-searching, self-questioning literary movement which uses as subject matter its own doubt and belief in the value of its message',[6] we can with no further hesitation call *Great Expectations* a modern novel, but it does not follow that the hero of this modern novel is himself a modern hero; and, paradoxically, the question that remains to be solved concerning Pip is precisely whether he is not an old-fashioned hero in a very modern novel.

Or, to use Robert's terminology, is he still at the end the modern Oedipal 'bastard' that we first discovered on his father's grave or has he not regressed into the more archaic type of the Romantic 'foundling', reading backward, in this event, his *Entfremdungsroman* or 'family romance'?

The 'family romance' in the Freudian theory is a story which the child makes up for himself 'as a correction of actual life',[7] a day-dream which serves 'as the fulfilment of wishes' during the early years of his life when he has to free himself from parental authority and which might be compared to a serial story in two main episodes, each corresponding to a new stage in the child's mental and psychic development.

The first episode begins with the child's disappointment with his parents after an early period of idolatry. As he grows up and comes to realize that he is not, or no longer, the sole object of parental care and loving-kindness, has to face the necessity of sharing his father's and mother's dispensation of love, food and security with unwanted siblings, and as he furthermore 'gets to know other parents and compares them with his own, and so acquires the right to doubt the incomparable and unique quality which he had attributed to them',[8] he feels betrayed and humiliated and embarks upon a compensatory dream in which he re-writes his life-story and imagines himself to be a lost child adopted by strangers. He is the noble 'foundling' whose true parentage will of necessity be discovered some day and things will be set to right at last.

The second episode takes place when the child grows aware of a sexual difference between his genitors and realizes that only his father's parental authenticity can be a matter of doubt. He then focuses on his father his genealogical uncertainty and takes on a new part as 'bastard' child of a familiar mother and of some distant, preferably aristocratic, father. This new-born bastardly Oedipus, having thus rid himself of his father, can keep the mother to himself and live in perfect bliss with her.

If, as Freud invites us to do in 'Creative writers and day-dreaming',[9] we consider that fiction, especially popular romance, is primarily based on wish fulfilment, we may assume with Marthe Robert that the two heroic types of the family romance have quite naturally found their way into literary works of fiction: the found-ling, a romantic dreamer, has developed into the fairy-tale hero, relying on benefactors, benevolent uncles and fairy godmothers; the bastard, a realist, is the hero of modern fiction, pugnacious, self-reliant and solitary. Among Robert's long list of 'bastards', whether real or fictitious, we may select Empire-builders like Napoleon, colonists like Robinson Crusoe, or lesser figures of ambitious young men like Rastignac or Julien Sorel.

If we now try to sort out Dickens's heroes according to these criteria, we will find few pure types and plenty of overlapping. Oliver Twist, the lost child whose sole *raison d'être* is to find his origins, will appear as the ideal, almost paradigmatic 'foundling', and no 'bastard' in spite of his illegitimate birth; but bastardy is as much a moral quality with Freud as 'true legitimacy'[10] is with Dickens.

At the other end, the legitimate, high-born Charles d'Evrémonde, alias Darnay, who, in hatred of his father, renounces his patrony-mic, his patrimony and his fatherland and opts for self-reliance in a democratic country with no thought of ever reconsidering his choice, will qualify as the ideal 'bastard'.

David Copperfield, the runaway child who fights his way up into society, makes his own fortune and achieves literary success after the fashion of his creator, is very much on the bastard side, though, in seeking the help of his aunt Betsey, who acts as surrogate and foster parent, the young Oedipus shows that he cannot entirely resist the old attraction of Telemachus for some protective parental figure.

The double temptation is in fact shared by many other Dickens heroes, none so well as John Harmon who early quarrels with his much hated father, leaves home and country with no intention ever to return, yet comes back, years later, at the news of his father's death, attracted by 'the accounts of [his] fine inheritance', though 'shrinking from [his] father's money 'and' [his] father's memory',[11] changes his mind on setting foot in London, passes himself for dead, takes on a pseudonym (thus performing a symbolic parricidal gesture), proves to himself that he can work for a living and needs no financial support, lets, meanwhile, other people come into his inheritance, and, after more than 700 pages of masquerading and tribulations, eventually takes possession again of his 'rightful name and ... London house',[12] ambiguously asserting himself both as the son of his father and as the heir of the latter's servant. With the notable exceptions of Oliver and of Darnay, the Dickens hero is very self-contradictory and it is significant that Dickens's last completed novel should offer such a glaring example of ambivalence, for it shows that to the last Dickens was desperately trying to settle his own oedipal conflict and was still working on this disturbingly inexhaustible theme, the father/son relationship, which is at the heart of his fictional matter.

The Dickens novel might in fact be described as an oedipal novel with Telemachus in the leading role. The hero, in most cases, is a male orphan whose father died before chapter 1. No father-killer himself (the murder is always committed in his stead and for his benefit by the impenitently parricidal novelist), he will have to redeem the deed and feel guilty in spite of his innocence before, let us hope, coming to terms with the past and with himself. The movement is always away from the father and back again, back to his origins.

Structurally, *Great Expectations* follows this pattern. When, after long years of absence in Cairo, Pip comes back to his native place and visits his friends at the forge, he finds himself in the presence of another little Pip, his namesake and *alter ego*:

and there, fenced into the corner with Joe's leg, and sitting on my own little stool looking at the fire, was – I again!

'We giv' him the name of Pip for your sake, dear old chap,' said
Joe, delighted when I took another stool by the child's side ...
'and we hoped he might grow a little bit like you, and we think he
do' (lix, 490).

The next morning, he takes the child for a walk to, of all places, the
old churchyard where it all began:

> I thought so too, and I took him out for a walk next morning, and
> we talked immensely, understanding one another to perfection.
> And I took him down to the churchyard, and set him on a certain
> tombstone there, and he showed me from that elevation which
> stone was sacred to the memory of Philip Pirrip, late of this
> Parish, and Also Georgiana, Wife of the Above (ibid).

We have now come full circle and reached the end of the novel. Two
or three pages follow on the Estella/Pip relationship, but this love-
story is of such limited significance to the novel as a whole that
Dickens could rewrite its conclusion at will and reorientate it
without damaging the book or improving it overmuch. Altering or
suppressing the return of the son to the graves of his parents would,
on the contrary, have greatly impaired the meaning of the novel;
and when Dickens reworked his ending, he knew better than to
rework this scene and reconsidered only what came next.

This act of filial piety is really essential: it confirms to the reader
that *Great Expectations* is first and foremost the novel of a son and,
more important still, it reminds him that it is the novel of the son of
Philip Pirrip. This is all the more necessary as, in between, the
relationship between this son and this father is not openly made the
subject of the plot: it even seems erased, ruled out of the book. Pip,
unlike Oliver, has no reason to seek his father when he knows so well
where to find him. He has no reason either to hate or despise him, as
John Harmon or Arthur Clennam do their own fathers, and between
chapter 1 and the final chapter he never mentions him, never gives
him a thought. He has, we remember, never set eyes on him and no
one, as far as we know, ever told him anything about his physical
appearance or his character. The return of the prodigal son is therefore not a return to someone he ever knew, but to someone he
imagined in the days when he was a young epigraphist. His filial pilgrimage is a journey back towards some idea, or some ideal maybe,
early derived from a few words inscribed on a tombstone.

We might well also make the journey back to this first chapter, as the conspicuously self-referential narrator invites us to do, if we are to appreciate what exactly he is returning to. He is returning, of course, to his 'first fancies' which, on reflection, prove to have been rather stereotyped images of a fragile mother and of a strong, dark, impressive father, the sort of man that any boy would like to take after or to imitate to strengthen his own image of himself. He is also returning to the poetic appeal of their epitaph and to his misreading of its convoluted phrasing:

> At the time when I stood in the churchyard, reading the family tombstones, I had just enough learning to be able to spell them out. My construction even of their simple meaning was not very correct, for I read 'wife of the Above' as a complimentary reference to my father's exaltation to a better world (vii, 73).

A father in Heaven, a mother magnified by the magic formula which commemorates her – 'Also Georgiana. That's my mother' (i, 37) –, two people whom the popular, conventional poetry of an inscription have immortalized into almost mythical figures, such are the parents he is returning to.

These wishful representations do not, unfortunately, provide the whole picture. The child sobbing among the graves is also, as we have seen, a child who has been cruelly slighted by the very people whom he is so willing to idealize; he has been slighted by their death, their inability to provide for him, and even their lack of concern in not taking him with them like the other five little boys. The scene in the churchyard precisely takes place at a crucial moment of awareness when Pip is beginning to estrange himself from his genitors and to 'bastardize' himself, when, in other words, he has just set about adding a new episode to his family romance 'as a correction of actual life' or in retaliation for being mishandled.

But something strange occurs then. For the narrating agencies, who are dreaming on his behalf, help by beginning to write his family romance for him in order to turn him eventually into an adopted son. Instead of remaining a bastard for life, he will thus be given a chance of becoming a foundling and being provided for. But, left in the dark about the identity of his adoptive parent, he will also be given the liberty of projecting his parental ideals on whomsoever he wishes. As blind as Oedipus, he blindly goes on living his oedipal drama through vicarious relationships, imaginary experiences, adapting his dreams to these mysterious new circumstances, misplacing his affections and expectations, faithless to his origins, faithful to his ideals.

The romance begins as early as chapter 1, when Pip is still weeping on his father's grave. What once were David's fearful apprehensions and unavowed dream of seeing Lazarus Copperfield the Elder rise from the dead suddenly comes true at long last: '"Hold your noise!" cried a terrible voice, as a man started up from among the graves at the side of the church porch' (i, 36). Even before being identified as a convict 'in coarse grey, with a great iron on his leg', the newcomer is unmistakably recognized as 'the ghost of a man's' or for that matter of a boy's 'own father' (xxvii, 242) and the recognition is greatly helped by associations with the earlier novel: are we not, after all, reading a new episode of Dickens's huge 'Family Romance'?

Only years later, when the convict returns and proclaims himself to be Pip's 'second father' (xxxix, 337), will the reader grasp the full meaning of this ghostly apparition. But, meanwhile, the mystery attached to the event will not impair his innermost conviction that the man who sprang up as a father-figure might reappear some day as something like a father, a conviction often strengthened in the course of the novel by incidental, premonitory coincidences and narratorial side-lighting. Pip, for his part, will not see beyond the event itself until, some sixteen years later, 'the truth of [his] position' comes 'flashing' on him (xxxix, 336). And it is certainly the greatest dramatic irony of this first-person narrative that the hints dropped throughout for our benefit and information should come from the very man who, as a character, was primarily concerned, yet remained so long in the dark.

Another, concomitant, irony concerns the child's identity in its long unsuspected relation with the newcomer:

'Tell us your name!' said the man. 'Quick!'
'Pip, sir.'
'Once more,' said the man, staring at me. 'Give it mouth!'
'Pip, Pip, sir' (i, 36).

That an escaped convict should prove so eager to know the name of a child whom he has just met by chance and whom in all likelihood he will never meet again (there is at this stage no reason why he should) seems quite inexplicable, even goes against commonsense. This behaviour cannot be ascribed to vain curiosity or be taken for convict 'manners'. Yet the question is asked twice, as if the man wanted to make sure that he gets the answer right. The obvious explanation that comes to mind is that this verbal exchange meets dramatic requirements: Dickens wants to secure the future of his story and how could the sheep-farmer from the depths of Australia ever find the track of the boy unless he knew him by name?

But there is more to it than that. For, when Jaggers comes to the forge eleven years later to acquaint him with his good fortune, he does not merely satisfy himself that Joe Gargery's apprentice answers to the name of Pip, but he imparts to him the peremptory and sole condition demanded by his mysterious benefactor, namely that he should always go by that name:

'Now, Mr Pip,' pursued the lawyer, 'I address the rest of what I have to say, to you. You are to understand, first, that it is the request of the person from whom I take my instructions, that you always bear the name of Pip. You will have no objection, I dare say, to your great expectations being encumbered with that easy condition. But if you have any objection, this is the time to mention it.'

My heart was beating so fast, and there was such a singing in my ears, that I could scarcely stammer I had no objection.

'I should think not!' (xviii, 165).

In a novel so meticulously sifted by the critics, little attention has been paid to this strange demand. No explanation, of course, is offered by Jaggers. None will ever be offered by Magwitch either. But this is no sufficient reason not to give it proper consideration.

Magwitch's likely motivations seem easy enough to detect. The former runaway convict wants to express his gratitude to the boy who once brought him food, a file and a glimpse of humanity, and whose name in his memory stands (rightly or wrongly) for human fellowship. In asking him to stick to this name, he is trying, not unlike Miss Havisham, to stop the clocks and arrest time. His money will go to the little child as he knew him and as he wishes to imagine him always, unchanged, unspoilt by time, child-like, generous, loyal, and weak enough, moreover, still to require his protection.

Other, less noble motives may be hazarded. The social outcast who intends to have his revenge on the oppressive and unfair society that has victimized him ever since he was born may wish to confer respectability on a name that connotes destitution and misery, as he turns this little speck, self-dubbed 'Pip', into a moneyed gentleman. And his vicarious ambition seems gratified: 'I tell it, fur you to know as that there hunted dunghill dog wot you kep life in, got his head so high that he could make a gentleman – and, Pip, you're him!' (xxxix, 337).

But, more important still, Magwitch has decided to make Pip his son and heir: 'You're my son', he says, 'more to me nor any son. I've put away money, only for you to spend' (xxxix, 337). Under normal circumstances (especially in a Dickens novel), the new father would naturally wish to bestow his name as well as his fortune on his adopted child: once in Dover, David begins a 'new life, in a new name'[13] and it is as David 'Trotwood Copperfield' that he eventually inherits what little is left of his aunt Betsey's property; and in the novel we are considering, Estella, the chosen heiress, is named 'Havisham' (xxix, 263) after the name of her patroness and adoptive mother. But if a convict's money can be bequeathed easily enough (for *pecunia non olet*), how could a man who lives in banishment bestow a tainted name on someone he loves dearly and wishes to protect from such misfortunes and humiliations as he himself has had to endure? Not to mention the fact that he must long remain anonymous to ensure the suspense of his own plotting and that on his return he has to go by a false name. Besides, the name of 'Provis' that this *provi*dential father assumes for a pseudonym, if it corresponds well to the role of donor that he has assigned himself, would ill suit the one placed at the receiving end. If the adoptive father's liberality is unfettered, his power on onomastics is, as we see, very limited and his choice to have Pip stick to the name of 'Pip' may appear as a poor makeshift. It is, none the less, a means of strengthening the father/son relationship between him and his protégé: in compelling his adoptive son to renounce his rightful identity, Magwitch gets the upper hand of an old rival, Philip Pirrip the Elder, the dead and buried father. Should Pip, in growing up, decide to revert to the name of Philip Pirrip (a not unlikely hypothesis), the ghost of the real father would forever be in the way, a constant reminder of the laws of genetics, disturbingly suggestive of usurpation, whereas, thanks to a little clause in a legal document, he is ousted for good. Or should we say that it is 'as if it were all over with him' (v, 71)?[14] And does not the new father run the risk, in time, of being double-crossed by his own stratagem?

The question is well worth asking, given the rather paradoxical character of the benefactor's demand; for it is only, as we must realize, on the understanding that he will keep his bastard's or, more exactly, his semi-bastard's name that Pip is allowed to become a foundling. And, as the narrative proceeds, this request will prove indeed to have harboured one of the major ambiguities of the book, the enduring enigma being whether the foundling will turn out to be 'somebody's child', 'anybody's', or 'nobody's'.[15]

Jaggers, the man who takes 'nothing on its looks ... everything on evidence' (xl, 351), is unduly hasty in his judgement when he calls the demand of Pip's protector an 'easy condition'. On second reading it even sounds rather ironic, though whether the irony be the speaker's or the writer's is a conjectural matter. To be Pip by order is just as absurd as to play to order, and the hero finds himself once again in the impossible situation of one whose wish has become another's command; direly put to the test, he must from now on be at once free and obedient, true to himself and true to his word. Self-naming had made the child father to the man, but now that a man is father to the self-named child, the meaning of Pip's name is as double-edged as its graphic appearance, a mirror-image of itself.

Pip's name is officially made the touchstone of his moral strength and of his loyalty to himself and to the past. Unfortunately, the child has early learnt to distrust and disown himself. Hectored by grown-ups, rebuked and ordered about by his sister, always under the threat of Tickler, and the subject of the most contemptuous conversations, only solaced by Joe's spoonfuls of gravy and inefficient outpourings of love, how could he be expected to be strong and self-reliant? On the occasion of his first visit to Satis House, his weakness and diffidence already induced him to betray himself, even before crossing the threshold of Miss Havisham's dressing-room:

'Who is it?' said the lady at the table.
'Pip, ma'am.'
'Pip?' (viii, 88)

His name is returned to him like a slap on the face or a misdirected note: 'Not known at the address', says the question-mark. So deep is the humiliation, so strong the desire to be recognized and acknowledged that, with no hesitation, Pip disowns his name at once and places himself in the most disgraceful bondage: 'Mr Pumblechook's boy, ma'am. Come – to play', he explains. Not Joe's boy, or even Mrs Joe's, but Pumblechook's, of all men. Common-sense readers will argue that this is the best means for Pip of making himself known to the mistress of the place, since Pumblechook is the very man who recommended him to her and who has just brought him there. But was it necessary to put it that way, to create this grammatical dependence as if in testimony of some filial or menial connection with a most hated self-imposed benefactor? And when, a moment later, Pip is asked to play, why should he hit upon the 'desperate idea of starting round the room in the assumed character of Mr Pumblechook's chaise-cart'? (viii, 88). The answer rests in one word: 'gigmanity'. For Pip who has seen so little of the world, but heard so often his sister's praises of the man, the local corn-chandler is a paragon of gentility and his chaise-cart, by any conceivable stretch of imagination, the most enviable symbol of prestige. The chaise-cart is part and parcel of Pumblechook: 'Uncle Pumble-chook ... was a well-to-do corn-chandler in the nearest town, and drove his own chaise-cart' (iv, 55). Pumblechook's *own* chaise-cart clinches any argument: 'as Mr Pumblechook was very positive and drove his own chaise-cart – over everybody – it was agreed that it must be so' (vi, 72–3). Pumblechook's *own* chaise-cart is the proper vehicle to carry young boys with expectations up to town: 'you do not know', Mrs Gargery says to Joe, 'that Uncle Pumble-chook, being sensible that for anything we can tell, this boy's fortune may be made by his going to Miss Havisham's, has offered to take him into town to-night in his own chaise-cart' (vii, 82). Pumblechook's *own* chaise-cart is such an object of veneration that Pip feels 'unequal to the performance' of impersonating it on that memorable occasion, though he will succeed better on his next visit: 'I started at once, ... and we went away at a pace that might have been an imitation (founded on my first impulse under that roof) of Mr Pumblechook's chaise-cart' (xi, 113). (We note that the 'own' is dropped as soon as the imitation succeeds.)

This instance of self-betrayal is a minor offence compared to the next, which takes place after Pip has pledged himself to Jaggers always to bear the name of Pip. Only too pleased to be removed into the upper spheres of gentility, the young Rastignac has just arrived in London, where he will share house with Herbert Pocket, whom he has identified as 'the pale young gentleman' of Satis House: 'Will you do me the favour to begin at once to call me by my christian name, Herbert?' asks Pip's new friend. Pip assents quite willingly and in his turn introduces himself, though under a name more genteel-sounding than Pip: 'I informed him in exchange that my christian name was Philip' (xxii, 202). But, genteel as it may sound and authentic as it may be, Philip will not do: 'I don't take to Philip', Herbert replies, 'I tell you what I should like. We are so harmonious, and you have been a blacksmith – would you mind it?' 'I shouldn't mind anything that you propose', Pip answers, 'but I don't understand you'. Herbert then explains himself: 'Would you mind Handel for a familiar name? There's a charming piece of music by Handel, called the Harmonious Blacksmith.' 'I should like it very much', acquiesces Pip, who has already forgotten the 'easy' condition to his great expectations.

As on the previous occasion, Pip acts on the initiative of a social better: the 'bastard' will go by any name to rise in society. But, in so doing, he is also the victim of irony, lets himself be 'handled' by others and aligned with the comic or hateful characters to whom, as Sylvère Monod remarks, Dickens mischievously allots preposterous names ending in 'le'.[16] Drummle, Wopsle, Hubble, and even the venerable and respectable Pumble(chook). The musical reference, besides, is as jarring as it is harmonious: in rechristening Pip, Herbert unwittingly performs variations on the theme of social determinism, 'once a blacksmith's boy, always a blacksmith's boy'.[17]

Pip, of course, is deaf to these prophetic undertones. He even takes his new identity as a token of enfranchisement and is soon greatly helped in this delusion by curious circumstances. When he next goes down to the village by stagecoach, convicts are among his fellow-travellers and one of them he recognizes as the man who had once brought him the two greasy one-pound notes on behalf of his old fugitive friend of the marshes. The newly-made gentleman dreads mutual recognition and is happily relieved on realizing that his new name may prevent it:

'Good-bye, Handel!' Herbert called out as we started. I thought what a blessed fortune it was, that he had found another name for me than Pip (xxviii, 250).

The coach journey is nevertheless a journey back into the past, a nightmarish revival of Act 1, scene 1, as the convicts' conversation precisely runs on his own adventures in the marsh country and his connection with the man who since then 'got made a Lifer' (xxviii, 251). Throughout the journey, Pip is obsessed with the fear of being identified, as if the mask of pseudonymity was thinning down to transparency:

> After overhearing this dialogue, I should assuredly have got down and been left in the solitude and darkness of the highway, but for feeling certain that the man had no suspicion of my identity ... Still, the coincidence of our being together on the coach, was sufficiently strange to fill me with a dread that some other coincidence might at any moment connect me, in his hearing, with my name (xxviii, 251).

Reading this, we think we can hear Miss Havisham's voice still ringing from the distance: 'Good-bye, Pip! – you will always keep the name of Pip, you know' (xix, 184), she had said to him when he had come to take his leave before starting for London. In its immediate context, her 'you know' could be understood to mean 'I know' or, more precisely, 'I want you to know that I know'. Miss Havisham in that scene was, as Pip will later tell her reproachfully, leading him on to believe, and leading the Pockets on to believe, that she was his benefactress: 'In humouring my mistake, Miss Havisham, you punished – practised on – perhaps you will supply whatever term expresses your intention, without offence – your self-seeking relations' (xliv, 374). And she was described indeed as 'gloating on' the questions and answers that constituted the conversation, 'so keen was her enjoyment of Sarah Pocket's jealous dismay'. But the reach of the sentence goes much beyond the narrow bounds of petty family conflicts and the meanness of immediate psychological implications; in the broader context of the novel, the remark, after a time, acquires some autonomy and may read as a key sentence, possibly *the* key sentence of the novel, an ironic summary of the plot, a cruel epitome of the social fable. Dickens often entrusts his cynics with the task of lending their voices to his sternest messages, and it seems that in this novel Miss Havisham, a disillusioned, clear-sighted, cynical woman, has been assigned the part of prophet and truth-teller, though she performs it most ambiguously, behaving like Rousseau's *faux sincères* 'who wish to deceive in speaking the truth'.[18] What she knows, and what Pip will come to know, is that he is no foundling of hers and has no future except in his past and self-reliant bastardy.

But the crowning irony of Pip's fantastic journey down to the end of the night is that it ultimately takes him to the discovery, on reading the local paper, that he is a most ludicrous father-seeker:

> Our readers will learn, not altogether without interest, in refer-ence to the recent romantic rise in fortune of a young artificer in iron of this neighbourhood ... that the youth's earliest patron, companion, and friend, was a highly-respected individual not entirely unconnected with the corn and seed trade ... It is not wholly irrespective of our personal feelings that we record HIM as the Mentor of our young Telemachus, for it is good to know that our town produced the founder of the latter's fortunes. Does the thought-contracted brow of the local Sage or the lustrous eye of local Beauty inquire whose fortunes? We believe that Quintin Matsys was the BLACKSMITH of Antwerp. VERB. SAP. (xxviii, 252).

For all its preposterous, convoluted style, the paragraph that Pip lights upon as he rests at the local inn, holds much truth about his character and destiny. It cruelly reminds him that if Miss Havisham is to be his Ulysses, he must needs accept his old Mentor into the bargain and remain to the last 'Mr Pumblechook's boy'. It says in funny terms what the novel reveals in more heart-felt accents: the incompetent Oedipus is also doomed to be a pathetic Telemachus.

When 'our young Telemachus' discovers his 'real' father, he is quite dumbfounded and Oedipus wakes up again. Reluctant at first to recognize him, he is bound, after a time, to identify the man with a 'strange' face (xxxix, 332) as *his* convict: 'for I knew him! ... I could not have known my convict more distinctly than I knew him now ... I knew him before he gave me one of those aids, though, a moment before, I had not been conscious of remotely suspecting his identity' (xxxix, 333–4). But he immediately estranges him again as '*the* Convict' (336, my emphasis), 'some terrible beast' (337); words of hatred and rejection crop up, 'repugnance', 'abhorrence', 'dread':

'I recoiled from his touch as if he had been a snake', he writes (338). He is on the verge of fainting – 'the room began to surge and turn' (337) –, on the verge, that is, of performing a suicide in effigy, behaving as if, short of destroying the unwanted father, he wished to destroy the father's unwilling son. Even his sense of identity is shaken for a while: 'I hardly knew ... even who I was' (xl, 344).

This aggressive stage is short-lived, however, and, after a few days, Pip, quite reasonably, opts for a compromise: he decides simultaneously to renounce his benefactor's patronage (xli, 357) and to stand by the man who, at the peril of his life, has crossed the seas just to see him. But both his decision and the words he chooses to account for it betray fundamentally oedipal motivations. Fearing that, 'under the disappointment', Magwitch might put himself 'in the way of being taken', which, since he is a lifer, would mean death by hanging, he thinks it wise not to impart to him his intentions concerning the inheritance and explains himself as follows:

> I was so struck by the horror of this idea, which had weighed upon me from the first, and the working out of which would make me regard myself, in some sort, as his murderer, that I could not rest in my chair but began pacing to and fro (xli, 358).

If Dickens had read Freud, he would never have dared to write this sentence! But what post-Freudian reader can fail to react at the word 'murderer' in such a context? And, in expressing his fear of being the 'murderer' of the man who calls him 'my son', how could Pip fail to draw our attention to the parricidal drive of his nature and to remind us of Pumblechook's oracular words, 'Take warning, boy, take warning!', which had been uttered, as Pip had remarked at the time, 'as if it were a well-known fact that I contemplated murdering a near relation, provided I could only induce one to have the weakness to become my benefactor' (xv, 145). Pip, like Oedipus, is afraid of the oracle and his fears are even better justified because, unlike Oedipus, he has from childhood, and long before hearing the Pumblechookian warning, been obsessed with fears or visions of murder of a parricidal type.

The avuncular Pumblechook himself had been the victim of his very first imaginary murder of a near relation and would-be 'patron': at the end of the Christmas meal, having absorbed a glassful of the Tar which Pip had poured into the brandy bottle, the uncle had performed such 'an appalling spasmodic whooping-cough dance' that the miserable child, believing that his end had come, had immediately looked upon himself as his murderer: 'I had no doubt I had murdered him somehow' (iv, 59–60).

Then, there had been the hallucination at the end of his first visit to Satis House, when he had seen, or fancied that he saw, his new 'patroness'[19] hanging by the neck from a beam of the brewery (viii, 93–4). Then, there had been his fear (prompted by Pumblechook) of his having had a hand in his sister's murderous aggression (xvi, 148). All this, assuredly, was expressed in terms of apprehensions and nightmarish visions, but the phenomenon on each occasion could also be read as an inverted wish. And so can this new manifestation of the Oedipus complex. Pip's fear is even so extreme that, again like Oedipus, he does his best to make the murder impossible: 'I did not wish to be a parricide',[20] Oedipus explains to the Corinthian messenger who wants to know why he left the town where his parents live. Pip cannot run away (which would be the death of Magwitch) but, by giving up his financial expectations, he cuts off any filial bond that might link him to his provider. He will help the man, he will protect him, he will be true to him, even to the death, he will indulge his illusions, let him be a father, or rather let him take himself for one, he will act *as* a son, but knowing all the time that he is playing a part, with this secret like a barrier between them.

Even towards the end, when his 'repugnance' to Magwitch has all 'melted away', Pip writes: 'in the hunted wounded shackled creature who held my hand in his, I only saw a man who had meant to be my benefactor' (liv, 456). But 'had meant to be' is a far cry from 'had been'!

It must be conceded that there is ironic bitterness in this 'had meant to be' and that the convict's money would now be less unacceptable than it had been a few weeks earlier. Pip's prejudices have melted away with his repugnance as we gather from a conversation he has with Jaggers about the 'fate' of the convict's wealth on the day that follows Magwitch's recapture:

I imparted to Mr Jaggers my design of keeping him in ignorance of the fate of his wealth. Mr Jaggers was querulous and angry with me for having 'let it slip through my fingers,' and said we must memorialize by-and-by, and try at all events for some of it.

But, he did not conceal from me that although there might be many cases in which the forfeiture would not be exacted, there were no circumstances in this case to make it one of them. I understood that, very well. I was not related to the outlaw, or connected with him by any recognizable tie; he had put his hand to no writing or settlement in my favour before his apprehension, and to do so now would be idle. I had no claim, and I finally resolved, and ever afterwards abided by the resolution, that my heart should never be sickened with the hopeless task of attempting to establish one (lv, 458).

Hopeless the task would certainly be. Dickens has hurried things and plotted against his hero's possible change of mind, allowing just enough time for him to be cured of his prejudices and intolerance, yet not enough for him to get an inheritance to which he has no lawful claim.

For the novelist has no wish to spoil the meaning of his moral and social fable. During the third stage of his adventures, Pip's progress has been towards solitude and renunciation, and, after renouncing the convict's money, he has declined all forms of patronage, even from the person whom he had so long imagined to be his benefactress: 'Miss Havisham', he tells Wemmick, 'was good enough to ask me ... whether she could do nothing for me, and I told her No' (li, 421). Pip will get no money from anyone who is not related to him or 'connected with him by any recognizable tie'; and, by so doing, by thus giving up all thoughts of being a 'foundling', he will return to the beginning and accept himself as the son of a poor man.

The real father's poverty is actually sublimated by the death of the adoptive one. With no legacy to hand down to his would-be son, Magwitch in the prison dies like a pauper. In fact, he dies two deaths: his own, which rehabilitates him as a man, even as a gentle man, and the death of the father long buried in the churchyard, whose ghost he had been when he had first 'started up from among the graves' and whom he impersonates to the very last.

Now that the ghost has gone to rest for good, Oedipus is cured of his parricidal leanings and Telemachus can give up his quest. A timely fever will help the hero exorcize old dreams and borrowed identities and become himself again:

That I had a fever and was avoided, that I suffered greatly, that I often lost my reason, that the time seemed interminable, that I confounded impossible existences with my own identity . . . that I passed through these phases of disease, I know of my own remembrance, and did in some sort know at the time. That I sometimes struggled with real people, in the belief that they were murderers . . . I also knew at the time (lvii, 471–2).

Pip recovers from this cathartic malady to become, after his own terms, if not the Pip of older times, at least one very like him: 'I fancied I was little Pip again' (lvii, 476), he says. With Joe looking after him 'in the old unassertive protecting way', 'like a child in his hands', Pip is born again to himself.

But it would certainly be a gross misreading of the book to say that in this scene Pip finds a new father or that a son is born to Joe. The relationship between these two characters has never had that kind of ambiguity. Joe is assuredly a 'fatherly', even a 'motherly' man: he feeds, protects, nurses; but he is, and always was, too honest, too 'unassertive' and too much like 'a larger species of child' (ii, 40) ever to play father to his 'best of friends'. Significantly, when the stranger at the Three Jolly Bargemen enquired about their relationship, he felt unable to define it:

'Son of yours?'
    'Well,' said Joe, meditatively . . . 'well – no. No, he ain't.'
    'Nevvy?' said the strange man.
    'Well,' said Joe . . . 'he is not – no, not to deceive you, he is *not* – my nevvy.'
    'What the Blue Blazes is he?' asked the stranger (x, 105).

It is precisely because he is no prevaricator that Joe can be a mediator between the true and the false Pips. The moral touchstone of the book, he alone can help the hero find his true metal and his true identity. Joe is the father who might have been, not the father who was or ever pretended to be. And this is the reason why, at the end of the novel, he can still father a Pip of his own, a little Pip Gargery whose happy story will never be worth telling.

For repetition implies difference. 'There . . . was – I again!' exclaims Pip who has had a sudden vision of what he used to be like when he was living at the forge; but Joe is more matter-of-fact: 'We giv' him the name of Pip for your sake, dear old chap', he says, 'and we hoped he might grow a little bit like you, and we think he do' (lix, 490). Not Pip's double, but his mirror, Pip Gargery will merely help the son of Philip Pirrip to recognize and accept himself, draw the line between what is, what was and what might have been, and return to his origins.

Thus, Pip's Odyssey brings him back to familiar shores, where Pip is waiting for him. He will now learn 'for certain' that his 'true legitimacy' rests on his semi-bastardy, half Philip, half Pirrip, 'as if in the Family Romance there were some sort of secret pact between aesthetics and logic, stipulating that the Bastard can never betray the Foundling who survives within him without running the risk of a *literary* impoverishment – a loss of depth, ambiguity and poetry – and of losing at least some of the social advantages due to him'.[21] Oedipus will survive and learn self-reliance only in harbouring Telemachus somewhere in his heart of hearts, but their different roles will no longer be confused. For was it not Oedipus who had embarked on a foolish voyage, looking for imaginary fathers and accepting self-imposed ones? Was it not Telemachus who had lost his bearings, blindly murdering parental figures in his dreams and *actes manqués*? But this strange comedy of errors ends with the hero's wanderings when the Tale of Lost Illusions becomes the Novel of Regained Identity.

NOTES: CHAPTER 10

1 *Our Mutual Friend*, The New Oxford Illustrated Dickens (London: Oxford University Press, 1963), III, vi, 476.
2 See below, ch. 12, 'The sense of two endings', pp. 175–9.
3 *David Copperfield*, ed. Nina Burgis, Clarendon Dickens (Oxford, 1981), lxiv, 751.
4 B. Westburg, *The Confessional Fictions of Charles Dickens* (De Kalb, Ill.: Northern Illinois University Press, 1977), p. 119; Robert B. Partlow Jr., 'The moving I: a study of the point of view in *Great Expectations*', *College English*, vol. 23 (November 1961), p. 122.
5 G. Robert Stange, 'Expectations well lost: Dickens' fable for his time', *College English*, vol. 16 (1954), reprinted in George H. Ford and Lauriat Lane Jr (eds), *The Dickens Critics* (Ithaca, NY: Cornell University Press, 1961), p. 295.
6 Marthe Robert, *Origins of the Novel*, translated by Sacha Rabinovitch (Bloomington: Indiana University Press, 1980), p. 19.
7 Sigmund Freud, 'Family romances', translated by James Strachey, in *The Standard Edition of the Complete Psychological Works of Sigmund Freud* (London: The Hogarth Press, 1975), vol. 9, p. 238.
8 ibid., p. 237.

9   Freud, 'Creative writers and day-dreaming', translated by I. F. Grant Duff, in *The Standard Edition of the Complete Psychological Works of Sigmund Freud*. (London: The Hogarth Press, 1975), vol. 9, pp. 141–53.

10 *Bleak House*, eds G. Ford and S. Monod (New York: Norton, 1977), lxiv, 753.

11 *Our Mutual Friend*, op. cit., II, xiii, 366.

12 ibid., IV, xiv, 779.

13 *David Copperfield*, op. cit., xiv, 184.

14 What Pip says of the convict at the end of chapter 5 might also apply to his real father.

15 cf. *Little Dorrit*, ed. H. P. Sucksmith, Clarendon Dickens (Oxford, 1979), II, ix, 524 (about Tattycoram).

16 Sylvère Monod (trans.), *Les Grandes Espérances* (Paris: Garnier, 1959), Introduction, p. xxi.

17 Pip's social determinism is repeatedly underlined. An early instance is when Pip is 'surprised into crooning' Old Clem as he pushes Miss Havisham round the room (xii, 124); a late one is when Drummle speaks to Pip of the marsh country: 'Curious little public-houses – and smithies – and that' (xliii, 370).

18 J. J. Rousseau (about Montaigne), 'Ebauche des Confessions' in *Oeuvres Complètes*, Vol. 1, '*Les Confessions* et autres textes autobiographiques' (Paris: Pléiade, 1959) p. 1150: 'ces faux sincères qui veulent tromper en disant vrai'.

19 Both Pumblechook, 'self-constituted my patron' (xii, 125) and Miss Havisham, 'my patroness' (xxix, 253) are clearly meant to be perceived as father or '*pater*' figures.

20 Sophocles, *Oedipus the King*, line 1001.

21 M. Robert, op. cit., p. 112.

CHAPTER 11

Romantic Irony

Even making allowances for the moral and philosophical advantages of deprivation, the outcome of Pip's adventures is not entirely satisfactory. The 'sacrifice of so much portable property' (lv, 461), the unhonoured pledges of the title, the enigmatic, and anyway unverifiable, promises of the last sentence will leave any reader with a sense of frustration, and any Dickens reader with the puzzling realization that the story does not end like an old play.

G. K. Chesterton long ago summed up the situation: 'All his books', he says of Dickens, 'might be called *Great Expectations*. But the only book to which he gave the name of *Great Expectations* was the only book in which the expectation was never realised'.[1] A justifiably provocative remark on a provocative novel, though, like all sweeping statements, it cannot receive unqualified approval: if we took it literally, what should we make of the *Dombey* plot or of Rick Carstone's tragic fate?

Recent criticism has improved on Chesterton. *Great Expectations* emerges no longer as the 'only' but as the most outstanding illustration of Dickens's self-contradictions. The view almost unanimously held is that the providential myth – the 'Dickens Myth' as Geoffrey Thurley calls it – remained from first to last Dickens's narrative *pattern*, whereas the Great Expectations *theme*, 'so complacently approved in *Oliver Twist*',[2] soon became an object of suspicion and criticism.

The undermining process begins as early as *The Old Curiosity Shop*, according to Gabriel Pearson who reads Grandfather Trent's 'illegitimate dreams of wealth' as Dickens's 'first criticism'[3] of the theme. But real demolishing is more patently observable from *Martin Chuzzlewit* onwards as, book after book, and with growing acuteness, the structural principle of the Dickens novel becomes its own subject-matter. 'Expectations', a word conspicuously absent from *Oliver Twist*, that ideal 'Great Expectations' novel in which desires were fulfilled without even having to be expressed, occurs ever increasingly in the later novels, where it is always loaded with derogatory, ironic connotations. Often synonymous with 'greed', 'ambition', 'illegitimate hopes', it is, among other examples, the word carefully selected by Old Martin Chuzzlewit to inveigle Pecksniff: 'I confide in you to be my ally; to attach yourself to me by ties of Interest and Expectation';[4] it is also a favourite term with mealy-mouthed Uriah Heep: 'You have heard something, I des-say, of a change in my expectations, Master Copperfield, – I should say, Mister Copperfield?'.[5] A word of ill omen too, it often triggers off catastrophes and ironic reversals of plot: 'I have been bred up from childhood with great expectations', declares Martin Chuzzlewit, 'and have always been taught to believe that I should be, one day, very rich. So I should have been, but for certain brief reasons which I am going to tell you, and which have led to my being disinherited'.[6] 'It began when I taught him to be too covetous of what I have to leave, and made the expectation of it his great business',[7] complains Anthony Chuzzlewit, who finds himself hoist with his own petard on discovering that his son's cupidity outdoes his own. Serves him right, thinks the reader, always ready to applaud comic retribution. But with *Dombey and Son*, things take a more serious turn as the thwarting of Dombey's misdirected expectations costs the life of little Paul. And, with *Bleak House*, the Great Expectations theme acquires a radically tragic dimension: 'Rick, Rick!' cries Jarndyce to his ward (Pip's forerunner in many ways) in a vain effort to exhort him against building castles in the air, 'for the love of God, don't found a hope or expectation on the family curse! Whatever you do on this side of the grave, never give one lingering glance towards the horrible phantom that has haunted us so many years. Better to borrow, better to beg, better to die!'.[8] But Rick is no more able than Miss Flite, his ambiguously comic counterpart, to give up wishful thinking:

'My father expected a Judgement,' said Miss Flite. 'My brother. My sister. They all expected a Judgement. The same that I expect.'
    'They are all –'
    'Ye-es. Dead, of course, my dear,' said she …
    'Would it not be wiser,' said I, 'to expect this Judgement no more?'

'Why, my dear,' she answered promptly, 'of course it would!'
'And to attend the Court no more?'

'Equally of course,' said she. 'Very wearing to be always in expectation of what never comes, my dear Fitz-Jarndyce! Wearing, I assure you, to the bone!' ...

'But, my dear,' she went on, in her mysterious way, 'there's a dreadful attraction in the place ... There's a cruel attraction in the place. You *can't* leave it. And you *must* expect.'[9]

Drawn like her, irresistibly, by the magnet of expectations, Rick for years will pine and waste away, unheeding his guardian's warnings, until too late: 'I have to begin the world ... I have learned a lesson now',[10] he declares on his death-bed.

The Great Expectations motif has become with the years such a tragic theme that by 1860, when 'Expectations' is appointed, so to speak, eponymous hero of Dickens's new novel, the Dickens reader has been sufficiently educated to suspect that there is something in the wind. All the more so as, a year before, in *A Tale of Two Cities*, the novelist felt it once more necessary to make his stand very clear on the question:

... he had expected neither to walk on pavements of gold, nor to lie on beds of roses: if he had had any such exalted expectation, he would not have prospered. He had expected labour, and he found it, and did it, and made the best of it. In this, his prosperity consisted,[11]

his narrator declared about Charles Darnay. And, as Barry Westburg argues, Dickens is doubtless writing for a 'fit reader', 'somebody', that is, 'who has already read Dickens's earlier works; somebody who brings to each text a knowledge of its pre-texts'.[12] 'The later books ... can really only be partially understood ... unless their provenance out of the earlier is spelled out', also writes G. Thurley who describes *Great Expectations* as 'the Dickens myth raised to the surface, laid upon the table, dissected, criticized'.[13]

With its irony well advertised in its title and the subversion of its plot, *Great Expectations* is undeniably Dickens's most crucially self-critical and self-questioning novel. Yet it is not quite fair to bring it down to a mere parody of itself or to Dickens's own doctoral thesis on the Dickensian novel. Thurley's cruel surgical image, besides, does justice neither to the mood of the novel nor to its integrity. We get an impression that the critic himself has laid hold of the anatomist's scissors to clip off the wings of the 'Robber Fancy' and amputate the romantic half of the book.

For, paradoxical though it may be, *Great Expectations* is just as romantic as it is ironic. But this ambivalence, which is its greatest charm, is curiously ignored by commentators. Romance is analysed, if at all, merely in terms of the hero's mistakes, never of the reader's or the author's pleasure. Only irony is proper food for the critic, whose clear-sightedness it testifies to. This is to proceed as if the two notions were mutually exclusive, which they by no means are. The two poles of the novel's dynamic and dialectic principle, they must on the contrary be accepted as complementary forces working together at the incessant construction and de-construction of a story dangerously poised between utopia and reality.

This strange interplay of forces, reason and passion, belief and doubt, freedom and restraint, acceptance and refusal, challenges the critic as much as it appeals to the common reader, for it baffles definition. Faced with a similar problem – the difficulty of accounting for the special kind of subjective objectivity that he observed in the poets – Friedrich Schlegel found not one word but two, *Romantische Ironie*,[14] which he yoked together in perpetual conjugal enmity to describe the phenomenon. Short of a definition, 'romantic irony' remains the best description of the dynamic process which enables the artist to see how far he can go, to enjoy at once critical awareness and creative licence, to be eternally destroyer and preserver.

Great Expectations does not begin 'Once upon a time' – that 'Open Sesame!' of pure fiction which everybody knows to mean 'Never upon any time' – but on Christmas Eve, on a 'raw afternoon' and in a churchyard. A child whose name calls to mind the Jacks and Toms of fairy tales, though we know he could go by a normal identity if only he wanted to, meets a ghost-like man who is no ghost but a runaway convict. 'What fat cheeks you ha' got ... Darn Me if I couldn't eat them' (i, 36), exclaims the stranger who is no Big Bad Wolf either, but only a starving man. We find ourselves at once disquietingly placed half-way between romance and reality. 'We have encountered such inductions before', Harry Stone writes. 'We are reminded of ghost stories, nurses' tales, and eerie legends told at twilight.'[15] 'Reminded' indeed, but aware all the same that we are not in fairy-land.

'But,' Stone goes on to say, 'these do not all begin on Christmas Eve. The immediate model is at once more exact and closer at hand. The opening of *Great Expectations* is nothing more nor less than a redaction of the archetypal onset of Dickens' Christmas fairy stories: of "Gabriel Grub," *A Christmas Carol*, and *The Haunted Man*'.[16] This is certainly closer to the truth. The aptness of Stone's new analogy is even strengthened by the seasonal character of this induction: the first four instalments appeared in *All the Year Round* between 1 and 23 December 1860, harking back, as Katherine Carolan points out, 'both in timing of appearance and in subject matter to the seasonal books which had permanently linked Dickens with Christmas'.[17]

Severed from the rest of the book, the first five chapters (corresponding to the first three serials) would in fact make up a perfectly self-contained Christmas story, or rather a parodic version of one. For, as has so often been observed, the Christmas spirit is no longer there. From the moment when Pip was tilted and tilted again and 'the church jumped over its own weather-cock' (i, 37), it seems as if the world had gone topsy-turvy. Christmas has become a 'festive occasion' upon which there is no rejoicing for little children, no reprieve for hunted criminals, and nothing to be expected even from the most 'gentle Christian man'. As Pumblechook immolates Pip on the communion table during this gruesome parody of a Christmas dinner that we are invited to attend at the Gargerys', Joe's offers of gravy become less and less acceptable and, when it comes to downright butchery and bloodshed, his inefficient tokens of comfort are definitely declined: 'Joe offered me more gravy, which I was afraid to take' (iv, 58).

Joe is just as helpless in the presence of the convict. All he can offer is his bad grammar as the expression of fellow-feeling: 'We don't know what you have done, but we wouldn't have you starved to death for it, poor miserable fellow-creatur. – Would us, Pip?' (v, 71). And it is not accidental, as Thurley remarks, that, even though he is 'emotionally' on the side of the prisoner, he 'has already helped recapture'[18] him both as blacksmith and man-hunter.

In destroying the Christmas spirit, Dickens is also bound to destroy supernatural agencies. The Christ-like figure 'who had been soaked in water, and smothered in mud, and lamed by stones, and cut by flints, and stung by nettles, and torn by briars' (i, 36) when he is caught again is taken up into a god-forsaken place, 'the black Hulk lying out a little way from the mud of the shore, like a wicked Noah's ark' (v, 71). There is no more hope to be got from biblical than from popular mythology, no more divine harbour than elves or good fairies. We are in the godless world of nineteenth-century England, from which the devil himself has been driven out: there are no evil spirits, no ogres, no mischievous genii, only very bad men.

This is a dire prospect for lovers of romance. But 'pretence' is the saving grace that will help fiction survive the loss of faith. If Noah's ark, no matter how wicked, has no right of sanctuary in the British islands, a hulk may still be said to look like it. If speaking animals have disappeared from Dickensland, a guilty child may still hear the voice of his conscience speak through the nostrils of a 'black ox, with a white cravat on' and 'something of a clerical air' and greet him with a reproachful 'Holloa, young thief!' (iii, 48). Would-be ogres are still free to threaten little children: 'your heart and your liver shall be tore out, roasted and ate' (i, 38). Out-Heroders of Herod extemporizing on the swinishness of boys are still entitled to achieve frightful metamorphoses verbally:

'Swine,' pursued Mr Wopsle, in his deepest voice, and pointing his fork at my blushes, as if he were mentioning my christian name; 'Swine were the companions of the prodigal. The gluttony of Swine is put before us, as an example to the young ... What is detestable in a pig, is more detestable in a boy.'

'Or girl,' suggested Mr Hubble.

'Of course, or girl, Mr Hubble,' assented Mr Wopsle, rather irritably, 'but there is no girl present.'

'Besides,' said Mr Pumblechook, turning sharp on me, 'think what you've got to be grateful for. If you'd been born a Squeaker –'

'He *was*, if ever a child was,' said my sister, most emphatically. Joe gave me some more gravy.

'Well, but I mean a four-footed Squeaker,' said Mr Pumble-chook. 'If you had been born such, would you have been here now? Not you –'

'Unless in that form,' said Mr Wopsle, nodding towards the dish.

'... And what would have been your destination?' turning on me again. 'You would have been disposed of for so many shillings according to the market price of the article, and Dunstable the butcher would have come up to you as you lay in your straw, and he would have whipped you under his left arm, and with his right he would have tucked up his frock to get a penknife from out of his waistcoat-pocket, and he would have shed your blood and had your life ...'

Joe offered me more gravy, which I was afraid to take.

'He was a world of trouble to you, ma'am,' said Mrs Hubble, commiserating my sister (iv, 58).

Dickens's make-believe rests on modal variations, 'as ifs', 'likes' and 'woulds', and on his well-founded trust in his readers' power to create mental pictures and take them for the truth as do his very characters.

Instalment number 4 of the serial (chapters 6 and 7) brings us back to normality. In chapter 6 Pip is put to bed and Wopsle's clothes are put to dry, while chapter 7 provides information about life in the village, evening-school tuition and Joe's life before his marriage. Dickens, we understand, is now laying the foundations for a realistic novel.

But these newly acquired certitudes are at once shaken as chapter 8 takes us into Wonderland. An authentic Wonderland, for we are introduced to Satis House with no rhetorical warnings to suspend our belief; within the convention of literary fiction at least, Satis House is a real house with real dark, mysterious passages, where the clocks have really stopped and from which the light of day has really been shut out; and the mistress of the place really is a withered bride, really wearing a yellowed bridal dress and yellowed bridal flowers. Metaphorical language will, admittedly, enhance the 'as-TON-ishing' (xiii, 130) character of the place and of its inhabitants: beautiful, scornful Estella behaves 'as if' she were 'a queen' (viii, 86) and looks 'like a star' (viii, 89), and 'corpse-like' Miss Havisham (viii, 90), with her 'crutch-headed stick' will later be said to look 'like the Witch of the place' (xi, 113); but, even divested of such ornaments, the world Pip enters at the beginning of his adventures is more romantic by far than any of the places where Dickens's fairy-tale heroes end up and find shelter: Oliver's resting-place after the workhouse and the thieves' kitchen is no better than a cottage of the most traditional pastoral fashion; so is Esther's new Bleak House, and Bob Cratchit's castle remains to the end a poor Englishman's house.

But such is the paradoxical nature of *Great Expectations* that it has all the outward signs of romance, and yet is not a romance. All the fairy-tale motifs are there – the enchanted house, death-in-life, the captive Princess, the weird Witch-like lady – but the hero himself is not a fairy-tale hero. He has in truth no right to be one: literary conventions forbid it because he is also the narrator of his own story.

A fairy-tale hero must pay the price of overprotection that will ensure the happy ending: he has no say in what happens to him. Always a third person, he has to trust his fate entirely into the hands of the almighty narrating authorities. Comparing fairy-tale heroes and the heroes of realistic short-stories, André Jolles judiciously suggests that they might be defined according to the questions they arouse in the reader's mind: 'What is he going to do?' in the latter case, 'What is going to happen to him?'[19] in the former. Judged by these standards, Oliver Twist is a perfect fairy-tale hero. He progresses through life guided 'by a stronger hand than chance'[20] and takes no active part in his own adventures. He has the passivity, says J. Hillis Miller, 'of waiting, of expectation, of "great expectations" '.[21] His one bold action, asking for more, is imposed upon him as the result of drawing lots: 'it fell to Oliver Twist',[22] a phrase that seals his destiny and is the true index of his election. But, apart from this memorable utterance, he hardly ever says a word; his retorts, in fact, are so few and so short – 'Yes, sir', 'No, sir', in most cases – that, placed on end, they would amount to little more than a hundredth of the whole book. He is even strikingly absent from twenty-one chapters in the fifty-three that make up the novel. Yet, he remains all the while the sole object of other people's preoccupations and activities. Without his having to interfere or even show up, his problems are settled for him by benevolent men and women whose main object is, in Mr Brownlow's own terms, 'the discovery of [his] parentage, and regaining *for him* the inheritance of which, if this story be true, he has been fraudulently deprived'.[23] There is no telling even how much he knows of what is going on in his absence when these good people are discussing and furthering what Mr

Grimwig himself calls 'the life and adventures of Oliver Twist'[24] as if he were a hero of his own fiction, and, as far as we can judge, he has no awareness that his story is being recorded.

Oliver Twist and *Great Expectations* are often compared as exemplifying two diametrically opposed plot patterns, which they do, but the difference is also a matter of heroic status and narrative technique. Oliver might be described as a fairy-tale hero placed in an ordinary setting that has even gained the novel a reputation for its realism. Pip, on the contrary, is an ordinary hero placed, at least for a time, in a fairy-tale setting which, as story-teller, he himself contributes to making even more romantic than it is. Oliver plays no part in either forwarding the plot or relating his adventures. Pip is held responsible for all that happens and for the way it is told: a twofold responsibility whose two aspects are closely linked since Pip's chief difficulty as a character is to appreciate people and events at their fair value, whereas his main endeavour as a narrator is to show that he was in his youth a most incompetent reader of the book of his life.

'Reader' is not a far-fetched simile: from the moment he enters Satis House, Pip acts like someone who has inadvertently found his way into a work of fiction, which he improves, as he reads on, with his own marginal notes.

As long as he remains an outsider – the 'common labouring boy' who comes to play at Satis House for the day and goes back at night to the Forge, which he knows is his true home – his metaphorical embellishments are rather harmless and do not alter the meaning of the book. Neither, for that matter, does his fantastic account of how he 'got on up town' and 'what like' Miss Havisham is. He merely dyes black the ghastly white picture and gives back to the scene the true colour of 'melancholy' that so impressed him that he could not play. So true to the spirit of his experience is his dream-like version of it that he even condemns himself in his phantasmagoria to take his meal in banishment: 'And I got up behind the coach to eat mine, because she told me to' (ix, 97), says the boy who was fed 'on the stones of the yard', like 'a dog in disgrace' (viii, 92).

So far, Pip knows his place and his fibs are not untruths. Real misconstructions begin when he finds himself changed overnight into a young man with great, yet greatly unexpected, expectations and, urged by circumstances to take himself for a fairy-tale hero, forces his way into the wrong book and the wrong literary genre.

He has the givens of the plot: his great expectations, a mysterious benefactor. His imagination provides at once the missing information, finds the setting, names the other actor: Satis House, Miss Havisham. Hasty as it may be, and mistaken as it will prove, his choice is admirably true to the workings of desire and its inner contradictions. 'What I wanted, who can say? How can *I* say, when I never knew?' (xiv, 135–6), he had confessed not so long ago, describing the discontent of his 'restlessly aspiring self', a perverted, yet common form of desire that feeds on its own frustration. And what place could better satisfy this insatiable need than Satis House itself, the official abode of wish fulfilment where wishes are never fulfilled:

> 'Enough House,' said I; 'that's a curious name, miss.'
> 'Yes,' she replied; 'but it meant more than it said. It meant, when it was given, that whoever had this house, could want nothing else. They must have been easily satisfied in those days, I should think' (viii, 86).

Satis House is a wicked place, as Pip has learnt to his cost, a place where he has been humiliated, made to play, made to weep, made to love, and beggared always, but there is 'a cruel attraction in the place', just as there was in Chancery, and this is where, 'against reason, against promise, against peace, against hope, against happiness, against all discouragement that could be' (xxix, 253–4), he chooses to belong and play the leading part.

This cannot be done unless he revises his text and suits his similes to the occasion, which he does without the slightest hesitation: the 'Witch of the place' is with no further delay promoted 'fairy godmother' to justify his own magic transformation:

> 'This is a gay figure, Pip,' said she, making her crutch stick play round me, as if she, the fairy godmother who had changed me, were bestowing the finishing gift (xix, 183).

When he leaves her, she has become '*my* fairy godmother' (p. 184, my emphasis), though she still has 'weird eyes' and her magic wand still is the witch's 'crutch stick'.

Such tricks, if they provide an interesting insight into the nature of the human heart and into the art of self-delusion, are totally out of place in a would-be fairy tale. A fairy-tale hero has no business and no power to delude himself in that way. He lives surrounded by characters endowed with well-defined functions, 'helpers', 'donors', 'opponents',[25] and he is never mistaken for long as to which is which. Neither is the reader who tells good from evil with unerring intuition, no matter how hard villains try to deceive him, for the narrator himself has a firm hold on the text and leaves no room for incertitude. But a first-person narrative permits the double mystification and the shared uneasiness as to which 'as if' is the right one.

Through the agency of his narrator, Dickens actually compels us to read *Great Expectations* as we do 'mystery tales' or 'uncanny stories'. Contrary to 'fairy tales', such narratives are usually written in the first person precisely in order to create mixed feelings in the reader,[26] uneasily torn between suspicion about the tale and regard for the teller: the reported events sound unbelievable, but the reporting 'I' ought to be reliable as first-hand witness of the facts, and will be all the more so if he writes apologetically, which he often does, recording in particular his own past incredulity and astonishment on first experiencing the strange phenomena that he now feels impelled to relate without omitting to add as a saving clause: 'Was there ever such a fate!' (xli, 357).

Reliable in this narrow sense, but never authoritative, Pip's narrative gives us imperfect and contradictory information: facts, hints, mere surmises from which we cannot fairly sort out *the* truth. We are *told* by Pip that Miss Havisham is his benefactress but given no proof of it; we are *shown* disturbing coincidences and made to suspect some connection between the hero's progress and his shameful past; and we have, of course, strong premonitions that the convict will reappear, for what would become of literature if characters were lost on the way? But it is not until we discover with the hero himself that Provis is the 'donor' (xxxvi, 307) that we know the real story. Reading an ordinary ironic novel, we would have been taken long ago into the narrator's confidence. Reading a fairy-tale, we would merely ascertain that our guesses were right or our wishes properly fulfilled.

Our surprise is assuredly nothing compared to Pip's astonishment on discovering the identity of his benefactor, but our forebodings were not foreknowledge properly speaking: when the moment of revelation comes, we know just as much and just as little as the hero does, we have received no side information from the homodiegetic narrator, as we might have if he had been an outsider, and we have been placed in no superior position from which to 'look down'[27] on the hero and wait for the catastrophe with amused anticipation, which is common practice in traditional third-person novels. When, for instance, in *Daniel Deronda*, Gwendolen Harleth eventually discovers the existence of her Jewish rival and of a world beyond her own, we have long been introduced to Mirah and to Jewish society, thanks to George Eliot's double plot, and we have been trained from the first to appreciate the heroine's moral shortcomings through the narrator's strictures and ironic portrayal. But in this novel, all the premonitory signs of plot reversal were perceived in time by the hero himself and are plainly reported as part of his own experience, not as narratorial exclusive knowledge. And our only superiority over Pip rests in our readiness to interpret these strange coincidences and recurrences, while the protagonist prefers to ignore them or rule them out of his memory. Thus, the unsolicited appearance at the Three Jolly Bargemen of the stranger who stirs his rum-and-water with Joe's file and bestows upon him the two one-pound notes leaves Pip 'stupefied by this turning up of [his] old misdeed and old acquaintance' (x, 107) and he goes to bed overburdened with guilt for being 'on secret terms of conspiracy with convicts'; but then, to our surprise, he calls this 'old misdeed' 'a feature in my low career that I had previously forgotten' (how could he?) and he tries hard to forget it again, endeavouring at once to replace the nightmare by sweeter dreams: 'I coaxed myself to sleep by thinking of Miss Havisham's, next Wednesday' (x, 108). It will never occur to him to interpret this visit as the harbinger of his own convict's return or, later, to associate his great expectations with this early instalment of money. Denegation is his usual reaction when the past haunts him too disturbingly, as the following two examples show:

> If I had often thought before, with something allied to shame, of my companionship with the fugitive whom I had once seen limping among those graves, what were my thoughts on this Sunday, when the place recalled the wretch, ragged and shivering, with his felon iron and badge! My comfort was, that it happened a long time ago, and that he had doubtless been transported a long way off, and that he was dead to me, and might be veritably dead into the bargain (xix, 173).

I consumed the whole time in thinking how strange it was that I should be encompassed by all this taint of prison and crime; that, in my childhood out on our lonely marshes on a winter evening I should have first encountered it; that, it should have reappeared on two occasions, starting out like a stain that was faded but not gone; that, it should in this new way pervade my fortune and advancement ... I beat the prison dust off my feet as I sauntered to and fro, and I shook it out of my dress, and I exhaled its air from my lungs (xxxii, 284).

Our aloofness as readers leaves us much freer to face strange situations, dwell on the meaning of unexpected encounters and associations and put two and two together. As we are not personally involved in the story, we do not mind being caught in a web of connections and cross-references. We rather tend, on the contrary, to welcome them as possible clues to the mystery that we are trying to pierce, not unreasonably suspecting them to have been purposely sifted from a heap of recollections by the autobiographer as especially meaningful. In other words, we are not better informed than the hero but what information we get is better signposted and we are more receptive to it. So much so that, although we read the same story, we read quite a different book. The two books even belong to different fictional modes: in Northrop Frye's classification ours would come under the heading of '*low mimetic* mode' since 'the hero is one of us' and 'we respond to a sense of his common humanity'; whereas the hero's should be affiliated to 'naïve romance', which is 'closer to the wish-fulfilment dream'.[28] The latter affiliation is explicitly propounded by the narrator himself who, after being long behindhand in grasping the meaning of his life-story, proves a sharper critic than might have been expected and audaciously steals a march on the structuralists:

Betimes in the morning I was up and out. It was too early yet to go to Miss Havisham's, so I loitered into the country on Miss Havisham's side of town – which was not Joe's side; I could go there to-morrow – thinking about my patroness, and painting brilliant pictures of her plans for me.

She had adopted Estella, she had as good as adopted me, and it could not fail to be her intention to bring us together. She reserved it for me to restore the desolate house, admit the sunshine into the dark rooms, set the clocks a going and the cold hearths a blazing, tear down the cobwebs, destroy the vermin – in short, do all the shining deeds of the young Knight of romance, and marry the Princess. I had stopped to look at the house as I passed; and its seared red brick walls, blocked windows, and strong green ivy clasping even the stacks of chimneys with its twigs and tendons, as if with sinewy old arms, had made up a rich attractive mystery, of which I was the hero (xxix, 253).

The last and catastrophic stage of Pip's expectations is heralded by a new reference to literary fiction:

In the Eastern story, the heavy slab that was to fall on the bed of state in the flush of conquest was slowly wrought out of the quarry, the tunnel for the rope to hold it in its place was slowly carried through the leagues of rock, the slab was slowly raised and fitted in the roof, the rope was rove to it and slowly taken through the miles of hollow to the great iron ring. All being made ready with much labour, and the hour come, the sultan was aroused in the dead of the night, and the sharpened axe that was to sever the rope from the great iron ring was put into his hand, and he struck with it, and the rope parted and rushed away, and the ceiling fell. So, in my case; all the work, near and afar, that tended to the end, had been accomplished; and in an instant the blow was struck, and the roof of my stronghold dropped upon me (xxxviii, 330)

The allusion is to one of James Ridley's *Tales of the Genii*, 'The Tale of the Inchanters, or Misnar, the Sultan of the East'.[29] Ridley's book had been a great favourite with young Dickens, as it was later to be with young David Copperfield, and the story of Misnar had even so appealed to his childish imagination that, when still at Chatham, he had made himself famous in the family circle for writing a tragedy founded on it and entitled 'Misnar, the Sultan of India'.[30] All his life, the novelist retained a nostalgic fondness for the fabulous heroes and friends of his youth who had so often 'kept [him] company' and whose adventures had 'kept alive [his] fancy';[31] and it is significant that, after a long lapse of years, when, in his own fiction, he came to depict the predicament of a young man suddenly driven out of the world of romance, the subject should have triggered off an associative process that took him back to those early days of escapism into romantic illusion, suggesting to him this comparison with the very story from which he had derived his first notion of tragedy.

As Ridley's were popular tales, widely read among Dickens's contemporaries, there was no need for the novelist to press the analogy, but as they have gone out of fashion, it is not inappropriate today to offer a brief summary of the story in question. Misnar is a prosperous ruler, beloved by all except Abubal, his envious brother who, wishing most particularly to dispossess him of a recently built abode of unequalled magnificence, takes up arms against him and, with the help of two enchanters, finds himself 'in one Day ... Master of India; his Brother defeated; and his gaudy Pavilion wrested from him'.[32] Having settled at once with his companions in the coveted pavilion, Abubal gives a banquet there in celebration of his victory during the night that follows. Meanwhile, Misnar has sought refuge in the mountains with Horam, his faithful vizier. In the middle of the night, Horam wakes up his master and takes him to a cave among the rocks; there, removing a stone, he uncovers a strong rope, one end of which runs through the rocks while the other is fastened to an enormous ring of iron. Placing an axe in the hands of his master, Horam enjoins him to strike and sever the rope. The Sultan obeys without in the least suspecting what the consequences of his gesture will be. But the next morning a messenger apprises him of the death of his enemies 'crushed to Atoms'[33] by a ponderous stone artfully concealed in the roof of the pavilion and released from its confinement when the rope had been cut. Foreseeing rebellion, Horam, unbeknown to his master, had installed the apparatus to trap unwelcome visitors.

Seen in the light of this original context, the analogy does more than express the crumbling of Pip's hopes and castles in air; it implies no less than the well-deserved destruction of an impostor. The once 'Knight of romance' now identifies himself with the villain of a moral tale and, by so doing, invites us to reconsider our notion of heroism. Of course, we cannot deny him the right to remain 'the hero of [his] own life'[34] and we are bound to admit that if 'plot consists of somebody doing something',[35] he remains that somebody; but, now that he is no longer 'superior in *degree*',[37] we are faced with the difficulty pointed out by Frye 'in retaining the word "hero" '[38] to describe his new fictional status. Chesterton helps us out of this dilemma: '*Great Expectations*', he writes, 'may be called ... a novel without a hero ... I mean that it is a novel which aims chiefly at showing that the hero is unheroic'.[39]

Chesterton's expression 'aims at showing' is appropriate: Dickens's demonstration is achieved with almost pedagogical rigour. Aware that heroism, or the lack of it, is not just a matter of the hero's moral fortitude but of his 'power of action' and is strictly determined by 'the level of the postulates made about him'[40] as well as by environment, plot pattern, values at stake, forces at play, he simply sets two plots against each other, one supposedly real, the other supposedly imaginary, with the same character in the part of the hero. The result is that we get two heroic types in one person.

The following diagrams, based on Greimas's actantial pattern,[40] will help us visualize the discrepancy between these two plots and appreciate their respective and relative implications.

Pip's plot:

Sender	*Object*	*Receiver*
Miss Havisham	Money, gentility, Estella	One of society's arbitrarily chosen few
Helpers	*Subject*	*Opponents*
Jaggers (and Wemmick)	Pip	Sarah and Camilla Pocket Pip's old friends and acquaintances (including Joe and his convict) Drummle

Magwitch's plot:

Sender	Object	Receiver
Magwitch	Money, gentility, 'bright eyes'	A working-class child rewarded for a good deed

Helpers	Subject	Opponents
Jaggers (and Wemmick)	Pip	The Law Compeyson and Orlick

Let us examine the second pattern and see how it differs from the first.

Pip, of course, retains his central position in the diagram, being as before the subject of the quest; but, as a receiver, he undergoes a drastic change owing to the change of sender. In his imaginary plot, Miss Havisham had acted arbitrarily, like the God of the puritans, whimsically electing him as, once upon a time, Oliver Twist had been elected. In Magwitch's plot, he merely gets his due: a perfect type of the modern receiver, he must now face the consequences of his fall from grace and accept his new condition as responsible Victorian hero, far less prestigious and enviable than that of Hero by divine right.

The other major novelty is the almost entirely new cast of 'actants'. As Magwitch comes in, Miss Havisham has to go; and not only is she dislodged from the sender's square, but she disappears from the diagram altogether, having no part to play in the new plot either as helper or as opponent. It is quite clear that, had she never existed, or had he never met her, Pip's great expectations would have been just the same, and we have every reason to believe that he would have renounced them just the same on discovering his benefactor's identity. Only his bitterness would have been less acute.

The first consequence of Miss Havisham's departure, as Pip immediately perceives, is that Estella has no reason to stay as object of the quest: 'Miss Havisham's intentions towards me, all a mere dream; Estella not designed for me' (xxxix, 341). And it is one of the most dramatic ironies of the new plot that the new sender, having been kept in total ignorance of his daughter's fate, should be denied the right to place her on his prize list. All he can offer is to buy Pip 'bright eyes ... if money can buy 'em' (xxxix, 338).

With Estella no longer starring, *exit* Drummle, whose part as opponent belongs to another plot. *Exeunt* in their turn the ugly Pockets, who have nothing to fear from Pip's expectations because the prize-money is no property of their rich and much fawned-upon relative. And thus the world of Satis House entirely recedes into the background.

The real actants in the new drama, Magwitch, Jaggers, Wemmick, Compeyson, Orlick, belong either to the world of crime or to the world of the Law, two worlds at times so ambiguously connected as to seem but one and to justify Pip's impression that to be in the hands of lawyers is an experience strangely similar to that of being handled by a starving convict: 'As I sat down, and he preserved his attitude and bent his brows at his boots, I felt at a disadvantage, which reminded me of that old time when I had been put upon a tombstone' (xxxvi, 305), he says, recording one of his visits to his enigmatic guardian. Jaggers and Wemmick are actually the only pawns that are not moved on the chessboard or out of it: significantly, the lawyer and his clerk can play helpers to any cause in any plot, work on behalf of a lady or of a convict alike, only provided they are commissioned to do the job and financially rewarded for it. And the Law, when it eventually forbids the happy outcome of Magwitch's scheme, fulfils the same function as the two villains of the book.

Thus, from a narrowly structural point of view, Pip is the hero of a novel that turns out to be much more of the Newgate than of the silver-fork type, however earnestly he had wished it to be so. The Satis House episodes now appear as little more than a digression through Wonderland, a place fit to harbour the dreams and fears of a child, but not those of a grown-up. We had sensed this, in fact, from the start; but, only too glad to be admitted, and not locked out like Pumblechook, we had entered this secluded world with no thought of sorting out child truth from child fiction. Pip's fairy-tale associations had appealed to the child who survives in each of us and we had at once responded to the enchantment; but we had had no difficulty in facing adult truth again on returning to more ordinary places, whereas Pip's tragic flaw is precisely his inability to leave childhood well behind him on reaching the age of man. David Copperfield had believed at about the same age that life was 'like a great fairy story, which [he] was just about to begin to read';[41] but, for Pip, life is rather like a sequel to a tale which he has just finished reading and unreasonably wishes to read over and over again.

Admonition is not spared him, but remains of no avail. When he is removed from the enchanted house on getting apprenticed to Joe, he is clearly advised not to return there:

> 'Joe,' said I; 'don't you think I ought to make Miss Havisham a visit?'
>
> 'Well, Pip,' returned Joe, slowly considering. 'What for?'
>
> 'What for, Joe? What is any visit made for?'
>
> 'There is some wisits, p'r'aps,' said Joe, 'as for ever remains open to the question, Pip. But in regard of wisiting Miss Havisham. She might think you wanted something – expected something of her.'
>
> 'Don't you think I might say that I did not, Joe?'
>
> 'You might, old chap,' said Joe. 'And she might credit it. Similarly she mightn't.' . . .
>
> 'You see, Pip,' Joe pursued . . . , 'Miss Havisham done the handsome thing by you. When Miss Havisham done the handsome thing by you, she called me back to say to me as that were all.'
>
> 'Yes, Joe. I heard her.'
>
> 'ALL,' Joe repeated, very emphatically.
>
> 'Yes, Joe. I tell you, I heard her.'
>
> 'Which I meantersay, Pip, it might be that her meaning were – Make a end on it! – As you was! – Me to the North, and you to the South! – Keep in sunders!' (xv, 138).

But he goes back all the same, enthralled by the place and its inhabitants, even at the risk of passing for a beggar: 'Everything was unchanged, and Miss Havisham was alone. "Well?" said she, fixing her eyes upon me. "I hope you want nothing? You'll get nothing" ' (xv, 143). He goes again on his birthday and again is suspected of wanting or 'expecting' something: 'she gave me a guinea when I was going . . . I tried to decline taking the guinea . . . , but with no better effect than causing her to ask me very angrily, if I expected more?' (xvii, 152). Miss Havisham's contemptuous use of the word 'expect' should prevent all misconstructions when the expectations do come, but Pip has by then forgotten the message or chosen to ignore it.

Warned against misplacing his expectations, Pip is also warned

against misplacing his affections: 'You ridiculous boy,' Estella says
to him when they meet in London, 'will you never take warning?'
(xxxiii, 287). And later, at Richmond, the warning is reiterated
almost literally:

> 'Pip, Pip,' she said one evening ... 'will you never take warning?'
> 'Of what?'
> 'Of me.'
> 'Warning not to be attracted by you, do you mean, Estella?'
> 'Do you mean! If you don't know what I mean, you are blind.'
> (xxxviii, 319).

Not blind, but self-blinded, Pip confesses: 'Whatever her tone with
me happened to be, I could put no trust in it, and build no hope on
it; and yet I went on against trust and against hope. Why repeat it a
thousand times? So it always was' (xxxiii, 288). The impenitent
dreamer, 'visionary boy – or man?' (xliv, 377), goes on believing in
the stories of his own making as indeed we all do when in our
day-dreams we give credence to our falsehoods.

Felix culpa! Were it not for Pip's fictions and misconstructions,
Great Expectations would be a straightforward novel amounting to
no more than one of its plots. 'The Return of the Convict' – for such
might be the title of this edifying, sentimental drama – would not be
lacking in pathos and in romantic appeal, thanks to the mythical
figure of the outcast in the part of provider; but with no other plot
with which to mirror itself, it would be deprived of its ironic and
nostalgic dimension and the novel as a whole would lose much
aesthetically.

As things are, the 'real' plot, Dickens's, can never be read as a
self-contained story and Pip's dream pattern remains to the end
superimposed on Magwitch's, blurring the picture. Miss Havisham's shadow, in particular, hovers formidably over the sender's
square, making her absence so conspicuous that she gains in char-
isma what she loses in power and becomes active as a 'non-actant'.
'You made your own snares', she tells Pip when he reproaches her
with deceiving him, '*I* never made them' (xliv, 374); and how could
he gainsay it? And when he complains 'You led me on', she simply
corrects him: 'I let you go on', she says. 'Was that kind?' he asks;
but then all he gets by way of a reply is a question rhetorically
addressed to both reader and character: 'Who am I, for God's sake,

that I should be kind?' (xliv, 373). The answer, which we feel allowed or requested to provide, might well be, as was suggested before, that she is the ironist of the book, the contemptuous outsider who watches things from a distance, takes pleasure in not interfering, asks questions and gives no answers, and never speaks 'straight'[42] the better to deceive her interlocutors.

Irony is a cruelly subversive game, which requires victims and victimizers and leaves little room indeed for kindness, even on the part of the lookers-on: what reader could boast that he never enjoyed Miss Havisham's equivocations or that he never played Trabb's boy to the hero, never took advantage like 'that unlimited miscreant' (xxx, 266) of his position as someone 'whom no man could hurt; an invulnerable and dodging serpent who, when chased into a corner, flew out again between his captor's legs, scornfully yelping' (xxx, 267)? Yet, even granting that Pip deserves moral castigation, that all his faults and shortcomings make him often ridiculous and occasionally truly despicable, who could deny that he is, by and large, more sinned against than sinning and has a right to feel 'vaguely convinced', as he puts it, of being 'very much ill-used by somebody, or by everybody', even though he 'can't say which' (xvii, 157)?

'Vaguely convinced', 'somebody', 'everybody', 'I can't say which': this overdone understatement is rather puzzling, even suspicious. Surely, if he tried, Pip would have no difficulty in listing the names of all those who once wronged him, bullied him, misled him, told him what to expect or whom to love, and taught him to be dissatisfied with himself and his condition. But his reluctance to denounce certain people, Estella in particular, also leaves the sentence open to more general interpretations and allows us to exclude no one from the list of wrongdoers, least of all the hero's maker who engineered all the mischief. Might we not even read the remark as a disguised authorial intrusion and tongue-in-cheek *mea culpa*?

It will be argued, of course, that Dickens has nothing to reproach himself with, that the misfortunes and blemishes of fictitious characters cannot fairly be blamed on their creators and that such narrow-minded censorship would soon be the death of fiction-making. Sure enough. But Pip's case is rather special in that he is not just a character who happens to be good or bad or whatever: in his own endeavour to achieve his conversion from Romanticism to Victorianism, Dickens '*ill*-uses' him because he *uses* him and takes

him for his whipping-boy. Pip thus finds himself ridiculed for
sticking to Dickens's standards, which are in the process of being
discarded, and gets severely punished for the unpardonable anachronism of taking himself for Oliver Twist!

This seems all the more unfair on the poor lad as Dickens's
enterprise never really carries conviction. It is even quite remarkable
that, under the pretext of destroying romance, the novelist should
have allowed himself in this book, as in no other before, the right to
build a most romantic story, which his very *coup de théâtre* destroys
most romantically. So that, when romance is over and 'realism' has
taken over, irony loses its edge and takes on a new quality: mellowed and melancholy, it becomes almost elegiac.

Should he still be looking for literary analogies when he reaches the
final stage of his expectations, Pip would have hardly any choice left
but to identify himself with the hero of a *Bildungsroman* of the low
mimetic mode. This he does implicitly as he gives up his false
pretences and takes himself for what he is, an ordinary young man.
'the *eiron* ... who deprecates himself, as opposed to the *alazon*',[43]
now placed in the school of experience and adversity and making
good progress towards self-knowledge, self-denial and self-reliance.
Having learnt to dissociate money from gentility and renounced his
expectations, he soon gets rid of his class-consciousness, gives up his
expensive habits, leaves the Finches of the Grove to themselves, and
to all appearances is now cured of romance.

But Dickens is not. And when it comes to concluding, he is at a
loss what to do with his hero. He knows that, 'bred to no calling, and
... fit for nothing', moneyless and patronless, Pip has no prospect
before him but 'go for a soldier' (xli, 357), go back to smithying or
accept Herbert's offer to join Clarriker's House (though he might
take to novel-writing if only it occurred to him!); but he is also quite
reluctant to face the implications and the logic of his tale and, in the
closing chapters, we can almost hear him asking himself
remorsefully 'What have I done! What have I done!' The result is a
series of dead-ends and false starts which, at this stage, should be
better termed false endings.

Significantly, the first ending is thwarted even as it is engineered:
Pip goes back to the village with a view to working there and getting
married to Biddy, but he turns up on the very day of the girl's
marriage to Joe. Crestfallen rather than truly disappointed, he then

decides to leave his native place and to emigrate, sets out for Cairo where Herbert has settled and, 'within two months', in spite of his lack of professional training, is doing successfully as 'clerk to Clarriker', though 'many a year' will have to go round before he becomes 'a partner in the House' (lviii, 489).

This strand of the novel will in its turn tail off inconclusively: there is no telling whether, when he returns to the mother country after eleven years abroad, Pip will stay for good or go back to the East, with or without Estella, and, in either case, whether he will still be working for Clarriker. But whatever may happen later, the Cairo episode considerably alters the course of Pip's life and the meaning of Dickens's book: rather than being 'forced to build his fortunes again from scratch in the old village', Pip is given the chance of a lifetime when, in Humphry House's famous words, Dickens 'whisks him off to the East, where gentlemen grow like mushrooms'.[44] But this decision, in fact, testifies less to the novelist's 'colonial optimism'[45] than to his desire to make amends for what he has done; for, as much as 'to the East', Pip is whisked off 'to the land of the Arabian nights', a place of which Herbert, less foolishly than one might have thought, had for years on end sketched 'airy pictures' (lii, 428) and where it is a tradition with writers to play fairy godmothers to their blue-eyed boys.

The two paragraphs describing Pip's Egyptian years are assuredly most unromantic. Pip's promotion is presented as the result of his self-helping exertions and the stress is on work, 'industry and readiness'. But the hero is also all too obviously rewarded for the one 'good thing' he had done in once helping Herbert with his expectations money. And he is fortunate enough, besides, not to be paid back 'in his own coin': in Clarriker's crucible, Magwitch's money and Miss Havisham's have been melted into one metal so that, at a symbolic level, he now comes into a double inheritance.

So indeed had Herbert done before him! The gentleman by birth and the former blacksmith's boy, two modern aristocrats of virtue-turned-into-talent, are now placed on an equal footing: co-partners in the Firm, co-heirs to the money of a convict and of a lady. Such is Dickens's modern version of the old wish-fulfilment dream, a subtle compromise between a fable and a tale.

Great Expectations was to have been Dickens's ironic farewell to romance, but, when we close the book, we see 'no shadow' of his ever parting from 'her'. And it is certainly the crowning irony of this novel that the 'handwriting' forger (xlii, 362), the 'obliging stranger' who had passed off on his hero so many banknotes of his own manufacture, should now thus 'swindle' himself by this last 'sleight of hand' (xxviii, 247)!

G. K. Chesterton called the enterprise of writing *David Copperfield* 'a romantic attempt to be realistic';[46] we might call *Great Expectations* 'a romantic attempt to be ironic'. But this may be a pleonasm: for Kierkegaard at any rate, the two words are synonyms:

> I use the expressions: *irony* and the *ironist*, but I could as easily say: *romanticism* and the *romanticist*. Both expressions designate the same thing.[47]

NOTES: CHAPTER 11

1 G. K. Chesterton, *Appreciations and Criticisms of the Works of Charles Dickens* (London: Dent, 1911), p. 200.
2 Gabriel Pearson, 'The Old Curiosity Shop', in *Dickens and the Twentieth Century*, eds John Gross and Gabriel Pearson (London: Routledge & Kegan Paul, 1966), p. 83.
3 ibid.
4 *Martin Chuzzlewit*, ed. Margaret Cardwell, Clarendon Dickens (Oxford, 1982), x, 157.
5 *David Copperfield*, ed. Nina Burgis, Clarendon Dickens (Oxford, 1981), xxv, 323.
6 *Martin Chuzzlewit*, op. cit., vi, 94.
7 ibid., li, 780.
8 *Bleak House*, eds George Ford and Sylvère Monod (New York: Norton, 1977), xxiv, 302.
9 ibid., xxxv, 439–40.
10 ibid., lxv, 762.
11 *A Tale of Two Cities*, The New Oxford Illustrated Dickens (London: Oxford University Press, 1962), II, x, 123.
12 Barry Westburg, *The Confessional Fictions of Charles Dickens* (De Kalb, Ill.: Northern Illinois University Press, 1977), p. 187.
13 Geoffrey Thurley, *The Dickens Myth: Its Genesis and Structure* (London: Routledge & Kegan Paul, 1976), pp. 17 and 289.
14 F. Schlegel, quoted by Ingrid Strohschneider-Kohrs, *Die Romantische Ironie in Theorie und Gestaltung* (Tübingen, 1970), p. 7.
15 Harry Stone, *Dickens and the Invisible World* (London: Macmillan, 1980), 'The fairy-tale transformation', p. 298.
16 ibid.
17 Katherine Carolan, 'Dickens' last Christmases', *The Dalhousie Review*, vol. 52 (Fall 1972), p. 374.
18 Thurley, op. cit., p. 283.
19 A. Jolles, *Einfache Formen* [1930], quoted by Tzvetan Todorov, 'Poétique', in *Qu'est-ce que le Structuralisme?* (Paris: Le Seuil, 1968), p. 142.

20 *Oliver Twist*, ed. Kathleen Tillotson, Clarendon Dickens (Oxford, 1966), xlix, 335.

21 J. Hillis Miller, *Charles Dickens: The World of His Novels* (Cambridge, Mass.: Harvard University Press, 1958), p. 43.

22 *Oliver Twist*, op. cit., ii, 11.

23 ibid., xli, 281, my emphasis.

24 ibid., xiv, 89.

25 See Vladimir Propp, *Morphology of the Folktale* [Leningrad, 1928], translated by Lawrence Scott (University of Texas Press, 1958). On Propp's theory, see Terence Hawkes, *Structuralism and Semiotics* [1977], (London: Methuen, 1985), pp. 67–9.

26 cf. Tzvetan Todorov, *Introduction à la littérature fantastique* (Paris: Le Seuil, 1970), pp. 87–91.

27 Kierkegaard, quoted by Wayne C. Booth in *A Rhetoric of Irony* (University of Chicago Press, 1974), p. 29.

28 Northrop Frye, *Anatomy of Criticism* [1957], (Princeton University Press, 1973), pp. 34, 37.

29 James Ridley's *The Tales of the Genii* (1776) is an interesting specimen of literary deception from the period of *Ossian* and the forgeries of Chatterton. The full title was: *The Tales of the Genii, or the Delightful Lessons of Horam, the Son of Asmar*, faithfully translated from the Persian Manuscript and compared with the French and Spanish EDITION. Published at Paris and Madrid. By Sir Charles MORELL, formerly ambassador from the British Settlements in Indi to the Great Mogul. London. MDCCLXIV.

30 See Edgar Johnson, *Charles Dickens: His Tragedy and Triumph* (London: Victor Gollancz, 1953), Vol. 1, p. 23.

31 *David Copperfield*, op. cit., iv, 48.

32 Ridley, op. cit., p. 4.

33 ibid., p. 12.

34 cf. *David Copperfield*, op. cit., i, 1.

35 Frye, op. cit., p. 33.

36 ibid.

37 ibid., p. 34.

38 Chesterton, op. cit., p. 199.

39 Frye, op. cit., p. 33.

40 See A. J. Greimas, *Sémantique Structurale* (Paris: Larousse, 1966). For a summary of his theory, see Hawkes, op. cit., pp. 87–95. The 'actantial model', illustrated by the Quest for the Holy Grail, is as follows:

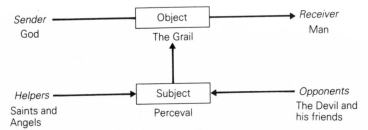

According to Greimas, these binary oppositions (Sender/Receiver, Subject/ Object, Helpers/Opponents) inform the fundamental structure of stories that may seem quite different on the surface, and the permanence of this dramatic syntax of narratives (or *énoncé-spectacle*, as he calls it) is 'guaranteed by the fixed distribution of the roles' (p. 173). 'At the surface level', Terence Hawkes explains, 'the structure of the enunciation-spectacle is manifested through the various *actants* who embody it' and who 'operate on the level of function, rather than content. That is, an *actant* may embody itself in a particular character (termed an *acteur*) or it may reside in the function of more than one character in respect of their common role in the story's underlying "oppositional" structure. In short, the deep structure of the narrative generates and defines its *actants* at a level beyond that of the story's surface content' (p. 89). It may therefore turn out that one character is given, simultaneously or successively, several actantial functions, just as several characters may be the embodiment of the same actantial function. An *actant* may also be an abstraction (God, the City) or an absent person.

41 *David Copperfield*, op. cit., xix, 233.
42 Booth, op. cit., p. 1.
43 Frye, op. cit., p. 40.
44 Humphry House, *The Dickens World* [1941], (Oxford Paperbacks, 1965), p. 156.
45 See Chesterton, op. cit., p. 132 (about *David Copperfield*).
46 ibid., p. 129
47 S. Kierkegaard, *The Concept of Irony* [1929], translated by Lee M. Capel (London: Collins, 1966), p. 212.

THE NOVEL
OF A NOVELIST

CHAPTER 12

The Sense of Two Endings

Modern readers of *Great Expectations* no longer read the same novel as Dickens's contemporaries. In 1874, when he came out with the third volume of *The Life of Charles Dickens*, Forster dealt the first blow to the wholeness of his late friend's book by revealing to the reading public the existence of an original ending, which he reproduced in a note.[1] It was a severe blow, but its effect was not immediate: for one thing, not everybody who had read *Great Expectations* read Forster; for another, those who did could still dissociate the two conclusions. As long as they were not strung together as they are now, the novel retained some of its integrity and readers could go on reading the version Dickens had intended for them. Then, in 1937, George Bernard Shaw, who edited and prefaced the text for the Limited Editions Club, decided to restore the original ending where it should have been, or so he thought at the time, and placed the second one in a Postscript intended for 'Sentimental readers who still like all their stories to end at the altar rails'.[2] Since then, editors have made it a practice to print both the revised and the cancelled endings (the latter usually in an appendix), thus forcing on the reader the embarrassing, Carrollian dilemma:

It *must* have been either the one or the other.
Which do *you* think it was?

Answers, of course, have not been wanting and are still proffered in plenty. Whether Dickens should or should not have let himself be persuaded by Bulwer to alter his conclusion, whether the one he opted for was the one he liked best, whether it was consistent with the drive of the novel are surely the most vexed questions in Dickensiana. And Edgar Rosenberg's conviction that the subject has 'generated enough talk in the last thirty years to call for some sort of moratorium'[3] is unlikely to bring an end to the debate: critics will go on agreeing to differ on this issue as long as *Great Expectations*, well-worn though it is, remains a favourite text for analysis.

Dickens had not expected or solicited the controversy. In rewriting the last page of his book, he had no intention of challenging his readers or presenting them with some anticipatory version of John Fowles's *The French Lieutenant's Woman*,[4] though he would have been quite capable of such 'modern' perversity: the construction in *Hard Times* of Mrs Sparsit's imaginary staircase, down which, in the course of two chapters, we track Louisa Gradgrind on her road to perdition until the omniscient narrator comes to a last-minute rescue and brings to light the 'real' version of the facts, is actual evidence that he *was* capable of it and that he could play at hide-and-seek with the truth of his fiction. With the death of Little Nell and the collapse of Dombey's dreams, he had in fact early made himself a speciality of cheating his readers – or his characters – of their expectations. And *Great Expectations* itself is, as we have seen, centered round the rivalry of two plots and therefore of two possible endings: it dramatizes the confrontation of 'what may be willed and what is predicted',[5] the various episodes literally corresponding to Frank Kermode's definition of *peripeteia*, 'a falsification of expectation, so that the end comes as expected, but not in the manner expected'.[6]

But the critical debate about the two 'endings' is another matter and the confusion between 'end of plot' and 'end of book' has been the cause of much misunderstanding. The word 'ending', which is normally applied to the closing pages of the book (in whichever version we prefer), is assuredly convenient and almost inevitable, but not quite appropriate. If 'ending' is to be taken seriously as belonging to the order of necessity and causality, it should be restricted to the description of the necessary, logical, inevitable outcome of the chain of causes and effects that constitutes plot, and plot in this novel ends before either of the two 'endings'.

Great Expectations, which has been rightly described as a 'highly plotted'[7] novel, is perceived from the start as an 'end-determined fiction'[8] and, in spite of appearances, it is and should be called a novel with a closed ending. A closedness which, admittedly, does not prevent protractedness: the plot begins to end the moment Magwitch returns and reveals the truth of Pip's position, and it goes on ending for the last third of the novel . . . or nearly so. It might be said to end, literally and figuratively, by instalments. It ends whenever there is a return to some beginning. It ends when the convict reappears. It ends when Pip decides to give up his financial expectations. It ends when Pip forgives Miss Havisham for what she has done. It ends when Pip discovers Estella's parentage. It ends when Magwitch dies and Pip is orphaned for the second time. It ends when Pip recovers from his illness and, under the ministering of Joe, becomes a little child again. It ends really and truly when the hero returns to his native place, then decides to emigrate. But there it stops ending. There we must draw the line. And this is where Dickens himself drew the line in his memoranda:

> Finds Biddy married to Joe.
> So goes abroad to Herbert (happily married to Clara Barley), and becomes his clerk.
> The one good thing he did in his prosperity,
> the only thing that endures and bears good fruit.[9]

Not a word is said either of Estella or of Pip's return to the home country. The last item of this briefing simply announces some moralizing epilogue on what the past has generated; the preterite in this sentence (the sign that all is over) is father to an enduring, happy-ever-after present, which seems to exclude any 'renewal of expectation', plotting or romance: this, says Peter Brooks, 'would have to belong to another story'.[10]

And even the first version of the epilogue, which offers no such renewal, is felt as extraneous and impertinent. What we get from now on is not 'ending' properly speaking, but some updating of what is no longer 'plot' but 'story' as defined by E. M. Forster, 'a narrative of events arranged in time-sequence',[11] or what Kermode terms 'chronicle' as opposed to 'history'.[12] We are no longer in the world of *kairos* or crisis, but in the world of *chronos*, a world where the clock goes 'tick-tick', not 'tick-tock'[13] any longer, a world where, as Brooks has it, 'plot is over':[14]

> As at the start of the novel we had the impression of a life not yet subject to plot – a life in search of the sense of plot that would only gradually begin to precipitate around it – so at the end we have the impression of a life that has outlived plot, renounced plot, been cured of it: life that is left over.[15]

Pip has been cured of plot. And so have we. And so has Dickens. What he offers us now is not one or two endings (or 'six' for that matter), but postscripts, winding-ups, 'fake full stop[s]'.[16] Brooks calls them 'finales',[17] but this is too grand a word; Milton Millhauser, also drawing his metaphor from the musical register, proposes the word 'coda',[18] an apt comparison, for it suggests something superfluous, an added piece, the sort of thing that, in a concert hall, we never hear properly because the uninitiated have already started clapping their hands, not suspecting that there is more to come. We do not clap our hands because we see the score, but we have stopped asking ourselves crucial questions. Our 'whys' have by now all been exhausted and there is only room left for a disenchanted 'what next?'

'What next' is, with one exception, the usual tidying-up which Dickens always believed he owed his readers as a matter of courtesy (or was it curtsey?). The only truly satisfactory episode in what now constitutes chapter 59 is, as we have seen before, Pip's visit to his father's tomb in the company of his young namesake. Martin Meisel rightly calls it 'the true ending of *Great Expectations*',[19] rightly, that is, provided we take it to mean the 'end of the novel', not the 'end of the plot'. The scene does not *belong* to plot: it is the *recognition* of plot, a sort of anniversary or commemoration of how it all began; it is the sign that Pip's memory is now at work giving shape to the past, ordering the plot of his life, and that he has already become an autobiographer.

Much has been written about the revised, 'conventional', 'happy' ending. But, barring the fact that marrying Estella is not necessarily every man's idea of a happy end (even if we take her word for it that she has changed for the better), the second postscript is by no means more conventional than the first. So-called 'unhappy' endings were in fact increasingly fashionable in the 1860s, therefore increasingly 'conventional'. Edwin M. Eigner, in a discussion of Bulwer's motives for persuading Dickens to cancel his first conclusion, goes even so far as to write:

Dickens was probably urged to forego what his friend considered a fashionable unhappy ending, designed to gain immediate popularity, and encouraged to substitute for it a conclusion more in keeping with what looked in 1861 like the time-tested rules of English narrative romance.[20]

Eigner's argument also undermines the commonly held view that Bulwer had pleaded against the unromantic end on crassly commercial grounds, fearing that it would have disastrous effects on the sales when the novel came out in book-form. Both novelists, Eigner further observes, 'had achieved great popular success with unhappy conclusions':

> Bulwer's all-time best-seller, *Rienzi*, had ended tragically, and the great heart-throb of English fiction before Little Nell had been provided by the death of Nadia in *The Last Days of Pompeii*. Clearly there was money to be made through tears.[21]

It should be remembered, besides, that less than a month before the two men discussed the ending of *Great Expectations* at Knebworth[22] they had exchanged correspondence about the conclusion of Bulwer's own *A Strange Story*, the novel that was to succeed *Great Expectations* in the columns of *All the Year Round*. And to Bulwer's questions as to whether he should kill Isabel, the heroine, Dickens had replied:

> As to Isabel's dying and Fenwick's growing old, I would say that, beyond question, whatever the meaning of the story tends to, is the proper end.[23]

At that stage, Bulwer had not yet hit upon the final title for his serial and thought of calling it 'Margrave, a Tale of Mystery'; but Dickens, in the same letter, advised him against the sensationalism of the word 'Mystery':

> I prefer 'Wonder' to 'Mystery,' because I think it suggests something higher and more apart from ordinary complications of plot, or the like, which 'Mystery' might seem to mean.

Judging by such unconditional declarations of principle, the 'proper end' of *Great Expectations* for Dickens would seem indeed to have been the one he eventually cancelled: it is 'more apart from ordinary complications of plot' than the revised ending and it is the one to which 'the meaning of the story' tends. And, though he wrote to Forster that he had 'no doubt the story [would] be more acceptable through the alteration'[24] (but it took him a fortnight to inform his friend of his decision), the letter he sent Bulwer on 24 June shows rather lukewarm conviction:

> I send you the enclosed, the whole of the concluding weekly No. of Great Expectations, in order that you may the more readily understand where I have made the change.
>
> My difficulty was, to avoid doing too much. My tendency, when I began to unwind the thread that I thought I had wound for ever, was to labour it and get out of proportion.
>
> So I have done it in as few words as possible: and I hope you will like the alteration that is entirely due to you.[25]

To Edgar Rosenberg this suggests 'acquiescence, not enthusiasm' and the remark 'is entirely due to you', he submits, might even be interpreted as 'a nice invitation to supply the unwritten "certainly not to me" '.[26]

Dickens is not reputed to have been a pliable man. He knew what he wanted, stuck to his principles and, being his own editor, had to take orders from no one. So why did he half-heartedly agree to make the alteration unless, for some reason, which still has to be established, he felt he had no choice but to follow his friend's advice?

To Forster he merely wrote:

> Bulwer ... so strongly urged it upon me, after reading the proofs, and supported his views with such good reasons, that I resolved to make the change.[27]

What were these 'views'? What were these 'good reasons'? And why did Dickens omit to expound them, especially to Forster, whom he so often took into his confidence and whose advice he so often sought on literary matters? Many hypotheses have already been advanced; all have been or can be disproved. The one that will be submitted here is just as tentative – and, no doubt, just as disputable – as previous attempts at solving the mystery.

The original ending of *Great Expectations* has in fact less originality than it is credited with. On 23 March 1861, Lever's *A Day's*

Ride at last came to a close and Potts, its Quixotic hero, made his last appearance. After touring the world, losing Blondel, his favourite horse, losing Catinka, a girl he had been infatuated with, and recovering from a long illness, the young man turns up in Paris, and the scene reads as follows:

It was about two years after this – my father had died in the interval, leaving me a small but sufficient fortune to live on, and I had just arrived in Paris, after a long desultory ramble through the east of Europe – I was standing one morning early in one of the small alleys of the Champs Elysées...

I crossed the road, and had but reached the opposite pathway, when a carriage stopped, and the old horse drew up beside it. After a word or two, the groom took off the hood, and there was Blondel! But my amazement was lost in the greater shock, that the Princess, whose jewelled hand held out the sugar to him, was no other than Catinka!

I cannot say with what motive I was impelled – perhaps the action was too quick for either – but I drew nigh to the carriage, and raising my hat respectfully, asked if her highness would deign to remember an old acquaintance.

'I am unfortunate enough, sir, not to be able to recal [sic] you,' said she, in most perfect Parisian French.

'My name you may have forgotten, madame, but scarcely so either our first meeting at Schaffhausen, or our last at Bregenz.'

'These are all riddles to me, sir; and I am sure you are too well bred to persist in an error after you have recognised it to be such.' With a cold smile and a haughty bow, she motioned the coachman to drive on, and I saw her no more...

I set off for England that night – I left for Wales the next morning – and I have never quitted it since that day.[28]

The chance meeting in the street after years of separation, the world-famous yet anonymous setting, the lady in the carriage, the servant in attendance, the estrangement between the two former 'lovers', all the ingredients of Dickens's first ending are there, and it is highly probable that unconscious remembrances of this text prompted Dickens's imagination when, within three months of his reading it, he came to write his own conclusion. But it is, to say the least, rather ironical that he should have got his inspiration from the

very novel that his own serial had so dramatically outshone. A
further irony is that Lever never even suspected it: the ending was
cancelled and he did not live to read it in Forster.[29]

Few people today, if any, read *A Day's Ride* and even at the time
of its serialization the novel was so unpopular that many subscribers must have given up reading it long before it reached its last
instalment. In 1874, when Dickens's original ending appeared in
Forster's *Life*, Lever's novel had fallen into oblivion and those few
who had read it through thirteen years before would not have
connected the two texts at such a distance. Quite understandably,
Dickens's borrowing thus passed unnoticed from early and later
commentators. Only George Bernard Shaw noticed it and remarked
briefly upon it: 'the passing carriage was unconsciously borrowed
from *A Day's Ride*', he wrote in his Foreword to *Great Expectations* in 1947. 'Dickens', he added, 'must have felt that there was
something wrong with this ending; and Bulwer's objection confirmed his doubt. Accordingly, he wrote a new ending, in which he
got rid of Piccadilly.'[30] The hint is worth following, though it is
more likely that Bulwer's 'doubt' preceded Dickens's. Bulwer, as we
know, was to be the next serialist in Dickens's magazine and he
must have been a most attentive reader of the two fictions that were
then being published there, doubtless comparing their merits and
demerits, their narrative devices and their treatment of similar
themes. Comparisons were all the more inevitable as Lever's novel
was in many respects a great expectations story: written in the first
person, it related the adventures of a young man who had embarked
on life with his 'mind filled with the marvels of Eastern romance',
'passed days in dreamland',[31] changed his identity, 'lived ... in a
fiction land of [his] own invention, with daydreams and fancies, and
hopes and ambitions all unreal',[32] in brief had much in common
with Dickens's Pip. So, when only a few weeks after finishing this
novel Bulwer received Dickens's manuscript for perusal, how could
he fail to notice the obvious points of similarity between the two
conclusions? It is easy enough, therefore, to imagine that he felt it
his duty to draw his friend's attention to them and argued persuasively against what would in more ways than one appear as a
most infelicitous form of plagiarism. If Dickens persisted in
publishing his conclusion, he ran the risk of being taxed with lack of
imagination or with lack of tact, or both. And, if such were the
arguments put forward by Bulwer, then we can understand why

Dickens had no wish to make them known to his other correspondents and why, in particular, he avoided consulting Forster on the judiciousness of the alteration.

This, surely, does not account for the radical change concerning the future of Pip and Estella. Dickens might have chosen to alter the setting, suppress the carriage, leave out the servant, yet retain the notion of lasting estrangement. But few settings were available if the meeting was to seem less accidental and, having opted for the ruined garden – the most acceptable alternative –, perhaps he felt that the shadow of another parting would not be in keeping with the nostalgia of the visitors and would, anyway, spoil the romantic atmosphere attached to the place. Or perhaps he simply decided to depart from the spirit of Lever's ending as well as from the letter.

The final ending, however, is not so unambiguous as some critics claim it to be. Those who hear the church-bells are very sharp of hearing, sharper than Dickens had wished them to be. For, if he had meant to say that Pip and Estella were intended to be married, he would have said it. The very last sentence actually went through several rephrasings and the first alteration was clearly intended to make the sense less explicit: in the manuscript it read 'I saw the shadow of no parting from her, but one', which, Rosenberg observes, 'would have carried a resonance uncomfortably redolent of the boozily pious till-death-us-do-part flourish on which *David Copperfield* ends'.[33] At proof-stage the last two words were struck out and in the serial version and editions prior to the Library Edition of 1862, the sentence went 'I saw the shadow of no parting from her', which was finally revised into the now familiar 'I saw no shadow of another parting from her'. Readers are disagreed as to which of these two formulations is the less equivocal; for Angus Calder the change was towards more ambiguity: the last version, he argues, 'hints at the buried meaning: "... at this happy moment, I did not see the shadow of our subsequent parting looming over us" '.[34] This is a bit far-fetched, though it is undeniable that the phrasing *is* ambiguous. Walter Dexter's contention that the ultimate version is the less equivocal is just as unconvincing.[35] The fact is that both versions are meant to be vague and enigmatic and Rosenberg's suggestion that the phrase was reshaped 'on "musical" grounds'[36] is by far the most satisfactory explanation ever given to the change.

Rosenberg's collating of the manuscript, galley-proofs and printed versions of the last ending has brought to light the many emendations, additions and corrections made by the novelist. Dickens was always a conscientious artist, but with the years he was increasingly attentive to the stylistic improvements of his texts. Reluctant though he may have been to rewrite his conclusion, it is quite obvious that, having decided to make the alteration, he wanted his 'pretty piece of writing',[37] as he called it, to be as pretty as possible when it went into print. No doubt he also wanted it to be even more 'acceptable' than when he had first drafted it; but the fear expressed in his letter to Bulwer of over-labouring the text and 'doing too much' would tend to suggest that his own notion of acceptability was not as precise as he might have wished, and his corrections show that to the last he wavered between saying too much or too little. Rosenberg, for instance, notes that 'a brief passage of dialogue' in which Drummle's widow makes veiled overtures to Pip ('since my duty has not been incompatible with the admission of that remembrance, I have given it a place in my heart'; lix, 492) was a last-minute addition, 'introduced at a very late stage in proofing'.[38] This would plead in favour of the marriage thesis, thus contradicting the vagueness of the last sentence; but it also pleads in favour of Dickens's lack of real interest in the subject (otherwise, he would have thought of it earlier) and of his lack of conviction: it seems as if he felt he had to interpolate the lines to make the idea of marriage more credible not only to his readers but also to himself.

It would seem, anyway, that he was more concerned with having Estella redeemed than remarried. Her change of heart, the one thing he retained from the cancelled version, is given still more emphasis in the new one. In the first ending this was expressed in indirect speech: 'she gave me the assurance, that suffering had been stronger than Miss Havisham's teaching, and had given her a heart to understand what my heart used to be'.[39] In the new postscript Estella's words are reported directly:

> ... suffering has been stronger than all other teaching, and has taught me to understand what your heart used to be. I have been bent and broken, but – I hope – into a better shape (lix, 493).

Estella thus is more present and more convincing, and, some would argue, more 'marriageable'.

But other considerations indicate that in fact the morally improved character, in either version, is not so much Pip's lost *bienaimée* or potential bride as his female counterpart. This is quite apparent if we consider the way Estella is brought in, in the passage that occurs just before Dickens made his major alteration. In the Gargery household there are two little children, a new Pip and a 'little girl', whose name is not revealed to us. Of course, it is out of the question to suggest that Biddy's daughter might have been called Estella; but, precisely, if the baby's name was made known to us, it would impair an analogy which is unmistakable:

> Biddy looked down at her child, and put its little hand to her lips, and then put the good matronly hand with which she had touched it, into mine...
> 'Dear Pip,' said Bibby, 'you are sure you don't fret for her?' (lix, 490).

'Her', also unnamed, never enjoyed matronly care and life has been as unfair to her as it has been to Pip. If Pip has been redeemed, why should redemption be denied 'her', the woman who once was a 'little girl', the half-sister somehow, Magwitch's daughter? 'A second chance for Pip requires a second chance for Estella', writes Martin Meisel.[40] The impression we get is that, in fact, Dickens had second thoughts about this character and suddenly felt it a duty to tidy up what might have been the Estella plot. But his second thoughts came too late, for there is no Estella plot. It is even particularly revealing that Estella did not find her way into the public-reading version of the novel, though, exceptionally, this version was a synopsis of the story, not the habitual selection of purple patches.[41] Estella is the heroine of a novel Dickens never wrote, and no ending, however gratifying, could possibly restore her to a place that she never held.

Critics may differ *ad infinitum* about the judiciousness of Dickens's change of mind and the nature of his motives, but one point on which they are bound to be unanimous is the importance of the change as such. The fact that *Great Expectations* should be doomed forever to be labelled as a 'double-ended novel' compels us to place it in a special category – 'Ambiguously ever after', says David Lodge[42] – and the anomaly calls for several comments.

The first comment that comes to mind, so very obvious indeed that no one ever makes it, is that neither conclusion, had it not been for the existence of the other, would have attracted such critical notice. As it happens, they have acted as foils to each other and been given far more importance than either would have deserved in its own right. Who discusses the appositeness of Sydney Carton's prophetic vision or of Bounderby's glimpses into futurity? We take those winding-ups as a matter of course; we take the alternative endings of *Great Expectations* as a matter of debate.

Dickens's change of mind further raises the false question of the author's sincerity and the true question of the novel's authenticity. A double ending would no doubt have been less remarked upon, and less remarkable, in a traditional third-person narrative; but the autobiographical form of the book, by giving the illusion of no ouside intervention, seemed to exclude faking. A man's life has no alternative endings and autobiography, however fictitious, ought to be linear, predetermined, conclusive. The discovery that such is not the case with Pip's life-story inevitably makes us suspicious of what we have been given to read. For the recognition that forces itself on us is not merely that the narrative 'I' was never a genuine one (Dickens, after all, never concealed the fact that he was the writer and Pip never signed his name on the cover of the book or at the bottom of the instalments): it is, more disconcertingly, that it was never even so much as *fictionally* genuine. A disguised 'he', Pip, as we now fully realize, was manipulated from beginning to end not only as a character but also as a narrator, made to record his life-story by using all the tricks of sensational novelists, suspense and prevarication, shilly-shallying conclusions, and, to crown it all, alternative endings ... The open-endedness of *Great Expectations* makes it a fake even as a fictional autobiography.

But then, we suspect our own reading: how far were we expected to believe in Pip and to believe him? Perhaps we have misread the book as Pip misread his text and Joe his wife's scribblings? Such considerations bring us to realize that there are degrees of credulity and that, if writing is 'a very complicated interweaving of truth and fiction',[43] reading is a very complicated interweaving of faith and disbelief. In fact, the great, if unsought, merit of the double ending is that it draws our attention to the novelistic character of the book, to the craft of fiction and to the craftsman, in other words to the fact that *Great Expectations* is not just a pseudo-autobiography, but a novel by a novelist, an artefact, the product of workmanship. Dickens knew it well: he wrote to Forster two months before completing his novel: 'All the iron is in the fire, and I have "only" to beat it out'.[44] Joe, the smith, says something very similar about his one piece of writing, the epitaph composed in memory of his father: 'I made it in a moment. It was like striking out a horseshoe complete, in a single blow' (vii, 77). Only, Dickens struck out two horseshoes when one would have been enough.

NOTES: CHAPTER 12

1   John Forster, *The Life of Charles Dickens* [1872–74], (London: Dent, 1966), Vol. 2, p. 441, note 141.
2   George Bernard Shaw (ed.), *Great Expectations* (Edinburgh: R. & R. Clark for the Limited Editions Club of New York, 1937), 'Editor's Postscript', pp. xxiii–xxvi.
3   Edgar Rosenberg, 'Last words on *Great Expectations*: a textual brief on the six endings', *Dickens Studies Annual*, vol. 9 (1981), p. 88.
4   See John Fowles, *The French Lieutenant's Woman* [1969] (London: Panther Books, 1971), ch. 45, p. 295, and David Lodge, 'Ambiguously ever after: problematic endings in English fiction', *Working with Structuralism* (London: Routledge & Kegan Paul, 1981), pp. 143–55.
5   Frank Kermode, *The Sense of an Ending* (New York: Oxford University Press, 1967), p. 85.
6   ibid., p. 53.
7   Peter Brooks, 'Repetition, repression, and return: *Great Expectations* and the study of plot', *New Literary History*, vol. 11 (Spring 1980), p. 521.
8   Kermode, op. cit., p. 6.
9   See above, ch. 2, 'Manuscript and memoranda', p. 20.
10 Brooks, op. cit., p. 522.
11 E. M. Forster, *Aspects of the Novel* [1927] (Harmondsworth: Penguin 1985), p. 44.
12 Kermode, op. cit., p. 51.
13 See Kermode, op. cit., pp. 44–5.
14 Brooks, op. cit., p. 524.
15 ibid., p. 522.
16 Kermode, op. cit., p. 145.
17 Brooks, op. cit., p. 521.
18 Milton Millhauser, '*Great Expectations*: the three endings', *Dickens Studies Annual*, vol. 2 (1972), p. 269.
19 Martin Meisel, 'The ending of *Great Expectations*', *Essays in Criticism*, vol. 15 (July 1965), p. 327.
20 Edwin M. Eigner, 'Bulwer-Lytton and the changed ending of *Great Expectations*', *Nineteenth-Century Fiction*, vol. 25 (June 1970), pp. 107–8.
21 ibid., p. 107.
22 'Dickens had arranged (on June 7) to spend a long weekend, from Saturday the 15th to Tuesday the 18th, with Bulwer-Lytton at Knebworth, no doubt both to submit the proofs of the final chapters to Bulwer ... and to discuss Bulwer's serial *A Strange Story*', writes Rosenberg, op. cit., p. 88.
23 Nonesuch *Letters*, Vol. 3, p. 221, 20 May 1861, to Bulwer.

24   ibid., p. 226, 1 July 1861, to Forster.
25   ibid., p. 225, 24 June 1861, to Bulwer.
26   Rosenberg, op. cit., pp. 103–4.
27   Nonesuch *Letters*, Vol. 3, p. 226, 1 July 1861, to Forster.
28   *All the Year Round*, vol. 4, 23 March 1861, p. 572 (ch. xlviii).
29   Lever died in 1872.
30   George Bernard Shaw, 'Foreword' to *Great Expectations*, The Novel Library (London: Hamish Hamilton, 1947), p. xvi.
31   *All the Year Round*, vol. 3, 15 August 1860, p. 441 (ch. i).
32   ibid., vol. 4, 16 March 1861, p. 548 (ch. xlv).
33   Rosenberg, op. cit., p. 94.
34   Angus Calder (ed.), *Great Expectations* (Harmondsworth: Penguin, 1965), Appendix A, p. 496.
35   See Walter Dexter, 'The end of "Great Expectations" ', *Dickensian*, vol. 34 (Spring 1938), p. 82.
36   Rosenberg, op. cit., p. 95.
37   Nonesuch *Letters*, Vol. 3, p. 226, 1 July 1861, to Forster.
38   Rosenberg, op. cit., p. 95.
39   See *Great Expectations*, op. cit., Appendix A, p. 496.
40   Meisel, op. cit., p. 329.
41   See above, ch. 3, 'The public reading version', p. 28.
42   cf. note 4.
43   *The Pilgrim Edition of the Letters of Charles Dickens*, Vol. 5 (Oxford: Clarendon Press, 1981), eds Graham Storey and K. J. Fielding, p. 569 [10 July 1849], to Forster.
44   Nonesuch *Letters*, Vol. 3, p. 217 [April] 1861, to Forster.

CHAPTER 13

Voices

Dickens, throughout his career, experimented on narrative modes and narrative voices, with a marked preference for the 'stance of overview',[1] which made him opt in most novels for the narrative convention of omniscience, omnipotence, omnividence, and also omnipresence; for his conception of the overseer is not that of some distant, unconcerned, objective, reporting deity. Dickens wants his narrator to be present, almost visible and tangible, to come down on earth and, occasionally, like the ancient gods, assume a human shape, be a shadow perhaps, 'cognisant of everything',[2] a dwarfish Mr Humphrey, an uncommercial traveller. He also wants him to be recognized as a character in his own right, even when anonymous and disembodied – which he is in most novels –, and to be everywhere recognizable as the authentic and unique performer of the Dickens texts.

This protean character, as a consequence, retains the same voice novel in novel out, a voice that draws attention to itself, to its gusto, its energy, its mannerisms, its love of incongruities, of unnecessary details, of intensified contrasts, of metaphor and anaphora, a voice that is garrulous, emphatic, loud, rhetorical, and that will not be confined to the task of telling, but provides at once information and form, commentary and style.

In *A Tale of Two Cities*, the novel Dickens wrote just before *Great Expectations*, the 'pervasive presence'[3] of the narrator's voice is felt as perhaps nowhere before. Dickens at the time was still under the influence and emotion of his theatrical involvement in Wilkie Collins's *The Frozen Deep* where he had played the leading part, an experience which he described interestingly as a form of collective literary creativity: 'I derive a strange feeling out of it', he wrote in January 1857, 'like writing a book in company'.[4] Conversely, writing the *Tale* was for him almost like acting in the privacy of his study: 'I must say', he told Mary Boyle, 'that I like my Carton, and I have a faint idea sometimes that if I had acted him, I could have done something with his life and death'.[5] And his famous preface points to a filiation between the two activities, play-acting and novel-writing:

> When I was acting, with my children and friends, in Mr. Wilkie Collins' drama of The Frozen Deep, I first conceived the main idea of this story. A strong desire was upon me then, to embody it in my own person; and I traced out in my fancy, the state of mind of which it would necessitate the presentation to an observant spectator, with particular care and interest...
>
> ... I have so far verified what is done and suffered in these pages, as that I have certainly done and suffered it all myself.[6]

No wonder that the narrator, highly strung, sensitive to the utmost, should do and suffer it all and should even so shamelessly exhibit the exquisite exhilaration of suffering on the forefront of the stage. As early as page one, the voice shifts from impersonal reporting – '*It* was the best of times, *it* was the worst of times' – to personal involvement – '*we* had everything before us, *we* had nothing before us' –,[7] becomes a collective voice, identified with both actors and readers, bridging the gap between the past and the present. Later, even more daringly, the voice speaks in its own name: 'A solemn consideration, when *I* enter a great city by night, that ...'.[8] Throughout the novel, the voice plays on all the 'degrees of indirectness'[9] and all the 'degrees of affirmation'[10] with unparalleled virtuosity, mediates the discourse of the various actors, goes even so far at times as to steal their parts and, dropping quotation marks, to appropriate their words, erasing the otherness of others, rubbing out the borderland between the shown and the shower, between the time of the action and the time of utterance, shifting abruptly from the preterite to the historic present, destroying at once the concept of double temporality and the concept of difference:

> Out of the open country, in again among ruinous buildings, solitary farms, dye-works, tanneries, and the like, cottages in twos and threes, avenues of leafless trees. Have these men deceived *us*, and taken *us* back by another road? Is not this the same place twice over? Thank Heaven, no. A village. Look back, look back, and see if *we* are pursued![11]

Mimesis and diegesis are all one in such a scene. The obliteration of enunciation markers, the camouflaging (or metamorphosis?) of the narrative instance, the internalization of emotion, the suppression of verbs which turns the description into immediate perception, all contribute to establishing this 'variable or floating relationship' between narrator and characters which, a century later, Genette was to describe as typical of the 'contemporary novel' and modernist audacity.[12]

The very last scene of the novel offers an even more remarkable violation of the laws of narration and a glaring instance of ambiguity, when the narrator, on the authority of his omnividence and of his own immortality, personally gives utterance to the prophetic discourse which the now dead hero would have delivered 'if' he had been allowed to express himself at the foot of the scaffold: 'I see ... I see ... I see ...'. As the vision itself corresponds exactly to the conventional winding-up of the Dickensian novel, where the narrator dutifully informs the reader of what 'was to' happen to each and every one of the characters, as the narrator somehow plays his own part by proxy, we feel overcome by a 'pronominal vertigo',[13] unable to tell who is who, who usurped whose voice. Through the mutual annihilation of narrator and hero, this last page, though written in the autobiographical mode, is most disturbingly impersonal and a-temporal: the 'I' has lost its referential competence and the present tense has lost its temporal quality to become, quite paradoxically, a mode of non-existence, an 'absent', this verbal form that Aragon dreamt of, 'a tense ... not cast out of the present, neither past nor future, but an *absent* properly speaking, a language of what is not'.[14]

After taking such liberties, Dickens must have realized that the return to the traditional 'I' form of narrative, which he had abandoned for almost a decade (except for minor pieces), would be very exacting, inhibiting and frustrating. It excluded omniscience, implied restriction of field and solitary confinement within a single consciousness. The author of *David Copperfield* must have known, besides, that difficulties would arise that he had not had to face when writing his first confessional novel, namely the difficulty of hushing the authorial voice. For, being Dickens's first narrator-protagonist, David had been entirely free to express himself in the style that came spontaneously to his lips or from his pen, and if the voice happened, as it did, to sound like that of the author, the kinship was acceptable, even welcome to those readers who were perspicacious enough to receive the book as Dickens's disguised autobiography.

But a new autobiographer, with a different name and a different personality, would be expected to have a style of his own. This Dickens had clearly perceived when embarking on *Bleak House*: to avoid overlappings, he had even been cautious enough to give his heroine a style totally different from his own: inconspicuous, diffident, sentimental, subdued, unclever, lachrymose, female: 'I have a great deal of difficulty in beginning to write my portion of these pages, for I know I am not clever',[15] poor Esther complains on getting started, and what follows immediately verifies her declaration:

> Dear, dear, to think how much time we passed alone together afterwards, and how often I repeated to the doll the story of my birthday, and confided to her that I would try, as hard as ever I could, to repair the fault I had been born with ... I hope it is not self-indulgent to shed these tears as I think of it. I am very thankful, I am very cheerful, but I cannot quite help their coming to my eyes.
>
> There! I have wiped them away now, and can go on again properly.[16]

What reader, after such a start, does not feel relieved at the thought that she was given only a 'portion' of the narrative? All the more so as the other voice, stentorian, megalomaniac, male ... and familiar to boot, has already compelled recognition and admiration in the splendid overture. Esther will in fact prove more clever than we had expected: subtle, sensitive, a great master of the art of understatement, she will cover her allotted ground with finesse and competence. As she goes on with her narrative, she will naturally acquire self-confidence and her style will improve; but, even allowing for greater ease and assurance on her part, who can really believe that the self-same Esther has within a few pages become the portraitist of Mrs Jellyby 'looking far away into Africa straight through my bonnet and head'[17] or of Mr Turveydrop:

> He was a fat old gentleman with a false complexion, false teeth, false whiskers, and a wig. He had a fur collar, and he had a

padded breast to his coat, which only wanted a star or a broad blue ribbon to be complete. He was pinched in, and swelled out, and got up, and strapped down, as much as he could possibly bear. He had such a neckcloth on (puffing his very eyes out of their natural shape), and his chin and even his ears so sunk into it, that it seemed as though he must inevitably double up, if it were cast loose.[18]

Clearly, someone has trespassed on her territory and no Dickens reader can fail to identify the naughty intruder as the 'performing artist, displaying his verbal skills', the 'self-exhibiting master of language' who, according to Robert Garis, is everywhere overtly trying to 'dazzle us', 'leading us through our impulse to applaud to a continual awareness' of himself.[19]

If such intrusions were not avoided in a novel in which the handling of narrative had been neatly portioned out from the outset between two distinct voices, surely they would be even more inevitable in a one-person narrative. And they were not avoided. For Robert Garis, it is not even a matter of intrusion but downright usurpation:

> ... in this particular novel the whole performance comes to us as the full-scale impersonation of a single man and a single voice. The great virtuoso appears on stage in the theatrical disguise of a man called Philip Pirrip who purports to be telling us his story ... Dickens's impersonation of the voice and point of view of Pip is a theatrical mask which he manipulates with the utmost dexterity when it is needed. But it is not always needed, and when it is quietly laid aside the skilful reader experiences no inconsistency. No reader accustomed to Dickens's theatrical art has ever been offended or even mildly puzzled to find that much of *Great Expectations* is spoken by the typically Dickensian voice – that of an acknowledged and self-confident master of language and narrative technique who quite audibly and quite unremittingly seeks to amuse, excite, and move his readers. Who has ever 'believed' that the famous comic set-pieces – Trabb's boy or Mr. Wopsle's *Hamlet* – were the work of a man named Philip Pirrip, called Pip?[20]

Garis is not quite fair: to say that Dickens 'manipulates' his theatrical mask 'with the utmost dexterity' is simply to describe the art of fiction-making and might be said of any good novelist. No literary character was ever self-born and manipulation is no other than the basic law of characterization. Yet, there is no denying that some scenes, especially the comic ones, could easily find their place in any other Dickens book and vice versa. If Pumblechook changed places with Mr Chadband, if Mr Hubble changed places with Mr Snagsby, the Christmas dinner at the Gargerys' could well find its way into *Bleak House* and the Snagsbys' tea-party into *Great Expectations*. Mrs Joe's funeral might well have been Mrs Copperfield's, and Pip's account of Wopsle's pantomime is strongly redolent of the Crummles scenes in *Nicholas Nickleby*. Pip in these scenes merely allows himself to be the speaking-trumpet of his master's voice. It is to the author of *David Copperfield*, not to the narrator of *Great Expectations* that we must attribute a passage like this:

At last I came within sight of the house, and saw that Trabb and Co. had put in a funereal execution and taken possession. Two dismally absurd persons, each ostentatiously exhibiting a crutch done up in a black bandage – as if that instrument could possibly communicate any comfort to anybody – were posted at the front door; and in one of them I recognized a postboy discharged from the Boar for turning a young couple into a sawpit on their bridal morning, in consequence of intoxication rendering it necessary for him to ride his horse clasped round the neck with both arms. All the children of the village, and most of the women, were admiring these sable warders and the closed windows of the house and forge; and as I came up, one of the two warders (the postboy) knocked at the door – implying that I was far too much exhausted by grief, to have strength remaining to knock for myself.

Another sable warder (a carpenter, who had once eaten two geese for a wager) opened the door, and showed me into the best parlour. Here, Mr Trabb had taken unto himself the best table, and had got all the leaves up, and was holding a kind of black Bazaar, with the aid of a quantity of black pins. At the moment of my arrival, he had just finished putting somebody's hat into black long-clothes, like an African baby; so he held out his hand for mine. But I, misled by the action, and confused by the occasion, shook hands with him with every testimony of warm affection (xxxv, 298).

What is objectionable about a text like this is the timbre of the voice that is heard uttering it, its special texture or 'grain',[21] rather than the contents themselves. After all, the autobiographer is quite free, as narrator and story-teller, to write what he pleases, free even to digress, tell tall stories or play the part of public entertainer.

Digressions, however, are not so acceptable in *Great Expectations* as in *David Copperfield*: David's story is digressive by nature, because its narrator has a taste for 'meandering' and because, as Taylor Stoehr rightly puts it, 'David merely tells a story which sometimes involves him';[22] Pip's book, on the other hand, is much too intensely and narrowly autobiographical, in fact too little digressive, to allow at all for extraneous developments and Pip is at his best and most convincing when he talks about himself. This he often does superbly, and in his own voice. Or, rather, his own voices, for polymodality[23] is his favourite mode of expression, best suited as it is to confessional writings. A perfect example of polymodal narrative occurs precisely in the paragraph that comes immediately before the text describing Mr Trabb's 'funereal execution':

> It was fine summer weather again, and, as I walked along, the times when I was a little helpless creature, and my sister did not spare me, vividly returned. But they returned with a gentle tone upon them that softened even the edge of Tickler. For now, the very breath of the beans and clover whispered to my heart that the day must come when it would be well for my memory that others walking in the sunshine should be softened as they thought of me (xxxv, 298).

This subtle blending of voices and of emotions belonging to different periods in the narrator-hero's life certainly does not prepare us for what follows, which is so suddenly different in tone and manner. But a passage like this is also much more representative of the style of the novel than the comic purple patches: Pip's narrative, as we have had many occasions to note, offers innumerable instances of such complex dialogues between the knowing, mellowed, moralizing voice of the elderly narrator and the eager, ignorant, anxious voice of the hero still enmeshed in the action, and many are the pages that really give the illusion of being 'the work of a man named Philip Pirrip, called Pip'.

But, for all its subtlety, *Great Expectations* was also meant to be a sensational novel, a novel with a mystery plot, closer in that respect to *Bleak House* than to *David Copperfield*. And in the absence of an impersonal narrator, Dickens had to find a means of unveiling the mysteries surrounding the life of his hero and of rendering the theatricality of suspense, sensation, revelation.

If this had been genuine autobiography, the narrator would have taken sensation upon himself: he would simply have limited himself as long as possible to providing only what information he held at the time of the action, and the revelations would have come in due time in the form of narration. But, if novelistic sensationalism was to be preserved, the revelations had to intrude into the story from unexpected sources, and preferably in direct speech: theatricality requires that discourse should be transacted by word of mouth, which accounts for the abundance of dialogue in this novel.

Confessional writings give short shrift to dialogue: their authors quote only memorable remarks, words that wounded or soothed or otherwise affected them for life and often call for long commentaries. First-person novels abide by different rules: their narrators, by tradition, are endowed with exceptional memories, a keen sense of observation, and a fondness for quoting in full what they heard ages ago; and, having entered into a tacit contract with novelists, we accept these quotations, even of lengthy speeches, as perfectly accurate. Pip, whose memory is, of course, as reliable as tradition permits, is all the more to be trusted as, throughout the book, he appears as a most attentive listener and as a greedy questioner, always eager to glean information from those whom he suspects of holding some 'portion' of the truth he is so earnestly seeking: 'Will you tell me ...?' (xlix, 412), 'Is that all the story?' (xxii, 205), 'I want to know' (l, 419), he goes about saying, as anxious as Arthur Clennam to find the sense of a beginning, to know what happened before if he is ever to know what is going to happen next or what is likely to. The piecemeal answers he gets he eventually pieces together: Herbert tells him what he knows of Miss Havisham's misfortunes; Magwitch comes out with the main revelations concerning his expectations; Jaggers, willy-nilly, lets out the truth about Estella's origins and adoption. Portions of the past are thus conjured up by instalments as Pip's interlocutors act as the novelist's deputy narrators.

This function is authenticated by style and rhetoric: whatever

their degree of linguistic competence, the truth-tellers express themselves as professional narrators. The moment they begin making the
slightest revelation, they don their Sunday stylistic best and become
'story'-tellers: 'Dear me!' says Herbert, 'It's quite a story, and shall
be saved till dinner-time' (xxii, 200); 'Dear boy and Pip's comrade',
begins Magwitch, 'I am not a going fur to tell you my life, like a
song or a story-book. But to give it you short and handy, I'll put it at
once into a mouthful of English' (xlii, 360). But we know that
denegation is disguised affirmation and, indeed, Magwitch's
account is neither short nor handy. The convict, besides, although
he has never read a book in his life, has the intuitive knowledge that
story-telling must obey strict laws: 'My Missis as I had the hard time
wi' – Stop though! I ain't brought *her* in – ' he says, interrupting
himself on realizing that his narrative grammar has gone wrong
somehow, and Pip rightly comments: 'He looked about him in a
confused way, as if he had lost his place in the book of his remembrance' (xlii, 364).

The word 'book' is appropriate: no matter how ungrammatical
his 'mouthful of English' may be, Magwitch 'speaks like a book'. Of
all Dickens's tellers in this novel, he is certainly the most gifted, and
by far. Plot-maker and illusionist, he is also the great stylist of the
book; he has a feel for words and the balance of sentences, and if his
morphology is often faulty his syntax is not (or hardly ever):

'I've been done everything to, pretty well – except hanged. I've
been locked up, as much as a silver tea-kettle. I've been carted
here and carted there, and put out of this town and put out of that
town, and stuck in the stocks, and whipped and worried and
drove. I've no more notion where I was born, than you have – if
so much. I first become aware of myself, down in Essex, a thieving
turnips for my living. Summun had run away from me – a man – a
tinker – and he'd took the fire with him, and left me wery cold.

'I know'd my name to be Magwitch, chrisen'd Abel. How did I
know it? Much as I know'd the birds' names in the hedges to be
chaffinch, sparrer, thrush. I might have thought it was all lies
together, only as the birds' names come out true, I supposed mine
did' (xlii, 360).

His sense of rhythm, his sense of humour, his ability to entertain, to
hit on the incongruous or comic comparison, his clever handling of

alliterations, his constant awareness of his listeners, his rhetorical questions, his concern with the reliability of language (which, incidentally, reminds us of Pip's 'first impression of the identity of things'), all pronounce him a first-class story-teller.

This we had known, or might have guessed, from the very start. In the churchyard scene, Magwitch had already given us a foretaste of his talent as a novelist:

'... Now, I ain't alone, as you may think I am. There's a young man hid with me, in comparison with which young man I am a Angel. That young man hears the words I speak. That young man has a secret way pecooliar to himself, of getting at a boy, at his heart, and at his liver. It is in wain for a boy to attempt to hide himself from that young man. A boy may lock his door, may be warm in bed, may tuck himself up, may draw the clothes over his head, may think himself comfortable and safe, but that young man will softly creep and creep his way to him and tear him open. I am a keeping that young man from harming of you at the present moment, with great difficulty. I find it wery hard to hold that young man off of your inside. Now, what do you say?' (i, 38).

'I said', explains Pip, 'that I would get him the file'. What else could the child do, under the spell of the illusion-maker?

Magwitch, the inspired novelist, can persuade himself as much as others of the truth of his own fiction, yet acknowledge it as fiction:

'Why, see now!' said he. 'When a man's alone on these flats, with a light head and a light stomach, perishing of cold and want, he hears nothin' all night, but guns firing, and voices calling. Hears? He sees the soldiers, with their red coats lighted up by the torches carried afore, closing in round him. Hears his number called, hears himself challenged, hears the rattle of the muskets, hears the orders "Make ready! Present! Cover him steady, men!" and is laid hands on – and there's nothin'! (iii, 51–2).

The text is much too universal in its significance to be read as the speaker's simple endeavour to express personal emotions and re-create the fear of the small hours of the night. Magwitch's speech-act is in fact a kind of performative: he is not just reporting on fear, but creating fear poetically through his rhetoric, 'indulging'[24] in it, performing it as a collective experience that involves the whole race of escaped prisoners and, emotionally, whole generations of Dickens readers; for he is not merely addressing Pip here, but 'writing' for posterity. To call him a 'writer' is no doubt to stretch the meaning of words since he never puts pen to paper, but his style is certainly not that of the average interlocutor in everyday conversation and even less of the average convict. His speech sounds like a text read out to an audience and might deserve the speaker the title of 'oral writer'.[25]

All Dickens's tellers are in fact 'oral writers'. The pulpit rhetoric of Pumblechook's homily on Pork, sententious and aphoristic, is also, in its own way, on the borderland between the spoken and the written word; so is Joe's epitaph, 'written' in direct speech – 'Remember *reader*' (vii, 77, my emphasis) – ; so is Jaggers's style, always halfway between a lawyer's discourse and a legal document.

Dickens himself never drew the line between writing and speaking to an audience and 'audience'[26] is a word he often used to designate his reading public. His public readings themselves had, over the years, strengthened the confusion: the more he read his texts aloud, the more, so to speak, he 'wrote them aloud'. This is why the best tribute ever paid to the oral quality of his books occurs at the end of Evelyn Waugh's *A Handful of Dust*, where the hero gets trapped in the Amazonian forest by a man who compels him to read him Dickens's novels. Dickens would have appreciated this form of acknowledgement: he knew very well that his books and serials were often read aloud in family or parish circles and that, through the spoken word, his texts could reach the illiterate. The idea was so dear to him that he made it an important subject in his last novel, giving Boffin the treat that Magwitch merely dreams of in this one:

> '... And your books too ... mounting up, on their shelves, by hundreds! And you read 'em; don't you? I see you'd been a reading of 'em when I come in. Ha, ha, ha! You shall read 'em to me, dear boy! And if they're in foreign languages wot I don't understand, I shall be just as proud as if I did' (xxxix, 338).

The habit Dickens had of delivering public speeches, his frequent participation in amateur theatricals, his love of the theatre and

theatrical art, his melodramatic imagination had all contributed to
giving his style its special quality. Even his method of composition
suggests that for him writing was just another form of play-acting.
We know that he projected himself into his characters and identified
himself with them when in the throes of creation: Taylor Stoehr, in
a perceptive analysis of the 'Memoranda' book, draws our attention
to the fact that some characters who were later to be alienated into
'hes' and 'shes' were first conceived as 'Is', and this applies, as he
notes, to 'minor characters – even despicable ones – like Podsnap
and Henry Gowan, with whom we would suppose him to have little
sympathy'.[27] Dickens himself admitted that creation for him was
very close to hallucination: 'I don't invent it – really do not – *but see
it*, and write it down',[28] he once wrote to Forster, and George Henry
Lewes reports: 'Dickens once declared to me that every word said
by his characters was distinctly heard by him'.[29] In his edition of
The Public Readings, Philip Collins also reminds us of

> his daughter Mamie's famous account of how she was once
> allowed to sit in his study while he was composing: he would rush
> to a mirror, make 'extraordinary facial contortions' in front of it,
> at the same time 'talking rapidly in a low voice', and then go to his
> desk and write. It was, as it were, a private 'reading' as an
> immediate preliminary to writing.[30]

Dickens, as we see, might have said with Aragon 'I never wrote my
novels, *I read them*'.[31]

Dickens read his books to himself and he read himself into them:
'D for Dickens', the mirror said, as it said 'J-O Joe' to Joe: ' "Why,
here's a J," said Joe, "and a O equal to anythink! Here's a J and a O,
Pip, and a J-O, Joe" ' (vii, 75). The deciphering of his initials in a
printed text is for Joe the best – perhaps the only – incitement to go
on reading as it means self-discovery, and the more Js and Os he
finds the happier he is: 'One, two, three. Why, here's three Js, and
three Os, and three J-O, Joes in it, Pip!' 'I'm oncommon fond of
reading', he concludes:

> 'On-common. Give me ... a good book, or a good newspaper,
> and sit me down afore a good fire, and I ask no better. Lord!...
> when you *do* come to a J and a O, and says you, "Here, at last, is a
> J-O, Joe," how interesting reading is!' (vii, 76).

Dickens, who mirrored himself into his characters, impersonated them all, lent his voice to his narrators, gave his initials (reversed in one famous case) to his favourite heroes, had a first-hand experience of the narcissism he describes here. 'D for Dickens' is what he read on every page, D, the be-all and end-all of reading and writing, D, the letter at which Dr Strong is still labouring at the end of *David Copperfield* with little hope or need to go any further in his Dictionary, D, the letter which Pip is given for meditation, close observation and imitation when he first learns to read and write:

> that very evening Biddy entered on our special agreement, by . . . lending me, to copy at home, a large old English D which she had imitated from the heading of some newspaper, and which I supposed, until she told me what it was, to be a design for a buckle (x, 103).

After this initiation, what chance is left the poor boy of ever properly emancipating himself stylistically from his creator? And if he (partly) fails, can other, lesser characters be expected in fairness to succeed?

It should be observed, however, that stylistic emancipation has nothing to do with linguistic autonomy. Dickens's characters, in this book as elsewhere, have their idiosyncrasies of speech and linguistic mannerisms. We expect them as part of the fun of reading a Dickens novel and we do not get tired of them. No one gets tired of hearing Pumblechook call Mrs Joe 'Mum' or of seeing the post-office mouth of Wemmick shape the magic words 'portable property'. No one gets tired of Joe's 'What larks' or of his many eccentricities and verbal oddities. His characteristic 'which I meantersay', his knack of 'turning *which* into a mere equivalent of "and" or "and, in his respect" or "and, talking of that" ' has even earned Joe the 'oncommon' compliment of being regarded by Sylvère Monod as the 'pupil'[32] of Mrs Gamp. This title he actually deserves on more than just these grounds alone: his malapropisms – 'coddleshell' for 'codicil' (lvii, 474), 'purple lectic' for 'apoplectic' (vii, 77) – are quite worthy of his mistress's; his neologisms, his mispronunciation – de-diphthongizations, v/w shifts, droppings of h's – all that constitutes his 'private language'[33] or his idiolect testifies to true discipleship and a thorough analysis of his speech mannerisms would in fact consist in reproducing Monod's admirably meticulous autopsy of Gampese.

Language is also used, as in all Dickens's novels, to place characters socially: Magwitch certainly does not express himself like Herbert Pocket or Mr Jaggers; his 'pecooliar' way of speaking is recognizably lower-class English, his pronunciation is faulty, as the narrator's phoneticizings show, and, clearly, neither the 'deserting soldier ... what ... learnt [him] to read' nor the 'travelling Giant ... what ... learnt [him] to write' (xlii, 361) 'learnt him' his irregular verbs or the rudiments of grammar.

But language is not style and, if his accent and grammar differentiate the convict from his social betters, his narrative art is very close to theirs. In delegating the story-telling, Dickens also delegated the rhetoric that goes with it, so that, regardless of their origins, his tellers all resort to the same devices: they all make extravagant and hyperbolic use of apostrophes, anaphoras, exclamations and superlatives and, even in private, theirs is the rhetoric of public discourse. Magwitch begins his life-story as if he were Mark Antony addressing a crowd of Romans, Jaggers retains at the forge the solemnity of a lawyer at court: 'Now, Mr Pip', he says, 'I address the rest of what I have to say, to you' (xviii, 165). They hardly ever speak conversational English (which, incidentally, would be very tedious) but recite parts or read texts specially written for them: they are the novelist's appointed public readers.

Their handling of narrative also invariably rests on the Dickensian principle that a story must be told by instalments and they all resort to the 'guess-what' or the 'let's pretend' method. Even Joe, who is not much of a teller, finds the trick of delaying information on the one occasion when he is the bearer of news: before telling his wife the exact amount of her brother's premium, he raises the bidding tantalizingly:

> 'What would present company say to ten pound?' demanded Joe.
> 'They'd say,' returned my sister, curtly, 'pretty well. Not too much, but pretty well.'
> 'It's more than that, then,' said Joe ...
> 'What would present company say,' proceeded Joe, 'to twenty pound?'
> 'Handsome would be the word,' returned my sister.
> 'Well, then,' said Joe, 'It's more than twenty pound.' ...

'Then to make an end of it,' said Joe, delightedly handing the bag to my sister: 'it's five-and-twenty pound' (xiii, 131–2).

Magwitch, as plot-maker and co-novelist, is even better entitled than anyone else in the book to parcel out his story and deliver it in parts, sadistically enjoying the effect of each bit on his listener. He progresses step by step with his revelations, enunciating each new piece of information as if it were a term in an endless riddle:

'Might a mere warmint ask what property?' said he.
I faltered, 'I don't know.'
'Might a mere warmint ask whose property?' said he.
I faltered again, 'I don't know.'
'Could I make a guess, I wonder,' said the Convict, 'at your income since you come of age! As to the first figure now. Five?' ...
'Concerning a guardian,' he went on. 'There ought to have been some guardian, or such-like, whiles you was a minor. Some lawyer, maybe. As to the first letter of that lawyer's name now. Would it be J?' ...
'Put it,' he resumed, 'as the employer of that lawyer whose name begun with a J, and might be Jaggers – put it as he had come over sea to Portsmouth, and had landed there, and had wanted to come on to you. "However, you have found me out," you says just now. Well! However did I find you out? Why, I wrote from Portsmouth to a person in London, for particulars of your address. That person's name? Why, Wemmick' (xxxix, 336–7).

His almost forensic 'put it as' (Could it be a distortion of a clause often heard at the tribunal?) strikingly anticipates Jaggers's famous 'put the case that': the stylist has merely adapted his grammar to his locutor's station without tampering with the rhetoric of his narrative. And what Barbara Hardy says of the lawyer's formula is just as true of the convict's: it 'underlines the formality and provisional caginess of his narrative'.[34]

'The story of Estella's mother is told fully, despite the guard of its rhetoric', Barbara Hardy adds. 'Despite' or 'thanks to' the guard of the rhetoric, truth will out. Only, Dickens's truth-tellers curiously deal with the truth as if it were fictitious: 'Mind!', they seem to say, 'it is up to you to decide what to believe'. To Pip, who wonders why Compeyson did not marry Miss Havisham 'and get all the property', Herbert replies by suggesting that the man might have been married already. 'Mind!' he adds, 'I don't know that' (xxii, 206). Magwitch, as we have seen, modalizes his discourse with 'oughts', 'mights' and question-marks. And Jaggers, who had early warned Pip that he was no 'fortune-teller' (xxvi, 239), now brackets his revelations between two safety clauses: 'I'll put a case to you. Mind! I admit nothing' ... 'Do you comprehend the imaginary case?' (li, 424–5). This theatrical rhetoric of distantiation at once magnifies and alienates the discourse of the 'truth-tellers', verifying Maurice Blanchot's assertion that 'literature is an "as if" '.

NOTES: CHAPTER 13

1 Jonathan Arac, *Commissioned Spirits: The Shaping of Social Motion in Dickens, Carlyle, Melville, and Hawthorne* (New Brunswick, NJ: Rutgers University Press, 1979), p. ix.
2 *The Pilgrim Edition of the Letters of Charles Dickens*, Vol. 5 (Oxford: Clarendon Press, 1981), eds Graham Storey and K. J. Fielding, p. 622, [7 October 1849], to Forster.
3 J. Hillis Miller, *The Form of Victorian Fiction* (Notre Dame, Ind.: University of Notre Dame Press, 1968), p. 64.
4 Nonesuch *Letters*, Vol. 2, p. 825, 9 January 1857, to Sir James Emerson Tennant.
5 ibid., Vol. 3, p. 255, 7 November 1861, to Mary Boyle.
6 *A Tale of Two Cities*, The New Oxford Illustrated Dickens (London: Oxford University Press, 1962), p. xiii.
7 ibid., I, i, 1 (my emphasis).
8 ibid., I, iii, 10 (my emphasis).
9 Norman Page, *Speech in the English Novel* (London: Longman, 1973), p. 31.
10 Gérard Genette, *Narrative Discourse*, translated by Jane E. Lewin (Oxford: Blackwell, 1980), p. 161.
11 *A Tale of Two Cities*, op. cit., III, xiii, 339 (my emphasis).
12 Genette, op. cit., p. 246.
13 ibid.
14 Aragon, *Je n'ai jamais appris à écrire ou les incipit* (Geneva: Skira, 1969), p. 116.
15 *Bleak House*, eds. G. Ford and S. Monod (New York: Norton, 1977), iii, 17.
16 ibid., p. 20.
17 ibid., xxiii, 296.
18 ibid., xiv, 171.
19 Robert Garis, *The Dickens Theatre* (Oxford: Clarendon Press, 1965), pp. 63, 24.
20 ibid., p. 191.
21 cf. Roland Barthes, *Le Grain de la voix* (Paris: Le Seuil, 1981).
22 Taylor Stoehr, *Dickens: The Dreamer's Stance* (Ithaca, NY: Cornell University Press, 1965), p. 45.
23 On the notion of polymodality, see Genette, op. cit., pp. 198–9.
24 cf. J. L. Austin's definition of performatives in *How to Do Things with Words* (Oxford University Press, 1962; 2nd edn, 1975), p. 6.
25 For a similar approach see Robert Tracy, 'Reading Dickens' writing', *Dickens*

Studies Annual, vol. 11 (1983), pp. 37–59. But the overlapping is quite fortuitous: this chapter was written long before Tracy's essay came to my notice.

26 cf. Nonesuch *Letters*, Vol. 3, p. 169, 3 August 1860, to Bulwer.

27 Stoehr, op. cit., p. 44.

28 John Forster, *The Life of Charles Dickens* (London: Dent, 1966), Vol. 2, p. 272.

29 G. H. Lewes, 'Dickens in relation to criticism', *The Fortnightly Review*, 17 February 1872, pp. 144–5.

30 Philip Collins (ed.), *Charles Dickens: The Public Readings* (Oxford: Clarendon Press, 1975), p. lix.

31 Aragon, op. cit., p. 47.

32 Sylvère Monod, *Martin Chuzzlewit* (London: Allen & Unwin, 1985), p. 62.

33 Dorothy Van Ghent, *The English Novel: Form and Function* [1953] (New York: Harper Torchbooks, 1961), p. 125.

34 Barbara Hardy, *Tellers and Listeners: The Narrative Imagination* (London: The Athlone Press, 1975), p. 170.

CHAPTER 14

The Other Stage

In *Great Expectations* there are several characters – Pumblechook, Orlick, Wopsle and, to a lesser degree, Trabb's boy – who, to all appearances, play an important, albeit importunate, part in the life of the hero, whose various performances, whether comic or dramatic, are impressive and memorable, but who, when viewed in the strict light of utility and plot economy, would seem to be totally unnecessary. If we look up *The Oxford Companion to English Literature* for instance, we observe that none of their names is mentioned in the summary of the novel given there and that only 'Joe's uncle, the impudent old impostor Pumblechook' has found his way into the list of 'Other notable characters in the book', which is appended to it.

The exclusion from the summary is easy enough to account for. Pumblechook has hardly anything to do with the plot except introduce Pip to Satis House, which any walk-on actor might have done. Wopsle's one and only connection with the action proper consists in identifying the spectator sitting behind Pip during his pantomime as the convict with the mauled face, which Pip might well have done for himself if he had happened to look behind him. Trabb's boy is assuredly one of Pip's three rescuers in the sluice-house scene, but his role as guide to Herbert and Startop is more symbolic than truly indispensable. Sensational as it may be, Orlick's aggression of Pip miscarries and even his assault on Mrs Gargery has no direct bearing on the subsequent events, except in so far as it leaves Joe free to marry Biddy; but then, Mrs Joe might just as well have died a natural death and, in any case, she might have been dead even before the novel began: her role in the opening chapters is already superfluous since she *has* brought up Pip by hand and now merely brandishes Tickler as a fetish, a reminder of her former part as foster-mother to the infant child.

Unnecessary as far as plot goes, these people, however, are not merely ornamental squiggles. They are necessary in more ways than one, necessary first and foremost to story and story-telling. Through them, Pip's story, instead of being merely told straightforwardly by himself, is foretold and side-told, parodied and magnified, analysed and annotated, staged and vicariously performed. Not truth-tellers but sooth-sayers, not reporters but commentators, not actants but actors, they might all be described as so many impersonations of some unofficial, slanderous narrative voice, which will make itself heard at all costs and which even Pip has no power to hush. To ignore them would be to ignore the irrational, unverifiable, metaphoric aspect of narration and to limit the novel to some imaginary 'authorized' version of the hero's biography.

But, 'authorial' at best, Pip's narration is never exclusive and always allows for the unsolicited discourse of those intruders. They may provoke him into outbursts of indignation, exasperation, disgust and loathing – he detests Orlick, the slouching Cain, has no patience with 'That ass, Pumblechook' (xii, 124), is aggravated with Wopsle's Roman nose and infuriated at the sight of Trabb's boy, the 'dodging serpent' (xxx, 267) – , but, if he indulges freely in remarks on what they are, he holds back from making comments on what they say, behaving somehow like a mere scribe who has no choice but to write what the novelist dictates.

What the novelist dictates is no other than the familiar Dickensian rhetoric of suspense, irony and ambiguity, of which the intruders are the deputy performers. Wopsle's function is that of the *aiodos*, the itinerant actor who moves from village to town, dogging the hero's footsteps, and threateningly performs the intertext, Collins's 'Ode on the Passions', Lillo's *The London Merchant* and Shakespeare's *Hamlet*. Trabb's boy is the ironist, mainly remembered for running along the street as a running commentary of Pip's social promotion, a living parody of Pumblechook's and society's 'May Is', the flippant deflator of hyperbole.

More willingly harmful, the duettists, Pumblechook and Mrs Joe, set the moral suspense going: they are to Pip what the gentleman with the white waistcoat was to Oliver Twist; they ask, and pretend to answer, the rhetorical questions of the narrative, 'Is the boy going to be hanged?', 'Will he be sent to the Hulks for asking questions?', 'Will he deserve bleeding by Dunstable the butcher?' Inconsistent in their predictions, they prophesy of awful things and of marvellous things to come: 'for anything we can tell, this boy's fortune may be made by his going to Miss Havisham's' (vii, 82), declares Mrs Joe, parroting Pumblechook's prognostications. They prompt the scenario of misplaced expectations, instil into the hero the poison of ambition and consequent dissatisfaction; they are the false prophets of the novel, caricatures of story-tellers, caricatures in fact of the novelist himself, who has grounded his novel on similar ambiguities and false premises. Eventually, they get what they deserve, what perhaps all novelists deserve: Mrs Joe becomes aphasic – 'her hearing was greatly impaired; her memory also; and her speech was unintelligible' (xvi, 149) – and when she tries to communicate through writing, 'extraordinary complications' arise and her messages are endless sources of misinterpretation. Pumblechook, in his turn, will be (temporarily) deprived of speech and have his mouth stuffed 'full of flowering annuals' by burglars 'to prewent his crying out' (lvii, 475).

Curiously enough, it is for taking part in the aggression of Pumblechook – a minor offence, one would think, compared to the murderous assault on Mrs Gargery and to the treacherous attack and near murder of Pip in the lime-kiln – that Orlick will be sent to jail. To Pip's astonishment, Mrs Joe never considers informing against her aggressor and even tries to conciliate him:

> I confess that I expected to see my sister denounce him, and that I was disappointed by the different result. She manifested the greatest anxiety to be on good terms with him,... she showed every possible desire to conciliate him, and there was an air of humble propitiation in all she did, such as I have seen pervade the bearing of a child towards a hard master (xvi, 151).

But, barring the fact that she has lost her use of speech, it would have been very difficult for poor Mrs Joe to convince the police of Orlick's culpability, considering, as we are told, that she was struck 'from behind' (liii, 437)! Much more astonishing is Pip's own attitude after the sluice-house episode:

> When I told Herbert what had passed within the house, he was for our immediately going before a magistrate in the town, late at night as it was, and getting out a warrant. But, I had already considered that such a course, by detaining us there, or binding us

to come back, might be fatal to Provis. There was no gainsaying this difficulty, and we relinquished all thoughts of pursuing Orlick at that time (liii, 442).

We are quite ready to accept Pip's good reasons for postponing his pursuit of Orlick 'at that time', but it is strange that he should bring no action against him later, when Magwitch is dead and no longer an obstacle to his going to the police. There is no obvious reason why, within a few months, he should have dismissed any thought of revenge against the man who attacked him so slyly and whom he now knows for certain to have been his sister's murderer. Does conscience make a coward of him?

What tentative answers can be given to the enigma of Pip's reticence must rest on an analysis of Orlick's function in the novel. For Robert Garis, the matter is simple and easily accounted for:

> The truth is that Pip has no continuing and developing relation-ship with Orlick, and that Orlick has only the sketchiest indepen-dent identity in the novel. Orlick is really only a name given to some actions; he is a theatrical handyman assigned certain tasks in the novel. This is acceptable in the Dickens theatre because these actions take care of feelings generated by the fable but never really engage Pip's attention.[1]

In other words, Orlick has been hired by Dickens as performer of violence and, when his task is over, he is simply dismissed into oblivion and, we feel inclined to add, into the county gaol, for morality's sake.

Garis's view of Orlick as 'a name given to some actions' is clever and convincing; but it does not follow that these actions 'never really engage Pip's attention'. This is certainly not the impression Pip tries to give in his recollections, and the pages devoted to Orlick, though supposedly written after a long gap of years, are couched in passionate terms suggestive of lasting hatred: 'if I could have killed him, even in dying, I would have done it' (liii, 437), he says: is this to be taken as a sign of unconcern? But it is Garis's conviction that 'Theatrical art is not an appropriate mode for dealing with the inner life'.[2] He therefore leaves it to the 'tedious parlour-analyst'[3] to ask himself idle questions about the hidden motives of Dickensian characters.

Concerned though he is for his part with the theme and treatment of guilt in *Great Expectations*, Julian Moynahan offers a no less disappointing explanation of Orlick's impunity. After remarking on the fact that Pip does not report Orlick's murderous assaults on himself and on his sister to the police, he merely concludes:

> Despite the fact that there is enough accumulated evidence to hang him, Orlick's end is missing from the book. Actually, it seems that Orlick simply evaporates into thin air after his punitive rôle has been performed. His case needs no final disposition because he has only existed, essentially, as an aspect of the hero's own far more problematic case.[4]

His reading of Orlick's role and of the 'ties of analogy'[5] that bind him to the hero might have inspired this critic with a more satisfactory interpretation of Pip's behaviour after his aggression. For him, Orlick is not just an 'exponent of violence'[6] as he is for Garis, but 'Pip's punitive instrument or weapon'.[7] Pip, he argues, was brutally handled by his shrew sister during his childhood and 'has the motive of revenge',[8] but it is Orlick who acts as his 'vengeful surrogate'.[9] The idea, of course, is not to present Orlick as some gallant avenger, but as the hero's dark *alter ego*: Dickens has split one man into two halves – the good and the bad – and given two names to two aspects of one complex personality.

This audacious, yet attractive theory has the advantage of accounting for the ambivalence of Orlick's words when, in the sluice-house, he confesses to having bludgeoned Mrs Gargery himself, yet accuses Pip of the crime: 'I come upon her from behind', he says, '*I* giv' it her!... But it warn't Old Orlick as did it; it was you' (liii, 437). 'Orlick', Moynahan comments, 'confronts the hero in this scene ... as a distorted and darkened mirror-image'.[10]

'Confronts the hero' implies in return that the hero *is* confronted. To make such a remark is to state the obvious, but the obvious has to be stated since Moynahan himself neglects these implications and deals with the confrontation as if the novelist had intended it for the mere puzzlement of readers and critics. It is worth remembering, therefore, that Orlick's psychodrama is first and foremost enacted in Pip's presence and for his benefit, so that no one should be better qualified than this privileged spectator to interpret its meaning.

Pip, of course, is unprepared to recognize himself in the mirror held up to him and flatly denies the accusation: 'It was you, villain', he retorts. But, surprisingly, a blunt denial is his sole reaction. We would expect him to argue, urge his interlocutor to explain himself or simply tax him with inconsistency. He does nothing of the kind. Nor does he make any personal attempt, even *a posteriori*, at working out the meaning of his aggressor's enigmatic discourse. Rather than investigate this puzzling affair, he behaves as if he wanted to hush it up, as if he was afraid of facing a disturbing truth, as if that other self which he has glimpsed in the looking-glass, whether he liked it or not, had to be rubbed out of his memory like a bad dream. His silence in fact is self-accusatory, the sign, it would seem, that he has obscurely identified himself with his sister's murderer, recognizing in him the man who has fulfilled his own unexpressed and long-unacknowledged wishes. After all, as he may now realize, he *had* the revenge motive.

Orlick, therefore, may well 'seem' to have 'simply' vanished into thin air towards the end of the novel, but the truth is that it is Pip who has deliberately ruled him out of his thoughts and out of his world: 'Your presence irks me', Oedipus said to Teiresias, 'gone, you will plague me no longer.'[11]

And when Moynahan suggests that Orlick's 'case needs no final disposal', it might be more exact to say that it is Pip who is unwilling to see his case fairly disposed of. On hearing from Joe that his near-murderer is locked in the county gaol, Pip does not jump for joy as he normally should; he hardly says a word, expresses no personal feelings and clearly avoids mentioning Orlick's name: 'Is it Pumblechook's house that *has been broken into*, then?' he merely asks (lvii, 475, my emphasis). Neither does he seize the opportunity of Orlick's imprisonment to give fresh evidence against the man who nearly killed him and was responsible for the death of his sister, though, surely, this would be a duty to her memory. But he is no more able to wreak vengeance on his sister's aggressor than was Hamlet to kill his father's murderer, dimly aware as he is, like Shakespeare's 'undecided Prince' (xxxi, 275), that in so doing he would punish a man for vicariously committing his own crimes. The Hamlet theme that runs through the novel cannot but confirm the hidden reasons for the hero's inability to 'take arms against a sea of troubles'. The oedipal inhibitions of Gertrude and Hamlet's son – which, without benefit of Freud or Ernest Jones, Dickens had intuited – throw light on the subconscious of the son of Philip Pirrip and foster-child of Mrs Joe.

The scene in the lime-kiln may strike us as crucial and cathartic, but it is certainly not unique of its kind. Built after a pattern that has by now become familiar even to the most inattentive reader, it is the last of a series of confrontations in the course of which Pip invariably finds himself trapped into making unpleasant identifications, forced to be the helpless spectator of himself as bad, criminal, guilty 'Naterally wicious' (iv, 57).

His badness, besides, is always of the same type: the badness of the bad son: 'Swine were the companions of the prodigal' (iv, 58), says Wopsle to the child whom Pumblechook's rhetoric is about to 'piggify'. The sexton's parable rests on a distorted recollection of St Luke's gospel,[12] and establishes a relationship between the swine and the swineherd which is unsupported by the biblical text but facilitates ambiguities and oblique indictments. As would-be 'companion' of the prodigal, Pig-Pip receives his own share of the latter's guilt, of his filial impiety, of his improvidence, of his ungratefulness. 'Be grateful', he had been warned a moment before, 'Especially ... be grateful, boy, to them which brought you up by hand' (iv, 57). But the company had agreed that boys are never grateful and the image of the prodigal, which is now associated with him, seems to doom him to everlasting ungratefulness. The subject, besides, is not totally unseasonable, for the scene takes place within only a few hours of Pip's first act of disloyalty to his kin: sealing a pact with a stranger over the tomb of his father, robbing his sister's pantry for the benefit of his 'fugitive friend' have already alienated him from parental authority. So that Wopsle's and Pumblechook's oracular utterances are both grotesque and pertinent; Pip's guilty conscience gives meaning to the speakers' words where none could be intended. *Male*diction becomes *pre*diction.

The passing reference to the prodigal will prove, later, to have worked also as long-term narrative, foretelling the son's ultimate drive back towards the father; but, on the spur of the moment, Pumblechook's threatening accents overshadow testamental optimism and his narrow-mindedness narrows the scope of his predictions to the earliest stage of the parable, the son's estrangement and exile. The emphasis, when we first read the scene (in the light of what little we know) is on the 'sonhood' of the son, on predictable transgression, on breaking away from the tyranny of unchosen kinship, on betrayal of origins.

Next, with the Barnwell scene, things go from bad to worse as the figure of the prodigal makes way for that of the parricide:

> Murder the worst of crimes, and parricide the worst of murders, and this the worst of parricides! Cain, who stands on record from the birth of time, and must to its last final period, as accursed, slew a brother favoured above him. Detested Nero by another's hand dispatched a mother that he feared and hated. But I, with my own hand, have murdered a brother, mother, father, and a friend, most loving and beloved. This execrable act of mine's without a parallel. O may it ever stand alone – the last of murders, as it is the worst![13]

It will be Pip's new ordeal henceforth to identify himself with the utterer of these words, an identification which might be short-lived, but which, given the circumstances, will last him a lifetime.

In a way, the ordeal ought to be more easily bearable than that of hearing personal remarks during the Christmas meal: unlike Pumblechook's improvisations, the words which now reach Pip's ears are read from a book and part of a show; but Pip's identification with the uncle-murderer is of a different nature from that of ordinary spectators. Identification with the heroes of drama is, as everyone knows, part of the game of theatre-going: people buy this right at the booking-office. But they doff their tragic masks on leaving the play-house and, during the performance, however caught up they may be by dramatic illusion, they are never as thoroughly involved as Brecht imagines them to be, were it only because theatrical architecture constantly reminds them that a stage is not the world.

The stage on which Wopsle performs his 'Murder of Gonzago' is unfortunately placed within the very recognizable world of Pumblechook's parlour (Pip will later rechristen it 'the Barnwell parlour', xix, 179) and, caught in the mousetrap set for him 'to be read at' (xv, 144), Pip is unprotected by anything like footlights, stage-curtain or orchestra pit from 'the identification of the whole affair with [his] unoffending self'. Yet, rarely was protection so badly needed, for, instead of being a willing suspension of the watcher's self-consciousness, the identification process is achieved here

through the actor's sole volition and persuasiveness: at the insti-
gation of Pumblechook, the 'Barnwell-parlour-analyst', it is Wopsle
who compels Pip to step on to 'the other stage' and become the
offending self of Lillo's drama:

> When Barnwell began to go wrong, I declare that I felt positively
> apologetic, Pumblechook's indignant stare so taxed me with it.
> Wopsle, too, took pains to present me in the worst light. At once
> ferocious and maudlin, I was made to murder my uncle with no
> extenuating circumstances whatever ... Even after I was happily
> hanged and Wopsle had closed the book, Pumblechook sat
> staring at me, and shaking his head, and saying, 'Take warning,
> boy, take warning!' as if it were a well-known fact that I contem-
> plated murdering a near relation, provided I could only induce
> one to have the weakness to become my benefactor (xv, 145).

This sadistic reversal of the usual identification pattern has unexpected, ironic effects: identification becomes downright metamorphosis, Pip becomes an impossible Barnwell, and tragedy becomes
comedy!

But comedy turns again to tragedy when Pip leaves the Barnwell
parlour only to discover on reaching the forge that the deed has
been committed:

> I became aware of my sister – lying without sense or movement
> on the bare boards where she had been knocked down by a
> tremendous blow on the back of the head, dealt by some
> unknown hand when her face was turned towards the fire –
> destined never to be on the Rampage again, while she was the
> wife of Joe (xv, 147).

'With my head full of George Barnwell', Pip goes on to explain, 'I
was at first disposed to believe that *I* must have had some hand in
the attack upon my sister' (xvi, 147). Here again, we think we can
hear Oedipus wondering 'Was I not born evil? Am I not utterly
unclean?'[14] The function of the Barnwell scene is very close indeed
to that of oracles and revelations in *Oedipus the King*. Admittedly,
no precise textual reference to Sophocles can be detected in this
novel and Oedipus does not seem to have ever belonged to the
novelist's imaginary world. Striking similitudes are none the less to

be noticed between the two heroes, their stories, their enigmatic connection with crime, their quest for the true father; both are the object of apparently ungrounded accusations, both react with a mixture of disbelief and disquietude, both, after vigorously claiming their innocence, start an inquiry, even at the risk of being found guilty: 'I thought I heard you say that Laius was killed at a cross-roads ... Where did this happen? ... How long ago? ... What was he like? ... Was he still in manhood's prime?'[15] asks Oedipus. And Pip wonders if the 'piece of evidence', a convict's leg-iron 'filed asunder some time ago', which was found on the floor beside his sister's body, does not somehow point to his guilt: 'Knowing what I knew', he says, 'I set up an inference of my own here. I believed the iron to be my convict's iron ... It was horrible to think that I had provided the weapon, however undesignedly, but I could hardly think otherwise' (xvi, 148). And he cannot help connecting this coincidence with 'that spell of [his] childhood', which again reminds us of Loxias' oracle.

But Pip is more lucky than his illustrious predecessor and, strange to say, it is Orlick who spares him the fate of being a new Oedipus: by assuming the murderous act and leaving the motive to his *alter ego*, by staging the revelation, by being mirror as much as mirror-image, Orlick reduces Pip's lot to that of being oedipal.

The confrontation in the sluice-house thus confirms, yet contra-dicts the scenes that foreshadowed it. What had been insinuated is now clearly stated: Orlick's accusations are brutal, direct, unmeta-phoric. But Pip comes out cleared of the crime, thanks to his double's double-talk ('*You* done it/ *I* giv' it her') and purged of all the violence in him by his double's aggression. Paradoxically, it is this tragic scene, not the tragi-comic ones, that marks the end of tragedy.

The lack of transition between the world and the stage much contributes to giving *Great Expectations* its uncanny, weird quality. Some 'real life' scenes are in fact more spectacular, unreal and nightmarish than theatrical representations. When he traps Pip on the marshes, Orlick, for instance, makes a real show of himself; he creates suspense, deliberately organizes the *mise en scène* of his would-be murder, closes the shutters, gropes his way about the room, strikes a light, disguises his voice, delays the action as if he was actually waiting for the rescuers' interruption on his imaginary stage as in some good horror play: 'The man', says Pip, 'was in no hurry' (liii, 434).

This man, who had come into the novel out of the blue, now clearly betrays his origins: he is the villain of melodrama and behaves in this scene as if he had escaped from the cheap boards of some East End riverside house to stage his own play on the misty, mysterious marshes. His words and imagery are lifted bodily from the stock repertory of sensational drama: '*I'll* let you go. I'll let you go to the moon, I'll let you go to the stars', he tells his victim, whom he calls 'Wolf' or 'Enemy', never 'young Pip' or 'young master' as in former days: 'Oh you enemy, you enemy!' he says. What journeyman ever expressed himself with such stagy grandiloquence? As he goes on playing his part, our credulity wavers: is it the truth? Is it a dream? Has Pip had one more hallucination? But even as we ask ourselves these questions, Pip tells us that the spectacle is on *his* side of the stage: 'His enjoyment of the spectacle I furnished, as he sat with his arms folded on the table ... had a malignity in it that made me tremble', he writes (liii, 435). As in a Woody Allen film, actor and spectator have changed places, anticipating the reversal of parts and pronominal merging of 'I' into 'You', 'You' into 'I', on which Orlick's accusations will rest so disturbingly.

The Woody Allen effect can be observed elsewhere in the book: during and after the Barnwell performance, as we saw before, and even more spectacularly, during Wopsle's Christmas pantomime. Towards the end of the performance, there suddenly occurs what Peter Brooks has already described as 'a curious mirroring and reversal of the spectacle, when Mr. Wopsle himself becomes the spectator'.[16] His part consisting mainly in being 'talked at, sung at, butted at, danced at, and flashed at with fires of various colours', Wopsle has 'a good deal of time on his hands', 'And I observed with great surprise', Pip notes, 'that he devoted it to staring in my direction as if he were lost in amazement'. From that moment on, Pip stops looking at the play and concentrates on Wopsle's eyes:

There was something so remarkable in the increasing glare of Mr Wopsle's eye, and he seemed to be turning so many things over in his mind and to grow so confused, that I could not make it out (xlvii, 397).

Right up to the end, Pip stares at the starer, believing himself to be the object of Wopsle's interest: 'I saw that you saw me', he tells him after the play. But Wopsle puts him right: it was another man, 'sitting behind you there, like a ghost' (xlvii, 398), whose sight had so fascinated him. Whose ghost, we wonder, a father's? Has he escaped from another play? But the ghost turns out to be, as Brooks has it, 'a "ghost" from the past',[17] the prisoner 'much mauled in the face' whose recapture Wopsle and Pip had attended together on a distant and memorable Christmas afternoon and who has now come back to haunt the stage-struck sexton's 'last new grand comic Christmas pantomime'. Once more, the real world has trespassed upon the world of make-believe.

'Make-believe' of course applies to intentions, not to achievements. Wopsle never ever creates the illusion of otherness in his impersonations and, whenever Pip goes to the theatre to see his 'gifted townsman' (xxxi, 274) play, it is 'Mr Wopsle' he sees exhibiting himself from beginning to end. During the *Hamlet* performance, it was 'Mr Wopsle' who had strutted forth as Prince of Denmark, 'Mr Wopsle' whose questions were greeted with 'peals of laughter', 'Mr Wopsle' who was 'descried entering at the turnpike' 'in a comprehensive black cloak', 'Mr Wopsle' who dusted his fingers 'on a white napkin taken from his breast' after returning the skull, 'Mr Wopsle' and no other who struggled with Laertes (xxxi, 275). And the Nautical drama and Christmas pantomime which Pip has just attended have offered him fresh opportunity to identify 'Mr Wopsle' under his many exotic disguises:

> This led to Mr Wopsle's (who had never been heard of before) coming in with a star and garter on, as a plenipotentiary of great power direct from the Admiralty, to say that the Swabs were all to go to prison on the spot, and that he had brought the boatswain down the Union Jack, as a slight acknowledgment of his public services. The boatswain, unmanned for the first time, respectfully dried his eyes on the Jack, and then cheering up and addressing Mr Wopsle as Your Honour, solicited permission to take him by the fin. Mr Wopsle conceding his fin with a gracious dignity, was immediately shoved into a dusty corner while everybody danced a hornpipe; and from that corner, surveying the public with a discontented eye, became aware of me.

The second piece was the last new grand comic Christmas

pantomime, in the first scene of which, it pained me to suspect
that I detected Mr Wopsle with red worsted legs under a highly
magnified phosphoric countenance and a shock of red curtain-
fringe for his hair ... But he presently presented himself under
worthier circumstances; for, the Genius of Youthful Love being
in want of assistance ... summoned a sententious Enchanter; and
he, coming up from the antipodes rather unsteadily, after an
apparently violent journey, proved to be Mr Wopsle in a high-
crowned hat, with a necromantic work in one volume under his
arm (xlvii, 396–7).

Whatever the character he tries to impersonate, 'Mr Wopsle' is as
unmistakably recognizable as 'Miss Jogg', the model, in Sir Leicester's *tableaux de genre*:

For he has his pictures, ancient and modern. Some of the Fancy
Ball School in which Art occasionally condescends to become a
master, which would be best catalogued like the miscellaneous
articles in a sale. As, 'Three high-backed chairs, a table and cover,
long-necked bottle (containing wine), one flask, one Spanish
female's costume, three-quarter face portrait of Miss Jogg the
model, and a suit of armour containing Don Quixote.' Or, 'One
stone terrace (cracked), one gondola in distance, one Venetian
senator's dress complete, richly embroidered white satin costume
with profile portrait of Miss Jogg the model, one scimetar superbly mounted in gold with jewelled handle, elaborate Moorish
dress (very rare) and Othello.[18]

Like bad painting, uninspired theatrical art fails to transcend what
it re-presents.
    But, when the play is over, a new performance takes place, and a
very successful one it is: 'You'll hardly believe what I am going to
tell you. I could hardly believe it myself, if you told me', Wopsle
warns Pip before starting. Pip, however, believes every word of it.
The man who, only a moment before, had cut such a poor figure as
the Enchanter has become a true magician and conjures up the past
in its minutest details: 'Mr Pip, you remember in old times a certain
Christmas Day...?' he asks. 'I remember it very well', Pip says.
'And you remember that there was a chase...?' 'I remember it all
very well.' 'And you remember that we came up with the two in a

ditch...?' 'I see it all before me' ... (xlvii, 398). But, significantly, this 'replay of the past',[19] which, for once, carries conviction, takes place outside the theatre.

Dickens's choice of an amateur actor,[20] and a very incompetent one, as main representative in the novel of the theatrical corporation is of course no accident. Wopsle's performances act as a foil to his own drama and the truly theatrical scenes always take place off-stage, when the play is over, or on the 'other stage' of the characters' dreamland. To give one more example, not a single scene of Waldengarver's *Hamlet* succeeds in moving Pip (except to laughter) and the identification process is quite excluded from a representation that only Partridge might have taken seriously; but, back home, during the night, Pip identifies himself with Shakespeare's hero and we are moved and worried by his mental representation:

> Miserably I went to bed after all, and miserably thought of Estella, and miserably dreamed that my expectations were all cancelled, and that I had to give my hand in marriage to Herbert's Clara, or play Hamlet to Miss Havisham's Ghost, before twenty thousand people, without knowing twenty words of it (xxxi, 278–9).

We worry about the dreamer's expectations, sensing that the dream is premonitory after the tradition of Shakespeare's tragedies. We worry even more on realizing that this new glimpse we are given of Pip's 'other stage' once more corroborates the other-staging of his ill-wishers.

Playing Hamlet to Miss Havisham's ghost is, we feel, no innocent dream. Pip, of course, holds back from interpreting it and, with no help from the dreamer, we are at a loss what to make of it. The image of the ghost that we picture to ourselves merely calls forth that other vision of the ghostly figure hanging by the neck, which Pip had once had in the brewery:

> A figure all in yellow white, with but one shoe to the feet; and it hung so, that I could see that the faded trimmings of the dress were like earthy paper, and that the face was Miss Havisham's, with a movement going over the whole countenance as if she were trying to call to me (viii, 94).

But are we supposed to connect the two hallucinations? In playing Hamlet to Miss Havisham's ghost, is Pip at long last answering the call of the imaginary corpse? And is it a love or a hate relationship he is trying to establish with his supposed benefactress? What is she to him anyway? Man or woman? Hamlet's father or some 'dear mother' like Claudius, the usurper? And what, in the first place, was the hanging body meant to suggest, execution or suicide? Had Miss Havisham been hanged as a criminal, like the pirate in Pip's first traumatic dream, or had she hanged herself like Jocasta? The 'parlour-analyst' would like to allegorize, but his questions are bound to remain unanswered. The only thing he knows for certain is that Pip's imagination is of the murderous order and that his private shows are no less overwhelming evidence of it than the shows put up by others for his reluctant self to watch. Surely, he never 'contemplates' murdering near relations or benefactors when in his right mind, but his visions and his nightmares point to parricidal impulses and desires which his waking self denies.

The many references to the theatre in this novel considerably add to its ambiguity: we may take them as a means of aligning Pip with famous tragic heroes or we may just as well consider them to be the externalization of the inner drama enacted in his subconscious. Their effect is double-edged: on the one hand, they give Pip a tragic dimension by making him the victim of fate as in Renaissance or Greek tragedy; on the other hand, they raise the question of the hero's guilt, which a plain story would have simply ignored.

What is at stake, of course, is the guilt of the psyche, the guilt, as it were, of Macbeth as long as he remains 'infirm of purpose', not the guilt of Macbeth after the deed is done. But are we allowed to pronounce Pip guilty, even of that guilt, on the strength of suspicions that were all conveyed metaphorically, through the not too reliable medium of dreams, hallucinations and obviously malevolent theatricals? Would not that be reading 'the Lord's Prayer backwards'? (xviii, 162)

Before we form an opinion, it might well be worth while returning to that scene at the Three Jolly Bargemen, in which Jaggers so powerfully expresses his warning against misreading and, even more precisely, against trusting too hastily the theatrical eloquence of amateur inquisitors. The scene takes place of an evening, when several villagers (including Pip) are assembled round the fire, 'attentive to Mr Wopsle', who reads the newspaper aloud to them:

> A highly popular murder had been committed, and Mr Wopsle was imbued in blood to the eyebrows. He gloated over every abhorrent adjective in the description, and identified himself with every witness at the Inquest. He faintly moaned, 'I am done for,' as the victim, and he barbarously bellowed, 'I'll serve you out,' as the murderer ... The coroner, in Mr Wopsle's hands, became Timon of Athens; the beadle, Coriolanus. He enjoyed himself thoroughly, and we all enjoyed ourselves, and were delightfully comfortable. In this cozy state of mind we came to the verdict Wilful Murder.

But a 'strange gentleman' (he will become Jaggers later in the chapter), who has attended the show with contemptuous attention, suddenly steps in and shakes them out of their 'cozy state of mind': 'Well!' he says to the company, 'you have settled it all to your own satisfaction, I have no doubt?':

> 'Guilty, of course?' said he. 'Out with it. Come!'
> 'Sir,' returned Mr Wopsle, 'without having the honour of your acquaintance, I do say Guilty.' Upon this, we all took courage to unite in a confirmatory murmur.
> 'I know you do,' said the stranger; 'I knew you would. I told you so. But now I'll ask you a question. Do you know, or do you not know, that the law of England supposes every man to be innocent, until he is proved – proved – to be guilty?' (xviii, 160–1).

Jaggers's lesson will not be lost on us: as he is not 'proved – proved – to be guilty', Pip will be declared innocent.

But uncertainty does remain. And, by letting evil-tongued showmen throw suspicions on his hero, Dickens knew very well what he was doing, aware as he was that, in Aristotle's terms, 'For the purposes of poetry a convincing impossibility is preferable to an unconvincing possibility'.[21]

NOTES: CHAPTER 14

1   Robert Garis, *The Dickens Theatre* (Oxford: Clarendon Press, 1965), p. 214.
2   ibid., p. 53.

3   ibid., p. 216.
4   Julian Moynahan, 'The hero's guilt: the case of *Great Expectations*', *Essays in Criticism*, vol. 10 (January 1960), pp. 72–3.
5   ibid., p. 69.
6   Garis, op. cit., p. 213.
7   Moynahan, op. cit., p. 72.
8   ibid.
9   ibid., p. 74.
10 ibid., p. 67.
11 Sophocles, *Oedipus the King*, lines 445–6.
12 See St Luke, XV, 11–32.
13 George Lillo, *The London Merchant* [1731] in *The Beggar's Opera and Other Eighteenth-Century Plays* (London: Dent, 1985), Act III, sc. vii, pp. 245–6.
14 *Oedipus the King*, lines 822–3.
15 ibid., lines 732–42, *passim*.
16 Peter Brooks, 'Repetition, repression, and return: *Great Expectations* and the study of plot', *New Literary History*, vol. 11 (Spring 1980), p. 518.
17 ibid.
18 *Bleak House*, eds G. Ford and S. Monod (New York: Norton, 1977), xxix, 357. See Anny Sadrin, 'Présence et fonction de l'art et de l'artiste dans *Bleak House*', *Annales Littéraires de l'Université de Besançon* (Paris: Les Belles Lettres, 1985), pp. 134–6.
19 Brooks, op. cit., p. 519.
20 On Wopsle and amateur actors, see V. C. Clinton-Baddeley, 'Wopsle', *Dickensian*, vol. 57 (Autumn 1961), pp. 150–9
21 Aristotle, *On the Art of Poetry*, translated by Ingram Bywater (Oxford: Clarendon Press, 1920), 25, III, p. 91.

CHAPTER 15

The Mirror of Death

None of the four characters who die[1] in *Great Expectations* dies a natural death: as in all good melodramas, death is dealt them like a blow, brutally, spectacularly. But of these four people, only one, Compeyson, the very bad one, is struck dead at once, damned irretrievably. The other three are granted a reprieve, given a chance, before they go, to be redeemed and forgiven and to find some peace on earth. Mrs Joe's last words, 'Joe', 'Pardon' and 'Pip' (xxxv, 302), raise her somewhat in the reader's esteem. Magwitch's deathbed scene, which spares him the gallows, rehabilitates him socially and morally, and his communing with his 'dear boy' brings him, at death's door, what life denied him.

Miss Havisham also is given respite. When we last see her, she is feverishly repentant, supplicating for pardon, rehearsing the same sentences over and over again, and Pip's parting kiss, if it does not soothe her instantaneously, is a kiss of forgiveness, the prelude, we assume, to regained serenity. But her last moments are not recorded and she is somehow given up for dead at the end of the chapter describing her accident. Her body, we are told, has received injuries which of themselves are 'far from hopeless' (xlix, 415), but her world has been destroyed, leaving her bare on a bare stage with no real chance of recovery. Even the outer world has already intruded into her private realm; no sooner have the flames turned the place into a wasteland, despoiling it of its properties and emblematic ornaments, than people have invaded it, people we had never heard of before, 'servants coming in with breathless cries at the door', then the surgeon 'with other aid' (xlix, 414), people who did not belong to the play and had so far been kept in the wings. But now the play is over, interrupted for ever. What remains of it is a parody:

> By the surgeon's directions, her bed was carried into that room and laid upon the great table: which happened to be well suited to

the dressing of her injuries. When I saw her again, an hour afterwards, she lay indeed where I had seen her strike her stick, and had heard her say that she would lie one day.

Though every vestige of her dress was burnt, as they told me, she still had something of her old ghastly bridal appearance; for, they had covered her to the throat with white cotton-wool, and as she lay with a white sheet loosely overlying that, the phantom air of something that had been and was changed, was still upon her (xlix, 415).

The shadow of her former self, 'changed', yet 'still' the same, Miss Havisham has no chance of surviving: lasting survival would imply a new birth into a new world, which after years of seclusion and mental alienation is totally inconceivable. By depriving her of her costume, of her décor and of her privacy, the fire has already mortally wounded the Miss Havisham we knew: the recluse and the actress. There is no need for the novelist to kill her a second time.

The recluse and the actress, paradoxical though it is, are not antinomic but complementary. But, before we analyse this strange complementarity, we must trace it back to the complex origins and long gestation of the character.

Tracing the ancestry of a character of fiction is an enterprise which is often unrewarding. But, in this particular case, several sources have been illuminatingly identified, especially by Martin Meisel[2] and by Harry Stone,[3] whose studies are full of remarkable insights into the workings of the creator's imagination and associative memory.

The oldest source detected by these critics, 'the fertile and dynamic nucleus',[4] as Stone calls it, on which other elements were later grafted, is 'a female invariably dressed in white, even to her shoes' who was 'well known to all perambulators of London'[5] in the days of Dickens's youth and who is now usually referred to as 'the Berners Street White Woman', from the description Dickens made of her in 'Where we stopped growing', his *Household Words* essay for 1 January 1853. The description runs as follows:

Another very different person who stopped our growth, we associate with Berners Street, Oxford Street; whether she was constantly on parade in that street only, or was ever to be seen elsewhere, we are unable to say. The White Woman is her name. She is dressed entirely in white, with a ghastly white plaiting round her head and face, inside her white bonnet. She even carries (we hope) a white umbrella. With white boots, we know she picks her way through the winter dirt. She is a conceited old creature, cold and formal in manner, and evidently went simpering mad on personal grounds alone – no doubt because a wealthy Quaker wouldn't marry her. This is her bridal dress. She is always walking up here, on her way to church to marry the false Quaker. We observe in her mincing step and fishy eye that she intends to lead him a sharp life. We stopped growing when we got at the conclusion that the Quaker had had a happy escape of the White Woman.[6]

This woman whom Dickens had seen in person, 'on parade in the street', he probably saw again impersonated, on parade on the stage. On 18 April 1831, Charles Mathews the elder, 'a great theatrical favorite'[7] of the young Dickens, opened in the twelfth of his annual 'At Homes' at the Adelphi. One of the sketches, a 'diapologue' entitled 'No. 26 and No. 27' or 'Next Door Neighbours', which he performed with Frederick Yates, featured two well-known London eccentrics, the Berners Street Woman in White and a woman in black often seen at the Bank and other public places. The two women in the playlet, Miss Mildew, 'the old eccentric Lady in White', and Mrs Bankington Bombasin, 'the eccentric old Lady in Black', were presented as regular clients of the London Expectation Office, where they came in search, one of a lost bridegroom, the other of a lost trustee. Much of the entertainment, says Meisel, was 'improvisation and inspiration' and what survives of the script is 'really no more than a scenario',[8] as we may judge from the following extract:

Miss Mildew the old eccentric Lady in White, enters/*Mathews*/ – She has lost her first love Forty Years before, on the day which was to be appropriated to her wedding, & she has worn the same clothes – Bonnet &c &c ever since – faded virgin white – She apostrophises her lover, (humourous pathetic style) states that she is followed in the street, but that it is in admiration of her figure – She goes to the *Expectation Office* in the hopes of learning what has become of her first Love – goes into office – ...

Enter immediately Mrs. *Bankington Bombasin/Yates/* the eccentric old Lady *in black* – She is also, on her way to the office – She
fancies that she is the heiress of vast wealth, describes it in all
sorts of fictitious shares &c states how her money is employed, &
is come now to the *Expectation Office*, to endeavour to make
enquiry after a person, supposed to have gone to the West Indies
40 years before; whose existence it is necessary to prove – as his
absence, has kept her totally out of her property – *Mrs. Bombasin*
enters Office.[9]

The missing bridegroom and the lost trustee turn out at the end to
have been the same person, a man 'recently come with his daughter
from Trinidad where he has made his fortune'.[10]

The similarities with Dickens's story and the conflation of themes
hardly need emphasizing and seem of themselves the proof that
Dickens attended the show; but, if he did, it must have been on the
opening night, because the sketch was cancelled at once, having met
strong disapproval from critics and spectators, who objected to
familiar London figures being ridiculed in a public place. Both
Meisel and Stone argue for the strong probability of Dickens's
presence at the Adelphi on that night: Dickens at that period
contemplated becoming an actor and 'went to some theatre every
night, with a very few exceptions, for at least three years', so he told
Forster, 'and always to see Mathews whenever he played'. When he
was about twenty, he writes in the same letter, he 'knew three or
four successive years of Mathews's At Homes from sitting in the pit
to hear them'.[11]

Another argument put forward by Meisel is that when, years
later, he wrote his *Household Words* essay, Dickens paired his
Woman in White with the Woman in Black who had inspired
Mathews to write his sketch. The portrait of this weird lady came
just before the other one:

There was a poor demented woman who used to roam about the
City, dressed all in black with cheeks staringly painted, and
thence popularly known as *Rouge et Noire*; whom we have never
outgrown by the height of a grain of mustard seed. The story
went that her only brother, a Bank-clerk, was left for death for
forgery; and that she, broken-hearted creature, lost her wits on
the morning of his execution, and ever afterwards, while her

confused dream of life lasted, flitted thus among the busy money-changers. A story, alas! all likely enough; but, likely or unlikely, true or untrue, never to take other shape in our mind.[12]

'The continued juxtaposition of the two women in Dickens' sketch', Meisel argues, 'suggests such an influence; so does his speculation on the White Woman's past and on the significance of her dress'.[13]

In his very perceptive study of Dickens's *Household Words* essay, Meisel also points out the moral polarization of the two characters: 'The Woman in Black is made entirely a victim of her unhappy past, the Woman in White entirely an embodiment of her distasteful present', he writes, 'the vanity of the Woman in Black is pathetic and the conceit of the Woman in White damnable'.[14] Dickens, it is true, has little compassion for the White Woman, whereas the other mad lady, a little Miss Flite already, 'with her wildly-seeking, never resting, eyes', is a 'poor soul'[15] much to be pitied. But Meisel is less convincing when he goes on to argue that this polarization clearly reappears in *Great Expectations* with Miss Havisham, the Woman in White, a conceited, self-absorbed, revengeful woman on the one hand, and Magwitch, the male version of the Woman in Black, victimized from childhood and most pitiable on the other. Dickens's influence on himself was never so systematic. Apart from being a victim, Magwitch has nothing in common with the Woman in Black, whereas much of this lady's story has gone over to Miss Havisham: the dead brother, the connection with forgery, the broken heart, the victimization, the very blackness which shows through the white bridal garments. This blackness, which will be later translated into Pip's fantastic narrative of a 'dark' woman sitting 'in a black velvet coach' (ix, 96–7), is perceived from the first and strikingly rendered when, looking for a word to express his feelings, the child, after several unsatisfactory attempts, hits on the word 'melancholy': 'it's so new here, and so strange, and so fine – and melancholy – ', he says; of course, he probably has no know-ledge of the word's etymology, but Dickens probably had: the word, which was not meant to go unnoticed, is well framed between two dashes and the narrator adds, as if to make sure that we do not miss the point: 'I stopped, fearing I might say too much, or had already said it' (viii, 89). A Black Woman in White, Miss Havisham is more complex than Meisel suggests.

Elements from Mathews's playlet also came into Dickens's novel: Magwitch's return seems to have been partly inspired by the return of the man from Trinidad and the two women's expectations of love and of wealth combined into Pip's Great Expectations of money and Estella.

Another interesting antecedent of Miss Havisham – first noted by Humphry House[16] and later expounded at some length by Harry Stone – is a certain Martha Joachim, whose life was briefly told in the first number of Dickens's *Household Narrative of Current Events* in 1850. This '*Wealthy and Eccentric Lady*, late of 27, York-buildings, Marylebone, aged 62', had recently been found dead in her house (with a walled garden) where she had lived as a recluse, 'dressed in white', for eighteen years, ever since her mother's death. But she had lost her reason years before, when her suitor 'whom her mother rejected, shot himself while sitting on the sofa with her, and she was covered with his brains'.[17] Her mental sanity may actually have been shattered even earlier when, in 1808 (she was ten at the time), her father, 'an officer in the Life Guards, was murdered and robbed in the Regent's Park'.[18] This new Woman in White, whom Dickens undoubtedly associated with the other one, brought fresh elements to the 'nucleus' – seclusion and wealth, and the connection with crime and violence – which were all to be incorporated into Dickens's final composition. Stone convincingly supports the thesis of a direct influence of the anecdote on Dickens's future novel with peripheral evidence, namely the presence in the same issue of the *Household Narrative* of several themes and items that were also to reappear most conspicuously in *Great Expectations*: an article dealing with transported convicts and emigrants to Australia; a discussion of what a true gentleman ought to be like; and a sensational section relating an accident that had nearly cost the life of a young lady whose gauzy dress had taken fire during a party and who had been rescued by 'One of the lads present', who had folded her in a rug and 'put out the flame before it had done any serious damage beyond scorching her arms severely'. The various items, Stone argues, were 'close enough to become forever entangled in Dickens' mind'.[19]

Many more claimants come knocking at the door of the Registrar's office to be acknowledged as legitimate ancestors of Dickens's Woman in White: a Miss Haverland in Ventnor,[20] a Mrs Navisham of Ordnance Terrace;[21] others whose names were more remote phonetically but who may be closer genetically: Miss Eliza Emily Donnithorne, an Australian lady recluse who, after being jilted by her future husband in 1856, 'kept her bridal clothes on' and left the wedding-breakfast to moulder away 'until nothing was left but dust and decay';[22] Miss Mary Lydia Lucrine, 'a maiden lady of genteel fortune', who was reported in *The Annual Register* for 1778 (which Dickens may have read) to have made a vow 'never to see the light of the sun again' after meeting with 'a disappointment as to matrimony';[23] an 'upper-class female recluse' murdered in Paris while Dickens was there in 1856;[24] an 'old-young woman' with 'weird gentility', dressed in 'faded black satin', whom Dickens had seen dancing at St Luke's Hospital for the Insane on Boxing Day 1851 and whose 'curious dance' he described in a *Household Words* essay;[25] Dirty Dick, 'The Dirty Old Man' of the 'Lay of Leadenhall';[26] Mad Lucas, a male recluse who lived next door to Bulwer Lytton at Knebsworth and who was to become the Tom Tiddler of Dickens's Christmas story for 1861.[27] Some or all of these people, and many others probably (including Dickens characters like Betsey Trotwood and Mrs Clennam) must in the course of years have been fused together until they crystallized into the character we know.

Wilkie Collins's *The Woman in White* was no doubt the occasion of this crystallization. The theatrical, 'extraordinary apparition' in the middle of the road, brightly lit by the moon, of 'the figure of a solitary Woman, dressed from head to foot in white garments'[28] on which the story opens, the very title of the novel which Dickens approved of so whole-heartedly – 'The Woman in White is the name of names, and very title of titles'[29] – no doubt conjured up two old recollections, the Berners Street Woman in White and Mathews's impersonation of her; while the story of Ann Catherick's confinement in an asylum must have triggered off sundry associations with recluses in white of the Martha Joachim type.

It is worth noting that Collins's heroine combined for the first time the two main characteristics of Miss Havisham, staginess and loneliness, which had been isolated traits of the real-life models. But this interrelatedness, which in Collins's novel remains superficial and incidental, becomes really central to Dickens's composition, and it is of a totally different nature in that it is *as* a recluse that Miss Havisham is theatrical: staginess and loneliness are built into her personality and it is this combination which makes her a truly original creation and not the mere aggregate that some source-hunters see in her.

Her seclusion itself is seclusion 'with a difference'. Unlike the demented solitary maidens, some of whose confined lives may have contributed touches to her creation, Miss Havisham does not live alone. She has an adoptive daughter, several people come and go at Satis House and some social life goes on there. Her confinement consists in not going out herself, letting in few visitors, and, above all, making a show of herself as a recluse for a limited audience: some occasional spectators, Pip and the Pockets, and two permanent ones, Estella and herself.

Nor is she fit for the asylum: though mentally deranged, she speaks quite rationally, is extremely clear-headed, even sharp-witted, cynical and self-composed and well in control of her alienation, at least intellectually. With the world turned hostile, she has exiled herself, but she has staged her exile methodically, with business-like determination: 'I sent for him', she says of Jaggers, 'to lay this place waste for me; having read of him in the newspapers, before I and the world parted' (xlix, 412). The lucid stage-manager and designer of her 'other stage', she then blocked up the windows, shut out the light of day, stopped the clocks, and deliberately turned her daily setting into scenery. This may be psychosis, but it is not raving or simpering madness.

In her essay 'Miss Havisham and Mr. Mopes the Hermit: Dickens and the mentally ill' Susan Shatto, evoking Dickens's well-known interest in mental abnormality, emphasizes the morbid attraction and 'algolagnic'[30] voyeurism that drew the novelist to St Luke's Hospital and similar places, incited him to 'look in curiously' at 'Hermit Lucas' and inspired several of his *Household Words* essays on eccentrics and lunatics. But the portrait of Miss Havisham, as Shatto also suggests, goes much beyond satisfying an unhealthy taste for the merely picturesque and for the anomalous; it is an in-depth study in psychopathology and the occasion for Dickens to reflect on the moral and social implications of seclusion and vanity.

Like ordinary theatrical alienation, the otherness of Miss Havisham's other stage rests on a discrepancy: the discrepancy between reality and its apprehension, between presence and re-presentation.

The objects surrounding her were already there before she and the world parted, and it is not by removing them that she has altered her setting but through a displacement of their use and significance.

They were there primarily as objects of consumption, clothes to be worn, food to be eaten; they are now the dead, fetishized images of what was once and is no more: the dispersed clothes will never be packed, the missing shoe will never be put on, the wedding-cake will never be eaten. Functional objects no longer, they have become mere signs. Their presence represents absence.

Signs they had been, of course, when they were living objects. As 'indices', they pointed to the imminent wedding, to the honeymoon and the feast in preparation; as 'symbols',[31] they stood for happiness, love and communion. But their semiotic function has also been perverted. They now indicate that the nuptials never took place and represent lasting sorrow, lovelessness and betrayal. 'Fetishization' has brought about a complete reversal of significance, turned a universally acknowledged system of social symbolism into a personal, anti-social semiotic network.

As witch of the place, Miss Havisham is the master of this codified deadness; but her authority does not obtain beyond the limits of her territory, a dressing-room, a dining-room. For her as for Mrs Clennam 'The world has narrowed to these dimensions'.[32] And even inside this private world, her power is limited. She is in control of the signified, not of the signifier: reality has been stronger than her will to arrest time and the objects have decayed, white has turned yellow, vermin have settled in the moulding cake. Unperturbed, however, she goes on living in the midst of this rottenness, as with an unburied corpse.

The refusal – metaphorical, of course – to bury the corpse of a loved person is precisely one of the symptoms of the psychosis that Freud describes in his paper 'Mourning and melancholia',[33] a text that might read as a perfect commentary on what is sometimes called 'the Miss Havisham syndrome',[34] even though Freud never had Dickens in mind when he wrote his essay.

'The correlation of melancholia and mourning seems justified' according to Freud 'by the general picture of the two conditions'. Both are characterized by 'a profoundly painful dejection, cessation of interest in the outside world, loss of the capacity to love, inhibition of all activity', yet one is normal, the other pathological. Although mourning involves 'grave departures from the normal attitude to life', it would occur to no one, Freud argues, 'to regard it as a pathological condition': it is the natural 'reaction to the loss of a loved person' and needs no medical treatment: 'We rely on its being overcome after a certain lapse of time'. This victory merely implies on the part of the suffering subject a 'work of severance' and the acceptance of reality, the recognition that the loved object 'no longer exists'. When the work of mourning is over and the libido has been 'withdrawn from its attachments to that object', the ego becomes free again, free even to 'adopt' a new object of love.[35]

In melancholia, on the contrary, the subject will not or cannot accomplish this work of mourning. His loss, for one thing, is not always perceived very clearly; his condition 'may be the reaction to the loss of a loved object', but the loss is often 'of a more ideal kind. The object has not perhaps actually died, but has been lost as an object of love (e.g. in the case of a betrothed girl who has been jilted)' and the melancholic, if he 'knows *whom* he has lost' does not know '*what* he has lost in him', so that 'melancholia is in some way related to an object-loss which is withdrawn from consciousness'.[36]

But the main distinction between mourning and melancholia concerns the subject himself:

> The melancholic displays something else besides which is lacking in mourning – an extraordinary diminution in his self-regard, an impoverishment of his ego on a grand scale. In mourning it is the world which has become poor and empty; in melancholia it is the ego itself. The patient represents his ego to us as worthless, incapable of any achievement and morally despicable; he reproaches himself, vilifies himself and expects to be cast out and punished.[37]

Listening to the confessions of his patients, Freud noticed that often their self-accusations were 'hardly at all applicable' to them whereas they did fit someone else, whom they loved or had loved, and he came to the conclusion that in melancholia 'self-reproaches are reproaches against a loved object which have been shifted away from it on to the patient's own ego'. 'Their complaints', he writes, 'are really "plaints" in the old sense of the word.' The slighted, disappointed subject has actually transformed the 'object-loss' into an 'ego-loss' by establishing an '*identification* of the ego with the abandoned object',[38] so that the ego itself has been altered by the identification.

Identification is on the part of the melancholic a means of refusing mourning. The lost object is integrated, absorbed into the ego, instead of being recognized as dead. Rather than face the 'work of severance' and let reality carry the day, rather than transform himself into a bereaved subject, the melancholic transforms the world and, to use the image of Nicolas Abraham and Maria Torok in their fascinating re-reading of 'Mourning *or* melancholia', he builds a 'crypt' in which to hide the unacceptable and unaccepted loss and to hide himself with it.[39]

For Freud and Freudians, as for Otto Rank, who first hypothesized the idea, the identification process is a form of regression to original narcissism:

> the object-choice has been effected on a narcissistic basis, so that the object-cathexis, when obstacles come in its way, can regress to narcissism. The narcissistic identification with the object then becomes a substitute for the erotic cathexis.[40]

With the unerring intuition of the 'street' psychopathologist[41] he is often said to have been, Dickens also connects narcissism and melancholia. When Pip enters for the first time the place that, a moment later, he will describe as 'melancholy', the first object he notices and points out to the reader is a looking-glass: 'But prominent in it was a draped table with a gilded looking-glass, and that I made out at first sight to be a fine lady's dressing-table' (viii, 87).

Thus brought into prominence, the word 'looking-glass', heavily loaded as it is by tradition with symbolism, at once alerts our attention. Will this glass be the mirror of self-love, introspection and self-knowledge, or, as so often in Dickens, the mirror of self-hate and *mis*knowledge, the discloser of hidden truths, the treacherous informer,[42] such are the questions that we ask ourselves before reading any further. 'Whether I should have made out this object so soon, if there had been no fine lady sitting at it,' Pip goes on to explain, 'I cannot say.' But the 'I cannot say' of the child clearly emphasizes the 'I can say' of the narrator who, through his casual remark, adds the connotations of conceit and vanity. Then comes the description of the 'fine lady'; then come Pip's remarks on the strangeness and melancholy atmosphere of the place; then, and only then, come reflections on the looking-glass:

> Before she spoke again, she turned her eyes from me, and looked at the dress she wore, and at the dressing-table, and finally at herself in the looking-glass.

'So new to him,' she muttered, 'so old to me; so strange to him, so familiar to me; so melancholy to both of us! Call Estella.'

As she was still looking at the reflection of herself, I thought she was still talking to herself, and kept quiet (viii, 89).

Whom does she see in the mirror? The Woman in White or the Woman in Black? The eternal bride or the skeleton in 'the withered bridal dress ... so like grave-clothes' and 'the long veil so like a shroud' (viii, 90)? Is it her ideal self she projects into the glass or, like the haunted man, 'an awful likeness of [her]self'[43] that she recognizes? Is it the attraction of Eros that draws her to the mirror? Or is it that of Thanatos? 'Both' is no doubt the answer. The mirror, the legend tells us, is the theatre of such conflictual desires: Narcissus dies of self-love. So does Lady Dedlock. So does Mrs Skewton.

But Miss Havisham's self-love, as we soon discover, is a form of self-hate. It is her wounded, her unloved, her deserted self that she has immobilized in front of the looking-glass; it is the forsaken bride that she likes to exhibit with this 'insistent communicativeness which' in the melancholic 'finds satisfaction in self-exposure':[44]

'Look at me,' said Miss Havisham. 'You are not afraid of a woman who has never seen the sun since you were born?'

I regret to state that I was not afraid of telling the enormous lie comprehended in the answer 'No'.

'Do you know what I touch here?' she said, laying her hands, one upon the other, on her left side.

'Yes, ma'am.' (It made me think of the young man.)

'What do I touch?'

'Your heart.'

'Broken!' (viii, 88)

On show in the candle-lit crypt, she had first reminded Pip of curiosities he had once been 'taken to see':

Once, I had been taken to see some ghastly waxwork at the Fair, representing I know not what impossible personage lying in state. Once, I had been taken to one of our old marsh churches to see a skeleton in the ashes of a rich dress, that had been dug out of a vault under the church pavement (viii, 87).

Miss Havisham, however, though she is there to be seen, is no waxwork effigy: 'Now, waxwork and skeleton seemed to have dark eyes that moved and looked at me'. She moves, looks, acts, *play-acts*. And she plays no less than two parts, two parts which at first sight might seem contradictory: she is the victim with the broken heart, she soon proves to be the victimizer who breaks hearts by proxy: 'You can break his heart', she suggests to Estella; 'Beggar him', she orders (viii, 89).

The victim is the masochist who gets satisfaction in cultivating her sorrow:

> She wants to make certain that her betrayal will be the whole meaning of her life, that nothing more will happen to change her destiny as it existed at the moment of betrayal. She does not want it to be possible for her to stop suffering, to forget, to turn her attention to other things and other people, and so cease to be the Miss Havisham who was cruelly abandoned on the day of her wedding.[45]

Thus writes J. Hillis Miller. And between the lines of his penetrating study we think we can hear Freud diagnosing 'a profoundly painful dejection, cessation of interest in the outside world, loss of the capacity to love, inhibition of all activity ... '

The victimizer is the sado-masochist whose ego has been altered by identification with her own victimizer. She is determined, says Miller, 'to make her whole life a reproach and a curse on Compeyson',[46] but the reproach is self-reproach, the curse is a curse on herself because she has debased herself into becoming the double of a man she hates and takes only bitter pride in her self-imposed, borrowed wickedness: 'Who am I', she will ask one day, 'who am I, for God's sake, that I should be kind?'; but she says this 'striking her stick upon the floor and flashing into wrath' and remains 'brooding after this outburst' (xliv, 373).

In such regressive forms of narcissism Freud came to see, under the influence of Karl Abraham, a regression to the oral stage of libidinal development:

> We have elsewhere shown that identification is a preliminary stage of object-choice, that it is the first way – and one that is expressed in an ambivalent fashion – in which the ego picks out

an object. The ego wants to incorporate this object into itself, and, in accordance with the oral or cannibalistic phase of libidinal development in which it is, it wants to do so by devouring it. Abraham is undoubtedly right in attributing to this connection the refusal of nourishment met with in severe forms of melancholia.[47]

With this connection in mind, we might well return to Satis House and, crossing the staircase landing, move from the room with the 'prominent' looking-glass where we first saw Miss Havisham to that 'other room' where we see her next and will see her last: 'The most prominent object', we read, 'was a long table with a table-cloth spread on it, as if a feast had been in preparation when the house and the clocks all stopped together' (xi, 113). So, this room too has its 'prominent' object, and this prominence again points to some symbolism, and again we anticipate symbolic ambivalence. The 'as if' suggests no less. The table laid for a feast which we know never took place, the traditional symbol of communion, will, we presume, call up the phantom of Judas. But what we get is far more weird and totally unexpected:

'This,' said she, pointing to the long table with her stick, 'is where I will be laid when I am dead. They shall come and look at me here.' ...
    'Matthew will come and see me at last,' said Miss Havisham, sternly, 'when I am laid on that table. That will be his place – there,' striking the table with her stick, 'at my head! And yours will be there! And your husband's there! And Sarah Pocket's there! And Georgiana's there! Now you all know where to take your stations when you come to feast upon me. And now go!' (xi, 113, 116)

The scene has the sacrilegious, obscene, surrealistic quality of Bunuel's parodies of the Lord's Last Supper. 'Take, eat', says the dead body lying on the table to its famished predators. With Christic masochism and unchristian motivations, Miss Havisham offers herself as a sacrifice to people she hates and despises. The Eucharist in her performance becomes a ceremony of lovelessness and damnation, and unholy sacrament.
    Besides being sacrilegious, this is a strange reversal of cannibalistic fantasy: literature dealing with cannibalism, (fairy-tales in par-

ticular), usually offers a different perspective. The point of view as a rule is that of the eater: 'I want to eat you', says the Ogre with hypertrophied, yet natural appetite. Ghoulism, vampirism, anthropophagy, for which Dickens had a lasting and morbid fascination, are in his novels common metaphors for voracity and greed for money: 'Make man-eating unlawful, and you starve the Vholeses',[48] Dickens writes in *Bleak House*; and one of the last remarks in *Our Mutual Friend* is to the same effect:

> 'Say, how did you leave the savages?' asks Lady Tippins.
> 'They were becoming civilized when I left Juan Fernandez,' says Lightwood. 'At least they were eating one another, which looked like it.'[49]

Great Expectations itself offers several examples of would-be cannibalism: Orlick's mouth waters at the thought of murdering Pip; Pumblechook greedily eyes the juicy Pork which the boy might have been converted into if he had been born a real squeaker; and Magwitch threatens in the first chapter, 'licking his lips': 'what fat cheeks you ha' got ... Darn Me if I couldn't eat em' (i, 36). The stress in all these cases is, as usual, on gluttony. The monstrous, masochistic anticipation of necrophagy in Miss Havisham's vision is a unique instance in Dickens of inverted cannibalism. For it is not so much the greed of the guests that is evoked as the victim's desire to satisfy their hunger. And this dream of the victim looking forward to being dismembered and devoured strikes us as more gruesome and far more anti-natural than the ogreish appetite of 'ordinary' man-eaters.

We do find in Petronius fragments describing the feelings of a testator in terms very similar to those of Miss Havisham:

> 'All those who come into money under my will, except my own children [*praeter libertos meos*], will get what I have left them on one condition, that they cut my body in pieces and eat it up in sight of the crowd.'

> 'We know that in some countries a law is still observed, that dead people shall be eaten by their relations, and the result is that sick people are often blamed for spoiling their own flesh. So I warn my

friends not to disobey my orders, but to eat my body as heartily as they damned my soul.'

'I am not at all afraid of your stomach turning. You will get it under control if you promise to repay it for one unpleasant hour with heaps of good things. Just shut your eyes and dream you are eating up a solid million [*centies sestertium*] instead of human flesh.'[50]

But the tone is different. We know Eumolpus, the speaker, less intimately than we do Miss Havisham and what he says sounds impersonal, almost aphoristic. Miss Havisham's fantasy, on the contrary, is so forceful and rendered with such passion that we are bound to take it as the pathetic and pathological expression of deep personal affliction. The vision is not just, as in *Satyricon*, that of a cynic but that of a self-tormentor. Contempt for the grotesque, toadying inheritors eager to 'pocket' her money cannot in itself account for the violence with which she imagines their feasting on her and, given the fact that it is the table laid out for her wedding-feast that she fancies she will be placed on, we cannot help connecting the dream with her monomania. The connection seems all the more justified as the man who deserted her, we must not forget, had first embezzled her money and has therefore much in common with the other predators.

This connection between Compeyson and the rapacious Pockets will actually be made by Pip himself on hearing Herbert's story of Miss Havisham's misfortunes:

'Miss Havisham was now an heiress, and you may suppose was looked after as a great match ...'...

'There appeared upon the scene – say at the races, or the public balls, or anywhere else you like – a certain man, who made love to Miss Havisham ... This man pursued Miss Havisham closely, and professed to be devoted to her ... He practised on her affection in that systematic way, that he got great sums of money from her, and he induced her to buy her brother out of a share in the brewery (which had been weakly left him by his father) at an immense price, on the plea that when he was her husband he must hold and manage it all. Your guardian was not at that time in Miss Havisham's councils, and she was too haughty and too much in love, to be advised by any one. Her relations were poor and scheming, with the exception of my father; he was poor enough, but not time-serving or jealous. The only independent one among them, he warned her that she was doing too much for this man, and was placing herself too unreservedly in his power. She took the first opportunity of angrily ordering my father out of the house, in his presence, and my father has never seen her since.'

I thought of her having said, 'Matthew will come and see me at last when I am laid dead upon that table' (xxii, 204–5).

The banishment of Matthew historically coincided with Compeyson's manoeuvres and disappearance. His return as best-hated guest will inevitably entail the fantasmic return of the man who was once best-loved, if only through associations and a transfer of hatred. Although he is never mentioned as one of the guests and is assigned no place at table, Compeyson is implicitly and vicariously present among the bride-eaters and the bride's fantasy cannot but appear as a revenge of her wounded pride and diseased imagination. It is her money, not her body Compeyson wanted, and this body, which he never possessed, is now offered as a money metaphor to the collective greed of the likes of him. Oral consumption will replace sexual consummation and Compeyson will get what he always wanted. This masochistic, suicidal substitute for sexual intercourse with the man she once idolized and now dearly hates is both an act of love and an act of hatred, but in this love/hate relationship with the lost partner, the fantasy of absorption corresponding, according to Freud, to the return to 'the oral or cannibalistic phase of libidinal development' is inverted into an unholy sacrifice and self-victimization.

The absorption in fact works both ways, since Compeyson has become part of his victim through identification. We are given here an interesting instance of the 'ambivalence' that is characteristic of melancholy 'in which hate and love contend with each other' and in which, 'by the circuitous path of self-punishment', the melancholic succeeds in 'taking revenge on the original object', thus satisfying 'trends of sadism and hate'.[51]

If circumstances compelled her to give up all thoughts of child-bearing, Miss Havisham has not renounced motherhood, as her adoption of Estella shows. But a psychotic woman is a psychotic mother and the story of her daughter's education is, in Pip's words, a 'grievous thing' (xlix, 411).

Even when the girl was first brought to her and she had no thought of using her as the instrument of her own revenge, it was the woman-to-be that she saw in the little child: 'when she first came to me', she says, 'I meant to save her from misery like my own. At first I meant no more' (xlix, 411). But this was meaning too much already and the formulation betrays the fundamentally narcissistic nature of this altruism. The girl was perceived from the first as the re-production of the mother's vulnerable, unprotected, gullible self of former days.

Natural reproduction, it must be granted, is itself rooted in narcissism. Nature, the conservative keeper of species, by replacing the same with the same (or the similar) encourages the narcissistic bent of genetic parents who are only too glad to mirror themselves in their living images. The laws of inheritance also reinforce the laws of nature, which they imitate, while education, the transmission of knowledge, rites, habits, tastes or principles, together with the all too symbolic transmission of identity, all contribute to strengthening self-contemplation in real parents. Though deprived of genetic narcissism, adoptive parents can also find some satisfaction in shaping the children who will inherit their name and fortune after their own ideals and after their own moral and social selves.

Miss Havisham's narcissism, unfortunately, is not of the self-loving but of the self-hating order and the image of her self that she soon decides to transmit to her daughter is that of the mummified woman immured in the crypt, the woman with a heart of stone. Like so many other Gorgons in Dickens,[52] she succeeds admirably in petrifying the girl's heart. She succeeds so well indeed that the imitation outshines the model: 'I am not all stone', Miss Havisham will say on considering, too late, the consequences of her acts. 'But perhaps you can never believe, now, that there is anything human in my heart?' (xlix, 408). The younger Miss Havisham on the other hand has no recollection of ever having had anything human in her heart: 'You stock and stone!... You cold, cold heart!' the Gorgon mother complains one day, yearning with love towards the girl whose 'self-possessed indifference' is not even willingly cruel:

'What?' said Estella, preserving her attitude of indifference as she leaned against the great chimney-piece and only moving her eyes; 'do you reproach me for being cold? You?'

'Are you not?' was the fierce retort.

'You should know,' said Estella. 'I am what you have made me. Take all the praise, take all the blame; take all the success, take all the failure; in short, take me' (xxxviii, 322).

And in a later scene, Estella will admit to Pip, who has just complained that her attitude 'is not in Nature': 'It is in *my* nature ... It is in the nature formed within me' (xliv, 376).

The Dickens novel is often self-referential, especially on such matters. We are reminded here of Louisa Gradgrind: 'What do *I* know, father, ... of tastes and fancies; of aspirations and affections; of all that part of my nature in which such light things might have been nourished?'[53] We are reminded of the many texts in which Dickens expresses himself on the damaging effects of misguided education. We think of the warnings of Charles Cheeryble:

Men talk of nature as an abstract thing, and lose sight of what is natural while they do so ... Parents who never showed their love, complain of want of natural affection in their children; children who never showed their duty, complain of want of natural feeling in their parents; law-makers who find both so miserable that their affections have never had enough of life's sun to develop them, are loud in their moralisings over parents and children too, and cry that the very ties of nature are disregarded. Natural affections and instincts, my dear sir, are the most beautiful of the Almighty's works, but like other beautiful works of His, they must be reared and fostered, or it is as natural that they should be wholly obscured, and that new feelings should usurp their place, as it is that the sweetest productions of the earth, left untended, should be choked with weeds and briars.[54]

We think of the narrator's aside in *Dombey and Son*:

It might be worth while, sometimes, to inquire what Nature is, and how men work to change her, and whether, in the enforced distortions so produced, it is not natural to be unnatural. Coop any son or daughter of our mighty mother within narrow range, and bind the prisoner to one idea, and foster it by servile worship of it on the part of the few timid or designing people standing round, and what is Nature to the willing captive who has never risen up upon the wings of a free mind – drooping and useless soon – to see her in her comprehensive truth!

Alas! are there so few things in the world about us, most unnatural, and yet most natural in being so![55]

'Unnatural nature', 'unnatural humanity' are the result of men's disrespect for God's creation or, worse, of their tampering with God's handiwork:

That she had done a grievous thing in taking an impressionable child to mould into the form that her wild resentment, spurned affection, and wounded pride, found vengeance in, I knew full well. But that, in shutting out the light of day, she had shut out infinitely more; that, in seclusion, she had secluded herself from a thousand natural and healing influences; that, her mind, brooding solitary, had grown diseased, as all minds do and must and will that reverse the appointed order of their Maker; I knew equally well. And could I look upon her without compassion, seeing her punishment in the ruin she was, in her profound unfitness for this earth on which she was placed, in the vanity of sorrow which had become a master mania, like the vanity of penitence, the vanity of remorse, the vanity of unworthiness, and other monstrous vanities that have been curses in this world? (xlix, 411)

The text, which is Dickens's, not Pip's, echoes almost word for word the remarks of the narrator of *Little Dorrit* on Mrs Clennam, that other recluse:

More than forty years had passed over the grey head of this determined woman, since the time she recalled. More than forty years of strife and struggle with the whisper that, by whatever name she called her vindictive pride and rage, nothing through all eternity could change their nature. Yet, gone those more than forty years, and come this Nemesis now looking her in the face, she still abided by her old impiety – still reversed the order of Creation, and breathed her own breath into a clay image of her

Creator. Verily, verily, travellers have seen many monstrous idols in many countries; but, no human eyes have ever seen more daring, gross, and shocking images of the Divine nature, than we creatures of the dust make in our own likenesses, of our own bad passions.[56]

As these several examples show, and as many others might, the question of man's creative potentialities tormented Dickens the Christian from first to last. Man, the creature, he maintains, has a duty of humility and of obedience to his creator. Made after the image of God, he has no right to reverse the order and make God after his image, no right to distort reflections on the looking-glass and worship idols of his own making. Parenting and educating are therefore two of Dickens's major preoccupations, for the power of parents to 'mould' malleable clay into what shape they desire amounts almost in his view to recreating God's creatures and he is constantly afraid lest man's creation should be miscreative.

Miss Havisham, as critics have often remarked, has a parallel in Magwitch: an outcast like her, like her a victim, Magwitch has, like her, adopted a child to serve his own revengeful ends. It is, says J. H. Miller, 'to see with his own eyes the gentleman he has made' and to let him 'know the real source of his transformation into a gentleman'[57] that he has returned from New South Wales: 'I've come to the old country fur to see my gentleman spend his money *like* a gentleman. That'll be *my* pleasure' (xl, 347), Magwitch himself declares shamelessly. But Pip, who had never before objected to being man- or woman-made, is suddenly horrified on discovering who his maker was. The identity of his creator alters and degrades his idea of himself; and to express his revulsion he resorts to no less than a reference to the creative myth of Mary Shelley's *Frankenstein*:

> The imaginary student pursued by the misshapen creature he had impiously made, was not more wretched than I, pursued by the creature who had made me (xl, 354).

The comparison, which falls back on itself at mid sentence, is curiously double-edged. At first reading, we tend to identify Pip with the 'imaginary student', the one who is being pursued by the monster, but then we come to realize that, being the one who has been made, he is also implicitly, albeit unwillingly, comparing himself to the 'misshapen creature'. The double meaning of the word 'creature' is also quite misleading; in the first half of the sentence it refers to the monster, Victor Frankenstein's creature, in the second half it designates Victor himself, the creaturely creator.

The ambiguity is traceable back to the mythic ambiguities of Mary Shelley's tale itself. For Paul A. Cantor, Frankenstein and the monster are both Adamic and Satanic creatures, both innocent and rebellious: 'Frankenstein does God's work, creating a man, but he has the devil's motives: pride and the will to power', and the monster, although he has 'something of Adam's innocence', is also 'impelled to his rebellion by Satan's motives: envy and the thirst for revenge'.[58] Master and slave to each other, they are also 'mirror images of each other'. 'As many readers have sensed', writes Cantor, 'they are the same being, viewed in different aspects, as creator and as creature'.[59]

In the Dickens version of the myth further ambiguities arise. For it is as if we had reached a new stage of the fable and the monster himself had become a creator. Magwitch, like Frankenstein, has 'the devil's motives: pride and the will to power', but he has also the motives of the creature, 'envy and the thirst for revenge'. He wants to revenge himself against his own makers for being 'misshapen', illiterate, 'a mere warmint' (xxxix, 336): 'The blood horses of them colonists might fling up the dust over me as I was walking; what do I say? I says to myself, "I'm making a better gentleman nor ever *you*'ll be!"' (xxxix, 339), he says. So that, unlike Frankenstein, he is proud of his achievement as a creator, proud to recognize in Pip his ideal double, the mirror-image of his dreams: 'If I ain't a gentleman, nor yet ain't got no learning, I'm the owner of such'. But Pip, who sees in his creator 'a terrible beast' and a monstrous creature, cannot be impelled by envy like Mary Shelley's monster; on the contrary, he is driven by fear and repulsion. He does not pursue his maker, but runs away from him, from his affection, from his admiration and above all from his monstrosity, which he thinks he might catch like some infectious disease. Worse, his tortuous syntax and his lexical equivocations would in fact seem to indicate that he has recognized in his 'second father' the uncouth, unread, 'rough common boy' (xliv, 378) he was before his metamorphosis into a London gentleman. In running away from his misshapen creator, he is running away from his once misshapen self.

There is one thing, however, that Pip is unaware of: it is that, in fact, 'the nature made within' *him* is very little the work of his newly met and unsought benefactor. The 'impressionable child' of the opening chapters had been remoulded into a new shape long before the creator of his fortune entered his life or even sent him his emissaries. Like Estella, Pip is first and foremost the creature of Miss Havisham. We must bear in mind that it was part of this woman's revengeful scheme to turn two beings, a girl and a boy, into doubles of her two selves, shape the former after her new, cruel, heartless, Compeyson-like self, and the latter after her former, sensitive, defenceless self with a heart to be broken. It is her influence that made Pip a discontented, aspiring, ungrateful fellow and to some extent the prejudiced young man who now recoils from the ungenteel maker of his wealth. The real Victor Frankenstein of Dickens's story, the impious miscreator, is the Witch of Satis House and Pip would have been well-advised if he had early run away from *her*.

Early running away from Miss Havisham would have spared Pip much suffering and much moral degradation. But he never felt the danger. Far from it. During the years when he believed this woman to be the maker of his fortune and of his genteel status, it never occurred to him to think that her creative work was other than beneficial and he often mistook regress for progress. And even once enlightened about the real nature of her motives and intentions, he remained blind to the destructive effects of her work and would have remained so if she herself had not suddenly awakened to the monstrous character of her achievement:

> 'Until you spoke to her the other day, and until I saw in you a looking-glass that showed me what I once felt myself, I did not know what I had done. What have I done! What have I done!' And so again, twenty, fifty times over, What had she done! (xlix, 411)

Miss Havisham is referring here to the scene when Estella informed Pip in her presence of her decision to marry Drummle and she saw with what 'ecstasy of unhappiness' (xliv, 378) he reacted to the news. The mirror he held up to her sent her images both of what she had been once and of what *he* might become. The sorcerer's apprentice became aware at that moment of the far-reaching consequences of her miscreative act: disappointment, she realized, might have similar effects on her creature as on herself and change him in his turn into a revengeful, world-hating, world-shunning man.

It is of some significance that the great melodramatic scene in which Miss Havisham asks to be forgiven for what she has done should take place 'not in her own room, but ... in the larger room across the landing' (xlix, 407). It was 'In the room where the dressing-table stood' (xliv, 372) that the living mirror suddenly disclosed truths which the gilded looking-glass on the draped table had kept to itself for so long. But now we have moved away from the part of the house that represented real seclusion and vain narcissism to the dining-room that symbolically stands, or ought to stand, for sociability. Assuredly, only parodies of social gatherings have taken place there so far, but now that the mirror symbolism has been renewed, we may expect the symbolism of the feast-table to be revalued also. And Miss Havisham's last crossing of the landing is indeed a journey away from selfishness to selflessness and from ceremonies of hate to a ceremony of love, which at last breaks the spell of revenge and vanity.

An actress to the last, she performs her new part with the utmost grandiloquence. But this grandiloquence, paradoxically, carries conviction, is even necessary for the catharsis to be accomplished both of the actors and of the spectator-readers. Repetition, exhort-ation, the rhetoric of exorcism can alone purge the speaker of her violence and of her resentment and work up her listener into pity and forgiveness. Overacting the change of heart can alone counter-act the overacted evil of so many years and ensure the double metamorphosis of creator and creature.

Pip is unquestionably the great beneficiary of the scene. Miss Havisham's repentance redeems her before she dies, but in teaching Pip forgiveness it spares him a fate like hers. In the following scene she will be burnt to death, but, trying to save her, he will so to speak be burnt to life. Purified by fire, he will henceforth be a new man, loving, tolerant, forgiving. The test, of course, will be his new attitude to Magwitch. His 'repugnance to him' from now on will melt away and he will see in him no longer a pursuer but a 'hunted ... creature', no longer a monster but 'a man', 'a man who had meant to be my benefactor', 'a much better man than I had been to Joe' (liv, 456–7). The gilded looking-glass had been a mirror of death, the living mirror will be a mirror of life.

NOTES: CHAPTER 15

1   There are five if we count Old Bill Barley; but do we?
2   Martin Meisel, 'Miss Havisham brought to book', *PMLA*, vol. 81 (June 1966), pp. 278–85.
3   Harry Stone, 'An added note on Dickens and Miss Havisham', *Nineteenth-Century Fiction*, vol. 10 (June 1955), pp. 85–6; 'Dickens' woman in white', *Victorian Newsletter*, no. 33 (Spring 1968), pp. 5–8; 'The genesis of a novel: Great Expectations', in *Charles Dickens 1812–1870*, ed. E. W. F. Tomlin (London: Weidenfeld and Nicolson, 1969), pp. 109–31, reprinted with slight additions and alterations as '*Great Expectations*: the factual matrix', in *Dickens and the Invisible World: Fairy Tales, Fantasy, and Novel-Making* [1979] (London: Macmillan, 1980), pp. 279–97; unless specified otherwise, references to Stone will be to the last title and edition.
4   Stone, 'An added note', p. 85.
5   *Morning Post*, 19 April 1831, quoted by Meisel, op. cit., p. 280.
6   'Where we stopped growing', *Household Words*, vol. 6, pp. 362–3.
7   Meisel, op. cit., p. 278.
8   ibid., p. 279.
9   Quoted by Meisel, ibid.
10 ibid.
11 *The Pilgrim Edition of the Letters of Charles Dickens*, Vol. 4 (Oxford: Clarendon Press, 1977), ed. Kathleen Tillotson, pp. 244–5, [?30–31 December 1844 and 1 January 1845], to Forster.
12 'Where we stopped growing', op. cit., p. 362.
13 Meisel, op. cit., p. 281.
14 ibid., p. 282.
15 'Where we stopped growing', op. cit., p. 362.
16 Humphry House, 'G. B. S. on *Great Expectations*', *Dickensian*, vol. 44 (Spring 1948), p. 69.
17 *Household Narrative of Current Events*, 1850, p. 10, quoted by Stone, op. cit., pp. 282–3.
18 ibid.
19 Stone, op. cit., p. 285.
20 A Miss Margaret Catherine Dick of 'Madeira Hall', Ventnor, is sometimes said to have been the original of Miss Havisham: 'Miss Dick, like Miss Havisham, had been jilted on her wedding day; had left the wedding feast untouched; and had turned night into day [sic], never leaving the house during daylight until her death' in 1879, 'when 52 year of age'. In 1860, 'the present "Roseleigh Cottage", Madeira Road, was built as a stable, saddle-room and coach-house for a Miss Haverland of Madeira Vale', writes Richard J. Hutchings, 'Dickens at Bonchurch', *Dickensian*, vol. 61 (Spring 1965), pp. 97–9. The well-named Misses Dick and Haverland may well have been fused into one in the novelist's imagination.
21 '... there must be some connection with Mrs. Navisham, who had lived at 5 Ordnance Terrace, Chatham, and who was the Old Lady of Our Parish in Boz's *Sketches*', writes Jack Lindsay, *Charles Dickens: A Biographical and Critical Study* (New York: Philosophical Library 1950), pp. 373–4. But, according to William J. Carlton, the lady's name was 'Mrs Mary Ellen Newnham': cf., ' "The old lady" in *Sketches by Boz*', *Dickensian* vol. 49 (September 1953), p. 149. An interesting instance of the way names can be distorted to support a demonstration.
22 S. Ryan, 'A possible Australian source for Miss Havisham', *Australian Literary Studies*, vol. 1 (December 1963), pp. 134–6.

23 Stanley Friedman, 'Another possible source for Dickens's Miss Havisham', *The Victorian Newsletter*, vol. 39 (Spring 1971), pp. 24–5.

24 On 'the French Duchess', see Harvey Peter Sucksmith, *The Narrative Art of Charles Dickens* (Oxford: Clarendon Press, 1970), p. 177.

25 'A curious dance round a curious tree', *Household Words*, vol. 4 (17 January 1852), pp. 385–9.

26 See 'The dirty old man', *Household Words*, vol. 6 (8 January 1853), pp. 396–7.

27 See Susan Shatto, 'Miss Havisham and Mr. Mopes the hermit: Dickens and the mentally ill', *Dickens Quarterly*, vol. 2, no. 2 (June 1985), pp. 43–50 and no. 3 (September 1985), pp. 79–84.

28 Wilkie Collins, *The Woman in White* [1860], (Harmondsworth: Penguin, 1974), p. 47.

29 Nonesuch *Letters*, Vol. 3, p. 115, 16 August 1859, to Collins.

30 See S. Shatto, op. cit. (June 1985), pp. 43, 49.

31 I am referring here to the 'categories' defined by Charles Sanders Peirce as follows:

'There are three kinds of representations.
First.   Those whose relation to their objects is a mere community in some quality, and these representations may be termed *likenesses*.
Second.   Those whose relation to their objects consists in a correspondence in fact, and these may be termed *indices* or *signs*.
Third.   Those the ground of whose relation to their objects is an imputed character, which are the same as *general signs*, and they may be termed *symbols*'. (*Principles of Philosophy*, *Collected Papers*, Cambridge, Mass.: Harvard University Press, 1965, Vol. 1, p. 295).

32 *Little Dorrit*, ed. Harvey Peter Sucksmith, Clarendon Dickens (Oxford, 1979), I, iii, 34.

33 Sigmund Freud, 'Mourning and melancholia', translated by Joan Riviere, in *The Standard Edition of the Complete Psychological Works of Sigmund Freud* (London: The Hogarth Press, 1975), Vol. 14, pp. 237–58.

34 Macdonald Critchley, 'The Miss Havisham syndrome', *The History of Medicine*, vol. 1, no. 3 (Summer 1969), pp. 2–6.

35 Freud, op. cit., pp. 243, 244 and 255.

36 ibid., p. 245.

37 ibid., p. 246.

38 ibid., pp. 248, 249.

39 Nicolas Abraham and Maria Torok, 'Introjecter–incorporer, deuil *ou* mélancolie', in *Destins du Cannibalisme, Nouvelle Revue de Psychanalyse*, no. 6 (Paris, Automne 1972), pp. 111–22.

40 Freud, op. cit., p. 249.

41 Dr J. Johnston Abraham speaks of 'Dickens' *street pathology*', which, he says, 'was often far better than that of the doctors of his time' (quoted by Shatto, op. cit., September 1985, p. 82). 'Dickens's psychiatric studies are as comprehensive and as varied as his observations on organic diseases', writes Lord Brain, 'Dickensian diagnoses', in *Some Reflections on Genius* (London: Pitman, 1960). Abraham and Brain's esteem was shared by Leonard Manheim and by A. and P. Plichet, 'Charles Dickens et ses observations neuro-psychiatriques', *La Presse Médicale* (Paris, 25 December 1956), pp. 2230–3.

42 On mirrors in Dickens's novels, see Fred Kaplan, *Dickens and Mesmerism* (Princeton University Press, 1975), pp. 106–38; and Anny Sadrin, *L'Etre et l'Avoir dans les Romans de Charles Dickens* (Lille-Paris: Didier Erudition, 1985), pp. 355–459.

43 *The Haunted Man, Christmas Books*, The New Oxford Illustrated Dickens (London: Oxford University Press, 1960), p. 330.
44 Freud, op. cit., p. 247.
45 J. Hillis Miller, *Charles Dickens: The World of His Novels* (Cambridge, Mass.: Harvard University Press, 1958), p. 256.
46 ibid., pp. 257–8.
47 Freud, op. cit., pp. 249–50.
48 *Bleak House*, eds G. Ford and S. Monod (New York: Norton, 1977), xxxix, 483.
49 *Our Mutual Friend*, The New Oxford Illustrated Dickens (London: Oxford University Press, 1963), IV, xvii, 816.
50 Petronius, *Satyricon*, translated by Michael Heseltine (London: Heinemann, 1961), p. 321.
51 Freud, op. cit., p. 251.
52 See A. Sadrin, op. cit., 'La Méduse', 478–87.
53 *Hard Times*, eds G. Ford and S. Monod (New York: Norton, 1966) I, xv, 77.
54 *Nicholas Nickleby*, The New Oxford Illustrated Dickens (London: Oxford University Press, 1960), xlvi, 595–6.
55 *Dombey and Son*, ed. Alan Horsman, Clarendon Dickens (Oxford, 1974), xlvii, 619.
56 *Little Dorrit*, op. cit., II, xxx, 754.
57 Miller, op. cit., p. 260.
58 Paul A. Cantor, *Creature and Creator* (Cambridge University Press, 1984), pp. 105–6.
59 ibid., p. 106.

CRITICAL SURVEY

CHAPTER 16

Prefaces to the Next

Sixteen years ago, Q. D. Leavis, starting from the indisputable observation that 'The ineptness of scholars as literary critics is a notorious fact', protested against 'the trend of American criticism of Dickens, from Edmund Wilson onwards, as being in general wrongheaded, ill-informed ... and essentially ignorant and misdirecting', condemned the 'Marxizing and other ideologically-slanted interpretations of Dickens', reviled at 'the simple-minded or the amateur psychologist', deplored that 'the young reader' in our decadent age should be 'further handicapped by crass misdirections from contemporary Dickens specialists', notably by 'the antics of critics searching for Freudian explanations' of Dickens, and helpfully provided us with instructions and a demonstration on 'How we must read *Great Expectations*'.[1]

There is no telling how many critical voices were hushed for ever after receiving such admonition and how much we lost into the bargain. Fortunately enough, some strong-minded scholars (or would-be scholars) survived the attack and, no doubt convinced that there might be more than one way of reading or re-reading the novel, made bold to go on expressing their views, some of which were actually indebted to Q. D. Leavis's provocative, yet thought-provoking chapter.

Reviewing *Dickens the Novelist* – not his own (1968)[2] but the Leavises' (1970) –, Sylvère Monod, exasperated by such peremptoriness, advocated more catholicity of approach and appended to his review a bibliographical note on 'How we *can* read *Great Expectations*';[3] this was a welcome invitation to further reading and an implicit encouragement to further writing on a subject unlikely to be so easily dismissed.

Great Expectations since then has indeed been submitted to constant critical reassessment, spanning the whole spectrum of recent and increasingly sophisticated methodology, and it has gone through the interpretation grids of Freudians and post-Freudians, structuralists and post-structuralists, linguists and narratologists, and even, though in homeopathic doses, Lacanians and deconstructionists, all of which has not prevented the personal response of the unmethodical reader or the old interest in biography, psychology, ethics and social history. In recent years numerous titles have been added to the already long list of essays, book chapters, introductions and dissertations, amounting, 125 years after the publication of the novel, to no fewer than 1114 entries in George J. Worth's *Great Expectations: An Annotated Bibliography* (1986)[4] which outshines Don Giovanni's *mille e tre*.

Worth's bibliography covers 'everything pertaining to the novel published in English from its first appearance in 1860–61 through the end of 1983'.[5] Three more years have elapsed since then and more titles have cropped up, some of which have already been itemized on Dickens studies checklists, which themselves require constant updating. Needless to say, a fair assessment of *Great Expectations* criticism is an impossible task within the limits of a few pages, and this chapter has no other ambition than to offer an overview of the main trends of past and present criticism.

To begin with the beginning, the first reviewers of *Great Expectations* were not unanimous in their reception of the book.[6] But a majority hailed it as 'a masterpiece' and 'a work of art': what they praised most was plot terseness, 'truthfulness and reality', credibility and/or imaginativeness, 'cheerfulness', and a return to the 'old *Pickwick* style' or to the '*Martin Chuzzlewit* and *David Copperfield* vein'. A good representative of this favourable approach is Edwin P. Whipple who praised the book with discerning intelligence as 'an artistic creation', a 'romance' in which the author had succeeded 'perfectly in at once stimulating and baffling the curiosity of his readers' and where observations were used as 'materials for his creative faculties to work upon': 'he does not record, but invents', he wrote.[7]

Others, much fewer in number (four out of the fourteen reviews we possess are utterly derogatory), were violently critical: they disliked the inconsistencies and exaggerations, improbabilities and sensationalism of plot and characters, regretted the 'fun of *Pickwick*' and the 'genuine pathos of *Oliver Twist*'. Particularly vehement was Mrs Oliphant, who read the book as the 'fatigued' work of a man 'bored with his own production'. To her, the fun was no fun, fancy was 'fancy run mad' and individual characters 'specimens of oddity run mad'.[8]

But, as we have seen, the rising sales of *All the Year Round* during the serialization of the novel testify to its immediate popularity with the general reading public. When the book came out in the summer of 1861, it sold enough in England to warrant five editions before the end of the year, and it met with similar success on the other side of the Atlantic. Robert L. Patten writes:

> Perhaps the most extraordinary testimony to the popularity of *Great Expectations* appears not in the ledgers of *All the Year Round*, nor even in the reviews, which hailed the restoration of Dickens's humour, but in the number, size, and kind of editions on both sides of the Atlantic that appeared within a few months of the novel's serialization.[9]

It is difficult to form an opinion on the reaction of Dickens's major rival novelists in the absence of written documents: 'one wonders', writes Worth, 'at the silence, at least in their published letters, of novelists like Eliot and Thackeray'.[10] Apart from Bulwer Lytton, who was lavish with eulogies (we must not forget that he had somehow fathered the new conclusion), and Forster, the staunch friend and admirer, who wrote that 'Dickens's humour, not less than his creative power, was at its best in this book',[11] only Carlyle is reported to have enjoyed the book and responded with 'roars of laughter' to Jane Welsh's readings of 'that Pip nonsense'.[12]

Not until the turn of the century did major authors, Gissing (1898), Swinburne (1902), Chesterton (1906),[13] express their admiration and enthusiasm, thus contributing to a revival of interest for a novel long neglected by commentators. During the thirty years following the death of the novelist it had received very scanty critical attention (though we must allow for the fact that the nineteenth century was not a critical age): we number no more than thirty entries in Worth for the years 1870–1900, twelve of which concern strictly 'down-to-earth' topographical matters. The only book worth mentioning is Forster's admirable *Life* (1872–4). And it is noteworthy that in his *Bibliography of the Writings of Charles Dickens* (1879),[14] James Cook ranged *Great Expectations* along with *Hard Times* among the novelist's 'Minor Works of Fiction', maybe only because these were two short novels compared to the 'baggy monsters' published in monthly parts. This view was shared as late as 1958 by R. C. Churchill, who wrote in the Pelican Guide to English Literature, *From Dickens to Hardy*: 'Hard Times and *Great Expectations* seem to me masterpieces of a minor order'.[15] But, by then, Churchill's was certainly a minority view.

The first forty years of this century were marked by few works of lasting critical interest, barring those of Gissing, Chesterton and Shaw (1937).[16] The 'Marxizing' study of T. A. Jackson, *Charles Dickens: The Progress of a Radical* (1937), affords historical rather than critical interest. Out of the 109 entries in Worth, no fewer than thirty-five are devoted to topography, mainly to the 'Cooling versus Higham' debate. But 1940, with George Orwell's *Inside the Whale*, soon to be followed by Humphry House's *The Dickens World* and Edmund Wilson's *The Wound and the Bow* (1941), was the beginning of a new era in Dickens criticism. K. J. Fielding goes so far as to speak of a 'critical revolution', which, he says, 'happened quietly but fast'.[17] The next decade was marked by Edgar Johnson's *Charles Dickens: His Tragedy and Triumph* (1952), Sylvère Monod's *Dickens Romancier* (1953) and Kathleen Tillotson's *Novels of the Eighteen-Forties* (1954), which all contributed to making Dickens a respectable author. By mid-century, Dickens, who had long been looked down upon by highbrows, had become food for academic thought, and his books were at last deemed worthy of being placed on University bookshelves.

The history of Dickens criticism has become since then a chapter in the history of general criticism. The history of *Great Expectations* criticism is itself in many respects a chapter within this chapter (a common practice with Dickens critics being to devote a whole book to the *oeuvre* and conduct their readers through chronologically ordered sections on the individual novels). *Great Expectations*, however, retains some 'critical autonomy' and a striking feature is the permanence of interest for a limited number of questions, possibly because, as Christopher Ricks remarks, 'The most important things about *Great Expectations* are also the most obvious':[18] plot, structure, the two endings, the hero's progress, Victorian issues, imagery and symbolism, characterization and narrative methods. Reading all the critics is like listening to many-voiced variations on the same themes or, to use a more Dickensian comparison, to a 'choral symphony'.

Plot was from the first, and still is, the major attraction of *Great Expectations*. E. P. Whipple, sensitive to the way 'the *dénouement*' was 'still hidden, though confidentially foretold', felt convinced that 'The plot of the romance is therefore universally admitted to be the best that Dickens has ever invented'.[19] But the meaning of the word 'plot' has evolved over the years: more or less synonymous with story at first, and then analysed in terms of its probability or of its romantic appeal, it gradually came to mean something closer to narrative strategy and is now analysed in terms of structural unity, intentionality and ordering. Significantly, Andrew Lang in 1898 called it Dickens's 'best plot':[20] Robert Golding in 1985 speaks of 'a masterpiece of construction'.[21] 'Fine', the adjective most often applied to it by early commentators, has been replaced by 'well-constructed', 'well-balanced', 'tightly organized'. And coherence has been more and more unanimously held to be a virtue, when some early readers thought it a blemish: the reviewer of *The Spectator* (20 July 1861) believed that Dickens was wrong to attempt 'a coherent tale' and had better 'ramble when he will and where he will'; a century later, G. Robert Stange praised the book for its lack of proliferation.[22]

Dickens's conciseness and coherence in this novel is usually held to have been the result of necessity: the weekly form of serialization prevented Dickens from indulging in digressions as he did in the longer monthly parts (A. Lang, 1898; Philip Collins, 1972; Ellen Casey, 1981).[23] The three-part division has also been recognized as the sign of careful planning and thematic ordering (John Butt, 1969; Q. D. Leavis, 1970);[24] but William Axton rightly argues that 'Within and behind this balanced three-part structural surface ... Dickens continued to develop a firm and decisive middle' and conceived his story 'as two halves' (1967).[25] Other structural patterns have been shown to give the novel its unity and formal shapeliness, such as 'symmetry', 'repetition' and the 'recurrence' of the theme of 'great expectations' (John H. Hagan, 1954).[26]

Even if there was no such 'recurrence' of the theme (as exemplified by characters like Wopsle, Herbert, Miss Havisham), 'great expectations' would be unmistakably recognized as the unifying element of the book: 'never was there a more wholly thematic plot-structure', says Q. D. Leavis, who also points to the 'irony which inheres in the title'.[27] 'The plot powerfully realizes the theme of false expectations and false values', writes Harvey Peter Sucksmith who, in *The Narrative Art of Charles Dickens* (1970), offers an excellent analysis of the 'structural irony' which 'pervades the novel and is already at work in the title'.[28] For Geoffrey Thurley, *Great Expectations*, a 'profoundly ironical' novel, 'is unique because it encapsulates the fable of every modern novel' (*The Dickens Myth*, 1976).[29] 'Myth', 'legend', 'fable', 'allegory', are the words that recur most often in discussions of the novel to express the unique linearity and centrality of an almost perfectly archetypal plot. The book has been described as 'Dickens's fable for his time' (R. Stange, 1954), a fable for all ages (Rowland D. McMaster, 1965), 'the myth of Paradise Lost' (Edgar Johnson, 1962), 'The Myth of the Self' (William H. Marshall, 1963), 'a social, moral, religious, mythical allegory' (Jean-Claude Amalric, 1973), 'an exemplary tale' (Barry Westburg, 1977), 'a fable of cultural emergence' (Robin Gilmour, 1981).[30] It has also been seen as Dickens's 'most ironic (and sophisticated) use of the conventions of the fairy tale' (Shirley Grob, 1964), Pip's 'upside-down vision' of *Sleeping Beauty* (Harry Stone, 1980) or of *Cinderella* (Michael C. Kotzin, 1972); and Edwin M. Eigner (1978) reads it as a novel in which 'the fairy tale motif of the bad wish' is 'fulfilled' and comes to be 'unwished' by the wisher.[31]

Inseparable from the theme of 'expectations' is the personality of the subject who expects. Studies of the leading structural theme are therefore studies of the hero's progress, though what this progress is is diversely analysed. For Humphry House (1941), Pip's story is right up to the end the story of 'a snob's progress'.[32] A snob's progress indeed, says C. Ricks, but the 'ungrateful snob' is 'eventually saved by his love for the convict who had been his unknown patron'.[33] A snob's progress by no means, says Q. D. Leavis, 'but the history of a successful progress towards spiritual freedom'.[34] For many it is a journey from deception and disappointment to acceptance, 'mature acceptance of the human condition' (Stange),[35] or just acceptance of 'the world for what it is' (Nancy K. Hill, 1981),[36] or, again, a journey from rejection to 'allegiance', from 'self-assertiveness' to 'self-sacrifice': 'By choosing his servitude to Magwitch, Pip transforms it into freedom', writes J. Hillis Miller.

'For Dickens, as for Kierkegaard, the self can only affirm itself through self-sacrifice' (*Charles Dickens: The World of His Novels*, 1958).[37]

'A book about growing up' (Robert Pattison, 1978), a *Bildungsroman* (Jerome H. Buckley, 1974), 'an inner, spiritual pilgrimage' (Grahame Smith, 1968), a 'quest-romance' (Lawrence Frank, 1984) are so many ways of accounting for Pip's 'pilgrimage of being'.[38] And to each definition corresponds a different way of assessing the hero's stature and the hero's autonomy. The young snob of House has little in common with Miller's 'archetypal hero',[39] Thurley's modern Oedipus Rex or Frank's 'romantic self'. For some critics Pip is just one more fictional hero, for others he is no less than a universal 'Everyman' (Dorothy Van Ghent, 1953)[40] or Dickens's version of Bunyan's Christian (Q. D. Leavis).[41]

House, like many early critics, judges Pip on moral and almost personal grounds, as if he were a real person. To be sure, Pip the narrator encourages his readers to do so by constantly passing unfavourable judgements on himself. A. E. Dyson remarks on his 'capacity for self-accusation' which 'is developed to the verge of morbidity' (1970);[42] and to Philip Hobsbaum '*Great Expectations* appears as a sustained exercise in self-castigation' (1972).[43] So much so that Pip has been said to prefigure George Silverman, one of Dickens's most guilt-ridden heroes; but whereas 'In Silverman's case a liberating vision is never achieved' (Dudley Flamm, 1970), Pip frees himself 'from his early conditioning and its burden of guilt and shame' (Q. D. Leavis).[44]

Next to 'expectations', 'guilt' is usually acknowledged to be the major theme of the novel. D. Van Ghent considers that the book has for its subject 'the etiology of guilt and of atonement',[45] and Robert Barnard names 'guilt' as 'The all-pervasive theme of *Great Expectations*' (1970).[46] But the question everybody asks is 'why does Pip feel guilty? What is he guilty of?' and the answers are quite varied. Lawrence Jay Dessner (1976) offers a Freudian explanation: Pip experiences the guilt of the orphan who feels responsible for the death of his parents and siblings and therefore 'wants punishment … as much as he wants love'.[47] For Colin N. Manlove (1980) Pip's guilt should be attributed to his ontological insecurity and a feeling that there is 'no place for him on this earth'.[48] Van Ghent's view of the problem is even more metaphysical: for her, 'every child, whatever his innocence, inherits guilt (as the potential of his acts) for the

condition of man. [...] the child is heir to the sins of the "fathers" '
and 'the world's guilt is his guilt'. But Van Ghent also tries to
conciliate her metaphysical explanation with her Marxist analysis
of a sinful society characterized by the 'dehumanization' of men, 'a
process brought about by industrialization, colonial imperialism,
and the exploitation of the human being as a "thing" '. Individuals,
she argues, are guilty of 'the sins of society' since everybody tends to
reify everybody else.[49] For Lionel Trilling, the guilt is also society's:
'The real thing is not the gentility of Pip's life but the hulks and the
murder and the rats and the decay in the cellarage of the novel'
(1951).[50] Robin Gilmour agrees that 'Pip's guilty conscience is the
link between cellarage and drawing-room in the novel', but he
disapproves of the terms in which the question is usually phrased
and refuses to consider Pip as a snob: 'The historical setting of the
novel provides the important clue to the nature of Pip's much-
discussed guilt. His predicament is representative of a social class in
the act of emergence'.[51] Julian Moynahan, in his influential essay on
'The hero's guilt' (1960), argues that Pip is unconsciously guilty of
acts of violence that are carried out by his criminal double, Orlick.[52]
Taking issue with Moynahan without naming him, Q. D. Leavis
maintains (not unlike Robert Garis) that Orlick is 'a character-of-
all-work' in the Devil's service who, in the sluice-house scene,
performs the part of Apollyon whom Pip has to face, together with
'the charges of his guilt', in his own Valley of Humiliation.[53] Q. D.
Leavis also makes a fine distinction between 'guilt' and 'shame', the
latter being 'a product of social distinctions', as opposed to the guilt
felt by the hero for being 'involved with crime'.[54] Pip himself, she
says, confuses the two notions, as when he speaks of 'the guiltily
coarse and common thing it was, to be on secret terms of conspiracy
with convicts' (x, 107–8). An interesting example of the dialogue
sustained between critics, regardless of time and space, is Robert
Newsom's essay 'The hero's shame' (1983) which, at twenty-three
years' distance, echoes Moynahan's 'The hero's guilt': Newsom,
who has read Q. D. Leavis, improves on the theme of 'social shame'
which, he argues, is the shame Dickens described in the autobiographical fragment, the shame of the young boy who was seen
working in the window at Warren's.[55] 'Shame' would then seem to
be the word Pip is looking for when he speaks of that 'smart without
a name' which he feels on being despised by Estella: 'I was so
humiliated, hurt, spurned, offended, angry, sorry – I cannot hit

upon the right name for the smart' (viii, 92); or it might also be said
to correspond to what R. Barnard calls 'guilt imposed' (which he
distinguishes from 'guilt assumed' and 'guilt transcended'):[56]
'shame' is the guilt imposed by Mrs Joe when she publicly enters 'on
a fearful catalogue of all the illnesses' Pip 'had been guilty of, and all
the acts of sleeplessness' he 'had committed' (iv, 59), or the guilt
imposed by Estella: 'Her contempt for me was so strong, that it
became infectious, and I caught it' (viii, 90).

The threefold object of Pip's quest – money, gentility, and Estella
– has also engaged the interest of many, if not all commentators.
Few have committed the mistake of considering these elements separately and those who do are all the more inexcusable as Pip himself,
the first critic of his novel, insists on the interconnection: 'Truly it
was impossible to dissociate her presence from all those wretched
hankerings after money and gentility' (xxix, 257). 'His relation with
Estella', writes Ross H. Dabney (*Love and Property in the Novels of
Dickens*, 1967), 'is not something between two persons...; it is
concerned with impersonal things – with class, with status, with
habits, occupations, gestures, and language standard in a particular
social milieu'.[57] And Grahame Smith, although he gives precedence
to the 'humanly destructive effects of money' in this novel as
elsewhere in Dickens, shows constant alertness to the fact that what
he calls, somewhat unfairly, Pip's 'greed for money' cannot be
discussed separately from class consciousness and personal feelings:
'Now we see Dickens merging the motif of money and gentility with
the most intimate of human emotions, that of love'.[58] His *Dickens,
Money, and Society* (1968) offers a very good study of the origins of
money and of the 'shame of a whole society', but it is regrettable
that he should not make it clear that the story is pre-Victorian and it
is rather surprising that he should have nothing to say about 'clean'
and 'dirty' money, a subject that is well analysed by C. Ricks and
Q. D. Leavis.[59]

On the question of gentility and gentlemanliness, R. Gilmour's
The Idea of the Gentleman in the Victorian Novel (1981) stands as
a major source for the study of background. It combines a detailed
look at Regency society with a perceptive analysis of Victorian
ideology and is rightly concerned with the notion of social mobility,
so often overlooked by other commentators. Laurence Lerner's
'Literature and social change' (1977) had earlier described *Great
Expectations* as 'a novel concerned with social mobility', pointing

to a confusion between the old fairy-tale wish to rely on godmothers and the new Smilesian ideal of self-help. He also argued very interestingly that only in a changing society could it be possible to feel ashamed or disdainful because new possibilities were offered to everyone, the possibility for instance of 'being less coarse'.[60] On the ambiguous idea of the 'gentleman', S. Monod early wrote perceptively about 'the false values on which the Victorian ideals of gentlemanliness rested: humbug ... smugness ... snobberies', concluding that 'Pip will never be a man before he has ceased to wish to become merely a gentleman, before he has discarded all his spurious ambitions' (1960).[61] Q. D. Leavis also has interesting things to say on Victorian ethics that made it a duty to rise socially, on the 'civilizing influence' of Herbert Pocket over Pip, on Joe's limitations and on the discrepancy between Dickens's and Magwitch's idea of a gentleman.[62] Who is the 'true gentleman' of the novel remains none the less a point at issue, the two candidates being Joe and Herbert: Hobsbaum considers that true gentlemanliness is embodied in Joe (1972),[63] James M. Brown considers that the model of gentility is not boorish Joe, 'a gentleman at heart', but Herbert, 'a gentleman in *both* heart and manner' (1982).[64]

As to Estella, she has received rather short shrift from the critics, apart from those bent on establishing connections with Dickens's private life. Ellen Ternan is often regarded as Dickens's source of inspiration. The idea was first launched by Thomas Wright (1935) and has been repeated since then by Edmund Wilson (1941), Hesketh Pearson (1949) and Jack Lindsay (1950).[65] The identification was mocked by Edward Wagenknecht in 'Dickens and the scandalmongers' (1950),[66] but rather unsuccessfully: 'It is inevitable that we should associate Pip's helpless enslavement to Estella with Dickens's desperate passion for Ellen Lawless Ternan', E. Johnson wrote in 1952: 'The very name "Estella" seems a kind of lawless anagram upon some of the syllables and initials of Ellen's name'.[67] Ada Nisbet in 'The autobiographical matrix of *Great Expectations*' (1959) argues that 'The novel can be seen to be the record of a brutal self-appraisal which centers on the three obsessive passions' of Dickens's own life, 'his passion for social status, his passion for money, and his passion for Ellen Ternan'; but she also submits the idea that 'The Estella who made fun of the boy Pip, and rejected him because he was "common", is more likely Maria Beadnell, Dickens's first love, who led him on but rejected him as an

unpromising suitor'.[68] It is Michael Slater's conviction that 'It is not
... to Ellen that we owe the powerful vision of frustrated love that
Dickens gives us in the most perfectly achieved of all his novels but
to Maria'. His argument is all the more convincing if one considers
that Pip is a projection of 'the young Dickens' and it is supported,
besides, by an interesting juxtaposition of an excerpt from chapter
38 and a letter to Maria of March 1833, which are very similar in
tone and phrasing (*Dickens and Women*, 1983).[69]

It would occur to no one to suggest that Pip is not infatuated with
Estella, since he tells us so, but it is difficult to agree with Pamela
Hansford Johnson that his passion is on a par with Bradley Head-
stone's for Lizzie Hexam (1970),[70] or with Ada Nisbet that '*Great
Expectations* is a novel about sex' and that Pip's 'fateful attraction'
to the girl is 'the deeply disturbing physical desire of a mature
man'.[71] If there are any sexual innuendoes in the book, they are to
be found in Miss Havisham's sado-masochistic definition of love:
'I'll tell you ... what real love is. It is blind devotion, unquestioning
self-humiliation, utter submission, trust and belief against yourself
and against the whole world, and giving up your whole heart and
soul to the smiter – as I did!' (xxix, 261). Pip merely says 'I loved
Estella with the love of a man' (xxix, 253), but sexual passion is
never brought to the fore; we never even see Pip courting Estella
and, enamoured as he may be, he never describes her physical
appearance. As a character Estella is in fact grossly delineated: 'As
the object of his desire', writes John O. Jordan (1983), 'Estella
remains an enigma. If her character does not appear to be fully
developed in the novel, it is because ... she most completely eludes
his grasp, in his narrative as in his life'.[72] The important thing about
Estella is that she is the person who first puts Pip to shame, that
'having inspired him with a sense of his own social inferiority, he
sees her as the exquisite representative of a higher kind of life'
(G. Smith),[73] that 'she is something to build on' (H. House).[74] It is
clear from the start, as Q. D. Leavis writes, that 'we are not to
expect a love affair or a love-interest in this novel',[75] or rather, in
John Kucich's terms, that 'From beginning to end, Pip's love for
Estella is fused with the deeper meaning of "expectations" '.[76]

Kucich, for his analysis of the Pip/Estella relationship, uses the
concept of 'expenditure' (George Bataille's concept of *dépense*), by
which he designates 'any human activity that involves the destruction of a limit'. 'Pip's desire for Estella', he writes, 'is, quite literally,

a desire for expenditure: Pip wants to break down the claustropho-
bia of selfhood and to release himself beyond the limits of identity
into the sphere in which Estella supposedly dwells'. 'Expenditure'
therefore is a crucial issue at the end of the novel, the ultimate
question being whether the 'desire to escape the pressure of ...
fundamental imprisonment' will be satisfied or not. The 'prominence' of Estella in either ending, Kucich argues, is the sign that Pip
is not 'cured of his desire'; the first ending 'betrays a final wish:
"that suffering ... had given her a heart to understand what my
heart used to be" ', the second ending answers this wish more
positively in so far as 'Estella represents a more painfully and
completely achieved selflessness ... than Pip can claim', so that she
is 'the final vehicle for Pip's integration of expenditure in love with
the restraint of self-knowledge and self-acceptance'.[77]

According to Kucich, 'The debate over the two endings of *Great
Expectations* – whether Pip should be allowed to marry Estella or
not – ' has obscured this larger problem.[78] But this is not a fair
account of 'the debate', which has borne, especially during the past
two decades, on other matters than just wedlock or celibacy. It is
true that many early commentators objected to the revised conclusion because, like George Bernard Shaw, they took it for granted
that the story ended 'at the altar rails', so that strong cases were
made out against the 'stock happy ending' (Oliver Elton, 1924)[79]
or, in J. Cuming Walters's words, against Dickens's 'weak conces-
sion to Lytton's namby-pamby sentimentality' (1911).[80] J. Butt and
K. Tillotson also consider that 'It was at least more appropriate that
Pip, who had lost Magwitch's money, should also lose his daughter,
than that he should marry her in the end' (1957).[81] For Dabney 'The
patched-on second ending is a great mistake' and Pip and Estella's
'marriage is pointless, purely a sentimental gesture'.[82] For Ricks 'it
is a matter of at least dismay that Dickens changed the original
ending and allowed Pip to marry Estella'.[83] Forster's reaction is not
so clear-cut and skirts round the marriage question: 'the first ending
nevertheless seems to be more consistent with the drift, as well as
natural working out, of the tale', he merely writes.[84] And Johnson's
is even more qualified: 'In love ... Pip's "great expectations" ...
have been disappointed and deceived, and ideally the story should
have ended on that loss', he says; but on the other hand the 'ending
of serene and twilight peace' has for him pleasant Miltonic
overtones and he concludes that 'It should close with that misty
moonlight scene in Miss Havisham's ruined garden, but, as Shaw

suggests, with Pip and Estella then bidding each other a chastened farewell'.[85]

It is worth noting that, as a rule, rejection is more unconditional than vindication: Gissing condemned Dickens for unwisely following 'Lytton's imbecile suggestion',[86] Shaw spoke of the 'botched up and tagged on' second ending (1937) and when he came to decide against the first ending as well, he did not hesitate to write: 'Dickens wrote two endings and made a mess of both' (1947).[87] But an increasing number of critics have tended in recent years to express themselves less bluntly and to speak of the revised ending as 'not inappropriate' (Richard J. Dunn, 1978).[88]

The arguments usually put forward in support of the new conclusion are not that 'Pip should be allowed to marry Estella', if only because a majority of critics today are not so sure that marriage is what Dickens meant. A. L. French (1979) is even convinced that 'Old Pip' is a bachelor and argues, like Angus Calder (1965), that 'He didn't see the "shadow", but it was really there'.[89] More numerous, however, are those who consider that the second ending holds out only 'ambiguous' hopes of 'domestic happiness' (G. W. Kennedy, 1974).[90] This ambiguity is particularly obvious to those who have given a close look at Dickens's various rephrasings of the last sentence: comparing the passage 'I saw the shadow of no parting from her' in the serial version and in the first book edition with the 1868 revision, 'I saw no shadow of another parting from her', Albert A. Dunn expresses his belief that 'The ambiguity ... was intentional'. Pip, he argues, 'is predicting a future', but 'what the future holds remains uncertain' and Dickens may well have meant to suggest that there would be no other parting because there would be no other meeting, though he left it for the reader to decide which interpretation to favour: 'Dickens was not writing an alternative, happy ending but one that still might satisfy sentimentalists like Bulwer and yet preserve a second sense that would satisfy himself and reinstate his original plan for the novel' (1978).[91] Had he been more attentive to these revisions, Douglass H. Thomson would not have ventured the absurd reading of 'another' as a 'pronoun': according to this critic 'One "shadow of another" who twice had "passed" from Estella's face is ... Molly. At the end, Pip's efforts to understand Estella ... are no longer obscured by this fleeting and "nameless" presence' (1984).[92] This reading in itself is far-fetched and irrelevant; but it is also unacceptable grammatically, considering the history of the phrase: there was no shadow of Molly in the 1861 version 'I saw the shadow of no parting from her'! Thomson would have been well-advised to read his predecessors, A. A. Dunn, who, like him, wrote for *Dickens Studies Newletter*, and, even better, Edgar Rosenberg's excellent and exhaustive study 'Last words on *Great Expectations*: a textual brief on the six endings' (1981).[93]

Neither E. M. Eigner (1970)[94] nor H. P. Sucksmith (1970),[95] who have paid some attention to his ideas about aesthetics and the art of fiction, would agree with A. A. Dunn that Bulwer reacted as a mere 'sentimentalist'. It is Sucksmith's conviction that Bulwer's arguments rested on a twofold principle, 'the need for idealization and for sympathetic characters', and that he probably pleaded in favour of a 'rhetoric of sympathy' to counterbalance the 'rhetoric of irony' that had pervaded the whole book: 'Bulwer may well have pointed out that the harsh ironic fate of the hero needs to be balanced by a more compassionate ending, that too severe a judgement on Pip would leave the reader with a cynical vision of life, alienate his sympathy, and spoil the final effect of the book'. This view, at any rate, is in keeping with much that has been written in defence of the revised ending. Marshall W. Gregory (1969) considers that it provides 'a final emphatic utterance of the values which have informed the whole rest of the novel' and shows that 'life *can* possess meaning and fulfilment'.[96] Robert A. Greenberg argues that 'Dickens's primary concern in the second ending was to establish the connection between present and past' and that the journey of both Pip and Estella ends 'in self-discovery' (1970).[97] For Q. D. Leavis 'Dickens's second thoughts produced the right, because the logical, solution to the problem of how to end without a sentimental "happy ending" but with a satisfactory winding-up of the themes'.[98] For John T. Smith (1971) the revised ending is not happy but more appropriate and less cruel.[99] For Lucille P. Shores (1972) it is 'not inconsistent with' the portrayal of Estella and it is not happy in the least.[100] Richard J. Dunn (1978) praises the 'autumnal' tone of the final paragraph.[101] David M. Craig (1979) thinks that the setting of the ruined garden 'unites the actual world, the world outside the Garden of Eden, with the pastoral garden of the imagination'.[102] On the whole, critics are agreed that 'happiness is not guaranteed' (Irwin Weiser, 1983),[103] but the second ending is felt to be more satisfactory on aesthetic and ethical grounds.

Another category of critics to be considered are those who think that the novel ends before the passage revised: Martin Meisel (1965), Richard A. Levine (1969), Milton Millhauser (1972), Peter Brooks (1980).[104]

Brooks is also concerned, like many recent critics, with 'the problems of closure, authority, and narratability' which 'show up in particularly acute form in any autobiographical narration'.[105] Alan Friedman (*The Turn of the Novel*, 1966) was probably the first critic to consider the conclusion of *Great Expectations* as a formal problem of closedness and openness, though he devotes only a few pages to the study of this novel.[106] Moshe Ron (1977) argues that the text 'works for its own destruction' and wonders if the sense of 'closure' and 'formal unity' at the end of the novel can 'be considered a triumph over the fundamental structure of alienation which launched this plot on its search for meaning'.[107] D. A. Miller (1981) and David Lodge (1981) both use *Great Expectations* as an example to illustrate a discussion of inconclusiveness in the traditional novel. Miller insists on 'the indeterminacy with which ... the function of Estella has been invested' and on 'textual ambivalence'; Lodge takes issue with John Fowles who maintains in *The French Lieutenant's Woman* that the dilemma of closing a novel is a specifically modern problem because 'The novelist is ... no longer the God of the Victorian Age, omniscient and decreeing'. 'There is plenty of evidence', replies Lodge, 'that Victorian novelists themselves had difficulty on occasion with the endings of their stories ... Perhaps the best-known example is that of Dickens's *Great Expectations*'.[108]

Less central to the understanding of the novel are the numerous studies of imagery and symbolism that cropped up in the 1960s and early 1970s, when all Dickens was sifted by the image and symbol hunters. But *Great Expectations* does not justify this sort of analysis as do *Bleak House* or *Our Mutual Friend*. R. Barnard himself begins his essay 'Imagery and theme in *Great Expectations*' by remarking that 'with the possible exception of the prison, *Great Expectations* contains no all-informing symbol'. His study of 'reiterated images and motifs' is therefore unsystematic and his awareness saves him from dogmatism. The essay has the further merit of considering the images in connection with the major themes of the novel: the prison

images throw 'a cloak of ambiguity over the question of guilt and
innocence', the 'chains of guilt and corruption' connect the characters, animal imagery illustrates parasitism (spiders) and the trans-
ference of guilt (dogs), but there is 'no carefully worked-out scheme
to be traced in this imagery', no 'neatly-planned bestiary'.[109]
John P. McWilliams Jr also offers an illuminating analysis of 'The
beacon, the gibbet, and the ship' (1972),[110] three outstanding
objects of the landscape in the opening scenes, which will gradually
interconnect into a complex cluster of symbols. For Taylor Stoehr
(1965), the spatial dimension furnishes 'the medium for ordering
and connecting details'. A novel, he admits, 'must *take place*, but in
Dickens place has an organizing function beyond that of mere
background'. In *Great Expectations* he singles out three 'symbolic'
places, the Forge, Satis House and Newgate, as alternatives to one
another and representative of Pip's inner conflict.[111] Not three but
four worlds are selected by Rosalee Robinson (1971), Satis House
and Little Britain, which are evil worlds, Joe's Forge and Wemmick's Castle, which are good.[112] London is seen by Donald H.
Ericksen (1970) as the 'archetypal City of Destruction',[113] an
opinion that is not shared by F. S. Schwarzbach, who stresses the
link between Newgate and Satis House, with its ruined garden, 'a
grim, ironic parody of the supposed pastoral qualities of the village',
and concludes that 'London in *Great Expectations* has no mono-
poly of corruption and evil' (*Dickens and the City*, 1979).[114] A
'second level of symbolism' is examined by Elizabeth MacAndrew
(1975), as opposed to the 'immediate' level represented by buildings
and institutions, namely a correspondence between the characters'
'states of being' and the weather, 'sunshine and rain, storm and
calm'.[115]

   But many studies of imagery are irritatingly exhaustive and systematic, and cannot be read without bringing to mind the image of
their authors shuffling and reshuffling their filing-cards. The 'hand
motif' is a case in point: M. H. Levine has counted more than a
hundred references to hands (1965) and Charles R. Forker's essay
on the subject (1961) is also crammed with such references; but the
word 'hand' often means no more than what it says, for it so
happens that, even in Dickens, characters as a rule have hands
rather than hooks; and a short paragraph in C. Ricks's essay is more
suggestive about the symbolic value of holding hands than the long
lists of stock-takers.[116]

The four elements have also received much attention: references to air, water, fire and earth have been catalogued and redistributed into moral categories. Water has been seen as the emblem of death and corruption, which it is in a way, but *Great Expectations* is not *Our Mutual Friend*. Fire is usually placed on the positive side, though it has been observed that it can burn and destroy.[117] So many interconnections have been found and used for so many purposes that demonstrations become more confusing than illuminating. Even the titles of essays interconnect, 'Hands and hearts', 'Hearts and hands', 'Fire, hand, and gate', 'Water and fire' ... [118] The importance of the fire imagery and of its ambivalence is certainly not to be denied, but John Carey in *The Violent Effigy* (1973) wisely reminds us that '*Great Expectations* is another novel which *plays* with fire' (my emphasis).[119] And Naomi Lightman (1986) renews the interest in this well-worn subject by focusing her analysis on 'the smith image', namely on the 'mythological dimension in Joe's calling' (Joe, she reminds us, was originally to be called 'George Thunder'), and on 'creative smithying'.[120]

Characters have also been subjected to the usual kind of attention, either singly or in pairs. Jaggers, the 'enigmatic' lawyer, the 'keeper of secrets', has attracted the attention of professional men as well as literary critics: he is usually credited with goodness, generosity and incorruptibility.[121] Wemmick's split personality has been the occasion of several essays. Often described as comic, his schizophrenia is taken very seriously by L. J. Dessner (1975), who sees in him the novel's 'most deeply imagined victim' and considers his alienation to be as 'self-destructive' as Miss Havisham's.[122] Wopsle's incompetence and amateurism as an actor is the subject of historians of the theatre, T. E. Pemberton (1888), J. B. Van Amerongen (1927) and V. C. Clinton-Baddeley (1961). His theatrical aspirations have also been shown persuasively by William F. Axton (1966) and by James D. Barry (1968) to underscore the theme of 'great expectations' and parallel Pip's career in burlesque fashion. Wopsle for these critics is somehow Pip's comic double.[123]

An interest in doubles and mirror-images, possibly originated by Moynahan's seminal essay on Orlick and Pip, gave rise to numerous pairings; the fashion was at its peak in the late 1960s, when all the young male characters were in turn seen as Pip's doubles: Trabb's

boy, according to Barry D. Bort (1966), 'exists as a reflection of'
Pip's 'pretensions to gentility'; Startop and Drummle are for
Richard J. Dunn (1967) personifications of Pip's conflicting forces
of good and evil; Herbert is Pip's 'good angel' and double for
Michael C. Kotzin (1983); and for Karl P. Wentersdorf, Orlick,
Herbert, Drummle, Startop, and, to a lesser degree, even Pepper,
'the Avenger', are all reflections of our hero (1966).[124] This doubling of characters has, of course, the advantage of recognizing (or
establishing) interconnections between the characters and of
pointing to the structural and thematic unity of the book,[125] but,
with everybody becoming everybody else's double, it becomes more
and more difficult to know who is who and what is what.

Of course, characters are bound together by relations other than
just those of analogy, and various patterns of relationships have
been discovered and explored. A predominant form of relationship
in this novel is often recognized to be that of oppressor to oppressed
and a most thorough, perhaps *the* most thorough analysis of the
question is to be found in A. L. French's 'Beating and cringing:
Great Expectations' (1974), which borrows its title from Jaggers's
remark about Drummle, 'A fellow like our friend the Spider ...
either beats, or cringes' (xlviii, 402): 'Much of the world of *Great
Expectations*', says French, 'sorts itself out into these two distasteful
categories'. French makes excellent points on the many situations in
which 'parents, or their substitutes, dominate and indeed determine
their children', on the Frankenstein activity of Magwitch and Miss
Havisham, on the domineering attitude of Mrs Joe towards her
husband, on bending and unbending, on taming and battering, on
the eventual reversal of parts, when 'the monster rounds on its
Frankenstein' and the slave becomes the master.[126] Among the
many other critics who have dealt with the creator/creature relationship, we may mention J. H. Miller (1958), Barbara Hardy (1961),
John Carey (1983) and L. Frank (1984).[127]

The quest for the true father and Pip's ambiguous relations with
the various parental figures placed in his way is an inexhaustible
subject that has been touched upon by most commentators, whose
remarks often overlap. An original contribution to the subject is
Albert Hutter's Freudian reading of Pip's ambivalent attitude to the
two father figures who, he submits, are the impersonations of the
two sides of '*the* father', Magwitch, threatening and castrating, and
Joe, benign and lovable. Magwitch and Jaggers constitute another

pair of father figures in Hutter's essay, corresponding to the two 'opposite but related sides to Victorian economic life – the dirty and the clean, the criminal and the legitimate'.[128] Another Freudian reading is G. Thurley's (1976), which shows Pip 'dominated' like Oedipus by a 'father figure' whom he meets 'at a cross-roads' of his life and by 'a version of the Terrible Mother', sphinx-like Miss Havisham: 'As the book moves to its conclusion, the hero slowly begins to overcome the mother, and to accept the father.'[129]

Another aspect of human relationships, love and hate, and its expression through the rituals of meals has been admirably appreciated by B. Hardy in 'Food and ceremony in *Great Expectations*' (1963), which analyses 'a series of related scenes' that bring out 'the moral significance of needs and hospitality' and establishes a comparison between true ceremonies of love and false ceremonies of hospitality.[130] Katherine Carolan's 'Dickens' Last Christmases' (1972) also deals with the Christian love rite turned upside down and reads the 'travesty of a Christmas feast' at the Gargerys' as mirroring 'Dickens' disillusionment with the hypocrisy and heartlessness of Victorian society'.[131] Heartlessness and cannibalism, 'the savage image of the eating of the heart', is also Anya Taylor's subject in 'Devoured hearts in *Great Expectations*' (1982).[132]

Language and style have surprisingly attracted little notice from the specialists. Joe has provided G. L. Brook (*The Language of Dickens*, 1970) and Robert Golding (*Idiolects in Dickens*, 1985) with examples of 'substandard speech' or 'non-standard idiom'; but Brook has no section on *Great Expectations* and Golding's book is disappointingly limited to commonplaces on personal style: Miss Havisham's 'mannered imperatives', Magwitch's 'rhetoric of emphasis', Wemmick's 'colloquialisms', Jaggers's 'aggressive interrogative mode'.[133]

The question of language as a means of communication has for its part been abundantly discussed. D. Van Ghent early launched the subject by describing the 'aloneness' of some characters who, like Joe, 'raptly soliloquize'.[134] Her analysis has been re-examined point by point and disproved by Ruth M. Vande Kieft (1961), who considers that 'there is genuine communication' in this novel and that Joe's 'obliquity of discourse' is no 'hindrance to finally successful communication'.[135] Two more essays on language and the tyranny of words ought to be mentioned here: Ian Ousby's 'Language and gesture in *Great Expectations*' (1977), which shows Pip as 'tyrannized' by language, especially when examined, cross-examined and 'catechized', and happier with Joe's 'innocent language of signs',[136] and Melanie Young's 'Distorted expectations: Pip and the problems of language' (1978), which distinguishes between the 'language of the heart' (Joe's) and the 'language of thought' (Jaggers's), between the 'language of fairy tale and romance' and 'the language of law', discusses Pip's tendency to romanticize and misconstruct the meaning of words, and argues that his journey from innocence to experience requires an 'initiation into semantics'.[137]

Although *Great Expectations* was hailed as Dickens's return to his best comic vein (and Dickens himself felt confident that his readers would 'not have to complain of' its 'want of humour'), the comic element is a subject to which critics have failed to do justice: 'Most discussion of *Great Expectations* nowadays', writes Philip Collins (1972), is 'portentously solemn';[138] and George Ford (1983) also remarks that for modern readers this novel is just 'another very sad book'.[139] Such statements are substantiated by P. Hobsbaum's perplexity: 'This, the grimmest of Dickens's books, was conceived as a comic extravaganza' (1972).[140] James R. Kincaid's *Dickens and the Rhetoric of Laughter* (1971) makes only one reference to *Great Expectations* and Walter Allen in 'The comedy of Dickens' (1970) merely cites Pip's fantastic whopper as an example of Dickens's taste for juxtaposing incongruities.[141] Henri Talon's courageous attempt at examining 'some aspects of the comic' in this novel (1972) ends up as a very serious study of Pip's 'self-mockery': 'the comic that Pip achieves at his own cost', he writes, 'is a counterpoint to the tragic in his story'.[142]

Neither tragic nor truly comic, *Great Expectations* eludes definition. Several attempts have been made at affiliating it to some specific genre, the romance, the fairy tale, the sensational novel (Walter C. Phillips, 1917; Philip L. Marcus, 1966).[143] Nina Auerbach (1975) links it to the picaresque tradition;[144] Jean McClure Kelty (1961) and Ann B. Dobie (1971) consider it to be a forerunner of the stream-of-consciousness novel.[145] Dickens, always his best critic, wisely called it 'a story'.

The confessional character of *Great Expectations* was long accepted as a narrative convention that required no commentary.

But a growing interest in narratology, a growing awareness of the fact that literature has itself for its own subject, and a growing concern in the inner life and the fictions of the self, which owes much to the attention Freud paid to the fictitious yet true stories of his patients, have in recent years changed the critical landscape of *Great Expectations*. During the past two decades, and especially the last one, an increasing number of critics have been asking themselves questions about the two Pips, the actor and the narrator, about his reasons for writing his autobiography and about the reliability of his 'confessions'.

A pioneering study was Robert B. Partlow Jr's 'The moving I: a study of the point of view in *Great Expectations*' (1961), which emphasized the 'strategic importance of the author's choice of a center' and of 'his mode of transmission'. Distinguishing between the 'I-as-I-was' and the 'I-as-I-am-now', he focused his attention on distance and closeness, on the various degrees of omniscience, on the shifts of point of view, on the handling of tenses and the ambiguity of the pronoun 'I'.[146] Since then, many critics, though using a different terminology, have given some attention to the problems of self-alienation and self-reconstruction: N. M. Visser (1977) opposes the 'narrating self' to the 'experiencing self', Moshe Ron (1977) and Steven Connor (1985) compare the 'narrating' and the 'narrated' Pips; W. J. M. Bronzwaer (1978) uses Genette's terminology, 'homodiegetic' and 'extradiegetic' narrator; so does Shlomith Rimmon-Kenan (1983).[147]

Such awareness involves an interest in time, memory and tense sequences. The stress has been put lately as never before on 'Dickens the Novelist of Memory', as K. J. Fielding once called him (1967)[148] and on the 'ordering of experience': 'Pip is made Pip in the telling', writes Joseph Gold (1972).[149] Henri Talon begins his essay, 'Space, time, and memory in *Great Expectations*' (1974), by quoting Nietzsche's beautiful remark 'Perhaps the long sentence of my life ought to be read backward. Before, when I read it normally, it did not make sense', and he goes on to explain that relating his life is for Pip 'essentially self-questioning', 'interpreting' and giving meaning to the past, though the meaning is not 'settled forever'.[150] 'It is all a question', says Moshe Ron, 'of looking back and *reading correctly*'.[151]

Several critics have wondered what purpose a 'moderately successful, middle-aged businessman' might have in adopting 'the mode of autobiography' (J. O. Jordan, 1983).[152] For Dianne Sadoff (1982), Pip in writing his life-story is performing a filial ceremony and paying off a debt to the dead father.[153] For Elliot L. Gilbert (1983), Pip wishes to explain how he moved 'from the Romantic prison of the secret life ... toward the Victorian prison of materialism': 'In the persistent nineteenth-century conflict between self-expression and solipsism, there could be no more complex or resonant figure than Pip, the passionate dreamer turned acquiescent realist who, choosing to renounce self, chooses also to tell the story of that choice'.[154] John O. Jordan suggests, among other things, that Pip wishes to justify himself in order not to be 'misremembered' as he once feared he might be, when he felt on the verge of death. But 'Like any historian of the self', Jordan writes, Pip can tell only 'his version of the truth' and, inevitably, he 'is constantly "bending" the shape of the past'.[155]

'Bending', 'choosing', 'ordering', 'reading', 'misreading', 'forging' are no doubt the keywords in contemporary criticism of *Great Expectations*. It has become a commonplace to say that remembering does not merely consist in reproducing but in recreating the past and that the 'memoirist' is a novelist. Hence the attention paid to the many metaphors of reading, writing and forging that earlier critics had not even noticed. 'The question of reading and writing ... is persistently thematized in the novel', says Peter Brooks.[156] Pip's self-deception is often equated with misreading or 'misperceiving' (C. C. Barfoot, 1976).[157] And it is certainly a sign of the times that, in a recent number of *Dickens Studies Annual* (1983), there should be two essays (besides Jordan's and E. L. Gilbert's) on reading and writing, Robert Tracy's 'Reading Dickens' writing' and Murray Baumgarten's 'Calligraphy and code: writing in *Great Expectations*', which are both concerned with the relation between oral and written language, the dangers of literacy and the problem of sincerity.[158]

Pip's fiction-making did not begin with his putting pen to paper. He was a novelist from the very beginning, when he began imagining, in Barry Westburg's terms, his 'fictions of the future' (*The Confessional Fictions of Charles Dickens*, 1977): 'The mode of consciousness that defines him', says Westburg, 'is "expectation" – his mind is typically directed toward the future rather than toward the past', but his 'dream of the future' is based on 'the denial of guilt', which is a denial of the past. In forgetting Magwitch, Pip has tried to 'disown' his guilty past and Magwitch must return 'because Pip has forgotten'. This return forces him 'to live his present as well as his future in a new relation to his past': 'remembering is a form of true knowing'. Westburg also points to the 'artificiality' of the novel, which he describes as a 'narrative being conscious of itself', a 'confession about fiction-making', a book in which 'imagination' and 'memory' are 'powers ranged against each other'. Hence the implicit analogy between 'forging' and 'writing' and a feeling conveyed throughout that 'something criminal and deceptive is associated with the power to use words'.[159]

For Steven Connor (*Charles Dickens*, 1985), Pip is a self-swindler because life compels him to be so: 'Pip rejects the secure and comfortable world of the "forge" for a "forged" narrative which he passes on to himself, as he acts out the desire of the Other in the chain of associations "forged" through the narrative'. Connor's Lacanian reading of the text is an attempt at defining how far 'identity is constructed by language and social life' and at following Pip's movement from 'the Imaginary Order' to 'the Symbolic Order'. The 'incursion of otherness' and violence into his life (Magwitch and Orlick) and his identification with Magwitch involve for Pip 'a loss of selfhood': '*Great Expectations* displays progressively Pip's alienation from himself', so that he finds himself 'acting out the desires of others', placed in a 'Symbolic relationship to the objects of his desire, because of the "desire of the Other" which is deflected through him'.[160]

Connor is an orthodox Lacanian. Westburg is no Lacanian at all. But their preoccupations are often very similar and so are many of their conclusions: on 'writing' as 'forging'; on language and prohibition; on the 'phallic' character of the convict's leg-iron and the 'sexual implications' of 'the secret burden' down the leg of Pip's trousers; on Pip's 'cry against ... the imprisoning fiction of destiny' (Westburg) and his recoiling from 'the apprehension of the loss or envelopment of the self in systems of signs' (Connor) when he dreams he is a 'brick in the house wall ... entreating to be released' from that 'giddy place' (lvii, 471).

In *Dickens and the Trials of Imagination* (1974), Garrett Stewart devotes only a few, but a few brilliant pages to Pip as an 'escape artist' and shows how his childish imagination and 'yearning fancy' are altered and distorted by the world of Satis House, how his 'dreams start converting themselves into lies' under its influence and its 'romantic deception', how his daydream is 'enslaved by expectations'. Satis House, Stewart writes, is 'a sort of pastoral rape, the violation of all authentic romance' and Pip's 'escape artistry' is a 'flight from self', a self which he only rediscovers after going through 'the trials of imagination', nightmares and feverish delirium.[161]

Lawrence Frank (*Charles Dickens and the Romantic Self*, 1984) often thinks on similar lines. Starting from Rousseau's and Freud's theories of the self, he writes beautifully about the 'fictive status of the self': 'we create the fiction of identity', he says, we are all 'narrative beings', novelists of ourselves. And he shows how Pip, even the narrated Pip, has always been narrating, '*creating* memory', as, for instance, when he decided that his visit to Satis House, not his encounter with a convict in the churchyard, was his most 'memorable day'. Not unlike Westburg, he speaks of Pip's 'loss of memory, a willed denial of the past' and of his 'misreading signs'. Not unlike Stewart, he shows how difficult it is for Pip to re-imagine himself after Magwitch's return, how he then tries to run away from himself and to dispel the past until he enters into the process of reconstituting his self.[162]

In spite of their different approaches, these four books often overlap, but, in spite of marked similarities, they do not overshadow one another: the older books are not old-fashioned, the more recent ones are not redundant. Maybe this verifies the statement Gayatri Chakravorty Spivak makes in her 'Translator's Preface' to Derrida's *Grammatology*: 'each act of reading "the text" is a preface to the next.'[163]

NOTES: CHAPTER 16

1   F. R. and Q. D. Leavis, *Dickens the Novelist* [1970] (Harmondsworth: Pelican, 1972), ch. 6. The first two remarks (pp. 9 and 10) are signed F. R. L., Q. D. L.; the last four (pp. 14, 20, 360, 415) are signed Q. D. L., as is the chapter on *Great Expectations*.

2   Sylvère Monod, *Dickens the Novelist* (Norman, Okla: University of Oklahoma Press, 1968).

3   Monod, 'Dickens et le grande tradition', 'Note bibliographique ou "Comment on *peut* lire *Great Expectations*" ', *Etudes Anglaises*, vol. 24 (Janvier–mars 1971), pp. 59–72.

4   George J. Worth, *Great Expectations: An Annotated Bibliography* (New York: Garland, 1986).

5   ibid., p. vii.

6   See Worth, op. cit., pp. 51–5; Philip Collins (ed.), *Dickens: The Critical Heritage* (London: Routledge, 1971), pp. 427–42; Norman Page (ed.), *Hard Times, Great Expectations and Our Mutual Friend*, A Casebook (London: Macmillan, 1979), pp. 94–100.

7   E. P. Whipple, '*Great Expectations*', *Atlantic Monthly*, 8 (September 1861), quoted in *The Critical Heritage*, pp. 428–30.

8   Mrs M. Oliphant, 'Sensational Novels', *Blackwood's Magazine*, 91 (May 1862), ibid., pp. 439–42.

9   R. L. Patten, *Charles Dickens and His Publishers* (Oxford: Clarendon Press, 1978), p. 288.

10 Worth, op. cit., p. xiii.

11 John Forster, *The Life of Charles Dickens* [1872–74] (London: Dent, 1966), Vol. 2, p. 287

12 See David Alec Wilson, *Carlyle to Threescore-and-Ten (1853–1865)* (London: Kegan Paul, 1929), p. 430.

13 George Gissing, *Charles Dickens: A Critical Study* (London: Blackie, 1898); Algernon Charles Swinburne, 'Charles Dickens', *Quarterly Review*, 196 (July 1902), pp. 20–39; G. K. Chesterton, *Charles Dickens* (London: Methuen, 1906).

14 James Cook, *Bibliography of the Writings of Charles Dickens and Many Curious and Interesting Particulars Relating to His Works* (London: Frank Kerslake, 1879), p. 26.

15 R. C. Churchill, *From Dickens to Hardy* (Harmondsworth: Pelican, 1958) p. 140.

16 George Bernard Shaw, 'Preface' to *Great Expectations* (Edinburgh: R. and R. Clark for the Limited Editions Club, 1937), pp. xxvi.

17 K. J. Fielding, 'The critical autonomy of "Great Expectations" ', *A Review of English Literature*, vol. 2, no. 3 (July 1961), p. 76.

18 C. Ricks, 'Great Expectations', in John Gross and Gabriel Pearson (eds), *Dickens and the Twentieth Century* (London: Routledge, 1962), p. 199.

19 E. P. Whipple, *The Critical Heritage*, p. 428.

20 A. Lang, 'Charles Dickens', *Fortnightly Review*, 64 (December 1898).

21 R. Golding, *Idiolects in Dickens* (London: Macmillan, 1985), p. 172.

22 G. R. Stange, 'Expectations well lost: Dickens' fable for his time' *College English*, vol. 16 (1954), reprinted in George H. Ford and Lauriat Lane Jr (eds), *The Dickens Critics* (Ithaca, NY: Cornell University Press, 1961), pp. 294–308.

23 A. Lang, 'Introduction' to the 1898 Gadshill edition; P. Collins, 'A tale of two novels: *A Tale of Two Cities* and *Great Expectations* in Dickens's career', *Dickens Studies Annual*, vol. 2 (1972), p. 340; E. Casey, ' "That specially trying mode of publication": Dickens as editor of the weekly serial', *Victorian Periodicals Review*, vol. 14 (Fall 1981), pp. 93–101.

24 J. Butt, 'The serial publication of Dickens's novels', in *Pope, Dickens and Others* (Edinburgh University Press, 1969), pp. 149–69; Q. D. Leavis, op. cit., p. 378.

25 W. Axton, ' "Keystone" structure in Dickens' serial novels', *University of Toronto Quarterly*, vol. 37 (October 1967), p. 47.

26 J. H. Hagan, 'Structural patterns in Dickens's *Great Expectations*', *ELH*, vol. 21 (March 1954), pp. 54–66.

27 Q. D. Leavis, op. cit., pp. 378, 375.

28 H. P. Sucksmith, *The Narrative Art of Charles Dickens: The Rhetoric of Sympathy and Irony in His Novels* (Oxford: Clarendon Press, 1970), p. 217.

29 G. Thurley, *The Dickens Myth: Its Genesis and Structure* (London: Routledge & Kegan Paul, 1976), p. 280.

30 R. D. McMaster, 'Introduction' to the Odyssey Press edition (New York, 1970); E. Johnson in *Dickens Criticism: Past, Present, and Future Directions: A Symposium with George H. Ford, Edgar Johnson, J. Hillis Miller, and Sylvère Monod* (Boston, 1962); W. H. Marshall, 'The conclusion of *Great Expectations* as the fulfillment of myth', *Personalist*, vol. 44 (Summer 1963), pp. 337–47;

J. C. Amalric, 'Some reflections on *Great Expectations* as an allegory', in *Studies in the Later Dickens* (Montpellier, 1973), pp. 127–33; B. Westburg, *The Confessional Fictions of Charles Dickens* (De Kalb, Ill.: Northern Illinois University Press, 1977), p. 180; R. Gilmour, *The Idea of the Gentleman in the Victorian Novel* (London: Allen & Unwin, 1981), p. 135.

31   S. Grob, 'Dickens and some motifs of the fairy tale', *Texas Studies in Language and Literature*, vol. 5 (1964), p. 572; H. Stone, 'The fairy-tale transformation', *Dickens and the Invisible World: Fairy Tales, Fantasy, and Novel Making* (London: Macmillan, 1980), pp. 322–3; M. C. Kotzin, *Dickens and the Fairy Tale* (Bowling Green University Popular Press, 1972); E. M. Eigner, *The Metaphysical Novel in England and America: Dickens, Bulwer, Melville, and Hawthorne* (Berkeley: University of California Press, 1978), pp. 136, 212.

32   H. House, *The Dickens World* [1941], (Oxford Paperbacks, 1965), p. 156, and 'G. B. S. on *Great Expectations*', *Dickensian*, vol. 44 (Spring 1948), p. 64.

33   Ricks, op. cit., p. 199.

34   Q. D. Leavis, op. cit., pp. 373, 394.

35   Stange, op. cit., p. 294.

36   N. K. Hill, *A Reformer's Art: Dickens's Picturesque and Grotesque Imagery* (Athens: Ohio University Press, 1981), p. 124.

37   J. H. Miller, *Charles Dickens: The World of His Novels* (Cambridge, Mass.; Harvard University Press, 1958), p. 276.

38   R. Pattison, *The Child Figure in English Literature* (Athens, Ga: University of Georgia Press, 1978), p. 122; J. H. Buckley, *Season of Youth: The Bildungsroman from Dickens to Golding* (Cambridge, Mass.: Harvard University Press, 1974), 'Dickens, David and Pip', pp. 28–62; G. Smith, *Dickens, Money, and Society* (Berkeley: University of California Press, 1968), p. 170; L. Frank, *Charles Dickens and the Romantic Self* (Lincoln, Nebr.: University of Nebraska Press, 1984), p. 176.

39   Miller, op. cit., p. 249.

40   D. Van Ghent, 'On *Great Expectations*', *The English Novel: Form and Function* [1953] (New York: Harper Torchbooks, 1961), p. 133.

41   Q. D. Leavis, op. cit., p. 417.

42   A. E. Dyson, '*Great Expectations*: the immolations of Pip', *The Inimitable Dickens* (London: Macmillan, 1970), p. 228.

43   P. Hobsbaum, *A Reader's Guide to Charles Dickens* (London: Thames & Hudson, 1972), p. 222.

44   Dudley Flamm, 'The prosecutor within: Dickens's final explanation', *Dickensian*, vol. 66 (January 1970), pp. 16–23; Q. D. Leavis, op. cit., pp. 367–73.

45   Van Ghent, op. cit., p. 130.

46   R. Barnard, 'Imagery and theme in *Great Expectations*', *Dickens Studies Annual*, vol. 1 (1970), p. 238.

47   L. J. Dessner, '*Great Expectations*: "the ghost of a man's own father" ', *PMLA*, vol. 91, no. 3 (May 1976), pp. 436–49.

48   C. N. Manlove, 'Neither here nor there: uneasiness in *Great Expectations*', *Dickens Studies Annual*, vol. 8 (1980), p. 63.

49   Van Ghent, op. cit., pp. 136, 128.

50   L. Trilling, *The Liberal Imagination* (London: Secker & Warburg, 1951), p. 211.

51   R. Gilmour, op. cit., pp. 119, 137.

52   J. Moynahan, 'The hero's guilt: the case of *Great Expectations*', *Essays in Criticism*, vol. 10 (January 1960), pp. 60–79.

53   Q. D. Leavis, op. cit., pp. 414–15; R. Garis, *The Dickens Theatre* (Oxford: Clarendon Press, 1965), pp. 213–14.

54   Q. D. Leavis, op. cit., pp. 385, 380.
55   R. Newsom, 'The hero's shame', *Dickens Studies Annual*, vol. 11 (1983), pp. 1–24.
56   Barnard, op. cit., p. 238.
57   R. H. Dabney, *Love and Property in the Novels of Dickens* (London: Chatto & Windus, 1967), p. 134.
58   G. Smith, op. cit., pp. 173, 174.
59   C. Ricks, op. cit., p. 201; Q. D. Leavis, op. cit., p. 398.
60   L. Lerner, 'Literature and social change', *Journal of European Studies*, vol. 7 (December 1977), pp. 231–52.
61   S. Monod, '*Great Expectations* a hundred years after', *Dickensian*, vol. 56 (Autumn 1960), pp. 139, 140.
62   Q. D. Leavis, op. cit., pp. 394, 387, 422, 408.
63   P. Hobsbaum, op. cit., p. 236.
64   J. M. Brown, *Dickens: Novelist in the Market Place* (London: Macmillan, 1982), p. 139.
65   T. Wright, *The Life of Charles Dickens* (London: Herbert Jenkins, 1935); E. Wilson, 'Dickens: The two scrooges', *The Wound and the Bow* (Boston: Houghton Mifflin, 1941); H. Pearson, *Dickens: His Character, Comedy, and Career* (New York: Harper, 1949); J. Lindsay, *Charles Dickens: A Biographical and Critical Study* (New York: Philosophical Library, 1950).
66   E. Wagenknecht, 'Dickens and the scandalmongers', *College English*, vol. 11 (April 1950), pp. 373–82.
67   E. Johnson, 'The tempest and the ruined garden', *Charles Dickens: His Tragedy and Triumph* (London: Victor Gollancz, 1953), Vol. 2, p. 991.
68   Ada Nisbet, 'The autobiographical matrix of *Great Expectations*', *Victorian Newsletter*, no. 15 (Spring 1959), pp. 10, 11.
69   M. Slater, *Dickens and Women* (London: Dent, 1983), pp. 73–5.
70   Pamela Hansford Johnson, 'The sexual life in Dickens's novels', in Michael Slater (ed.), *Dickens 1970* (London: Chapman & Hall, 1970), p. 185.
71   A. Nisbet, op. cit., p. 10.
72   J. O. Jordan, 'The medium of *Great Expectations*', *Dickens Studies Annual*, vol. 11 (1983), p. 80.
73   G. Smith, op. cit., p. 176.
74   H. House, 'G. B. S. on *Great Expectations*', op. cit., p. 67.
75   Q. D. Leavis, op. cit., p. 390.
76   J. Kucich, 'Action in the Dickens ending: *Bleak House* and *Great Expectations*', *Nineteenth-Century Fiction*, vol. 33 (June 1978), p. 102.
77   ibid., pp. 92, 102, 104.
78   ibid., p. 102.
79   O. Elton, *Dickens and Thackeray* (London: Edward Arnold, 1924).
80   J. Cuming Walters, *Phases of Dickens: The Man, His Message, and His Mission* (London: Chapman & Hall, 1911).
81   J. Butt and K. Tillotson, 'Dickens as a serial novelist', *Dickens at Work* [1957], (London: Methuen, 1968), p. 33.
82   R. H. Dabney, op. cit., p. 147.
83   C. Ricks, op. cit., p. 210.
84   J. Forster, op. cit., Vol. 2, p. 289.
85   E. Johnson, op. cit., Vol. 2, pp. 992, 993.
86   Gissing, op. cit., p. 171.
87   G. B. Shaw, 'Foreword' to *Great Expectations*, The Novel Library (London: Hamish Hamilton, 1947), p. xvi.
88   R. J. Dunn, 'Far, far better things: Dickens' later endings', *Dickens Studies Annual*, vol. 7 (1978), p. 234.

89 A. L. French, 'Old Pip: the ending of *Great Expectations*', *Essays in Criticism*, vol. 29 (October 1979), pp. 357–60. See A. Calder (ed.), *Great Expectations* (Harmondsworth: Penguin, 1965), p. 496.

90 G. W. Kennedy, 'Dickens's endings', *Studies in the Novel*, vol. 6 (Fall 1974), p. 283.

91 A. A. Dunn, 'The altered endings of *Great Expectations*: a note on bibliography and first-person narration', *Dickens Studies Newsletter*, vol. 9 (June 1978), pp. 40–2.

92 D. H. Thomson, 'The passing of another's shadow: a third ending to *Great Expectations*', *Dickens Quarterly*, vol. 1, no. 3 (September 1984), pp. 94–6. *The Dickens Quarterly* succeeded to *Dickens Studies Newsletter* in March 1984.

93 E. Rosenberg, 'Last words on *Great Expectations*: a textual brief on the six endings', *Dickens Studies Annual*, vol. 9 (1981), pp. 87–115.

94 E. M. Eigner, 'Bulwer-Lytton and the changed ending of *Great Expectations*', *Nineteenth-Century Fiction*, vol. 25, no. 4 (June 1970), pp. 104–8.

95 H. P. Sucksmith, 'Sympathy and irony: Dickens and Bulwer-Lytton', op. cit., pp. 110–19.

96 M. W. Gregory, 'Value and meaning in *Great Expectations*: the two endings revisited', *Essays in Criticism*, vol. 19 (October 1969), pp. 402–9.

97 R. A. Greenberg, 'On ending *Great Expectations*', *Papers on Language and Literature*, vol. 6 (Spring 1970), pp. 152–62.

98 Q. D. Leavis, op. cit., p. 425.

99 John T. Smith, 'The two endings of *Great Expectations*: a re-evaluation', *Toth*, vol. 12, no. 1 (Fall 1971), pp. 11–17.

100 L. P. Shores, 'The character of Estella in *Great Expectations*', *Massachusetts Studies in English*, vol. 3 (Fall 1972), pp. 91–9.

101 R. J. Dunn, op. cit., p. 234.

102 D. M. Craig, 'Origins, ends, and Pip's two selves', *Research Studies*, vol. 47 (March 1979), p. 25.

103 I. Weiser, 'Reformed, but unrewarded: Pip's progress', *Dickens Studies Newsletter*, vol. 14 (December 1983), p. 144. See also E. M. Eigner, 'The absent clown in *Great Expectations*', *Dickens Studies Annual*, vol. 11 (1983), pp. 115–33.

104 Martin Meisel, 'The ending of *Great Expectations*', *Essays in Criticism*, vol. 15 (July 1965), pp. 326–31; Richard A. Levine, 'Dickens, the two nations, and individual possibility', *Studies in the Novel*, vol. 1, no. 2 (Summer 1969), pp. 157–80; Milton Millhauser, '*Great Expectations*: the three endings', *Dickens Studies Annual*, vol. 2 (1972), pp. 267–77; Peter Brooks, 'Repetition, repression, and return: *Great Expectations* and the study of plot', *New Literary History*, vol. 11 (Spring 1980), pp. 503–26.

105 P. Brooks, op. cit., p. 504.

106 A. Friedman, 'The closed novel and the open novel', *The Turn of the Novel* (New York: Oxford University Press, 1966), pp. 25 and 49.

107 Moshe Ron, 'Autobiographical narration and formal closure in *Great Expectations*', *Hebrew University Studies in Literature*, vol. 5 (Spring 1977), pp. 37–66.

108 D. A. Miller, *Narrative and Its Discontents: Problems of Closure in the Traditional Novel* (Princeton University Press, 1981), 'Afterword', pp. 273–7; D. Lodge, 'Ambiguously ever after: problematic endings in English fiction', *Working with Structuralism* (London: Routledge & Kegan Paul, 1981), pp. 143–55.

109 R. Barnard, op. cit., pp. 238–51.

110 J. P. McWilliams Jr, 'The beacon, the gibbet, and the ship', *Dickens Studies Annual*, vol. 2 (1972), pp. 255–66.

111 Taylor Stoehr, *Dickens: The Dreamer's Stance* (Ithaca, New York: Cornell University Press, 1965), pp. 101–2.

112 R. Robinson, 'The several worlds of "Great Expectations" ', *Queen's Quarterly*, vol. 78 (Spring 1971), pp. 54–9.

113 D. H. Ericksen, 'Demonic imagery and the quest for identity in Dickens' *Great Expectations*', *Illinois Quarterly*, vol. 33 (September 1970), pp. 4–11.

114 F. S. Schwarzbach, *Dickens and the City* (London: The Athlone Press, 1979), pp. 188–9.

115 E. MacAndrew, 'A second level of symbolism in *Great Expectations*', *Essays in Literature* (Macomb, Illinois), vol. 2 (Spring 1975) pp. 65–75.

116 M. H. Levine, 'Hands and hearts in *Great Expectations*', *Ball State University Forum* (Autumn 1965), pp. 22–4; C. R. Forker, 'The language of hands in *Great Expectations*', *Texas Studies in Language and Literature*, vol. 3 (Summer 1961), pp. 280–93; C. Ricks, op. cit., pp. 208–9

117 See Paulette Michel-Michot, 'The fire motif in *Great Expectations*', *Ariel*, vol. 8, no. 2 (April 1977), pp. 49–69.

118 Jack B. Moore, 'Hearts and hands in *Great Expectations*', *Dickensian*, vol. 61 (Winter 1965), pp. 52–6; Harry Stone, 'Fire, hand, and gate: Dickens' *Great Expectations*', *Kenyon Review*, vol. 24, no. 4 (Autumn 1962), pp. 652–91.

119 J. Carey, *The Violent Effigy: A Study of Dickens' Imagination* (London: Faber & Faber, 1973), p. 14.

120 Naomi Lightman, 'The "Vulcanic Dialect" of *Great Expectations*', *Dickensian*, vol. 82 (Spring 1986), pp. 33–8.

121 On Jaggers, see: Andrew Gordon, 'Jaggers and the moral scheme of *Great Expectations*', *Dickensian*, vol. 65 (Winter 1969), pp. 3–11; Anthony Winner, 'Character and knowledge in Dickens: the enigma of Jaggers', *Dickens Studies Annual*, vol. 3 (1974), pp. 100–21; A. F. Dilnot, 'The case of Mr. Jaggers', *Essays in Criticism*, vol. 25 (October 1975), pp. 437–43; A. L. French, 'Mr. Jaggers', *Essays in Criticism*, vol. 26 (July 1976), pp. 278–82; Stanley Tick, 'Toward Jaggers', *Dickens Studies Annual*, vol. 5 (1976), pp. 133–49.

122 L. J. Dessner, '*Great Expectations*: the tragic comedy of John Wemmick', *Ariel*, vol. 6, no. 2 (April 1975), pp. 65–80. On Wemmick, see also: Noel C. Peyrouton, 'John Wemmick: enigma?', *Dickens Studies*, vol. 1 (January 1965), pp. 39–47; Barbara Lecker, 'The split characters of Charles Dickens', *Studies in English Literature*, vol. 19 (Autumn 1979), pp. 689–704; Mary Ann Kelly, 'The functions of Wemmick of Little Britain and Wemmick of Walworth', *Dickens Studies Newsletter*, vol. 14 (December 1983), pp. 145–9.

123 T. E. Pemberton, *Charles Dickens and the Stage* (London: George Redway, 1888), pp. 55–66; J. B. Van Amerongen, *The Actor in Dickens* (New York: Appleton, 1927), pp. 161–3; V. C. Clinton-Baddeley, 'Wopsle', *Dickensian*, vol. 57 (Autumn 1961), pp. 150–9; W. F. Axton, '*Great Expectations* and burlesque form', *Circle of Fire: Dickens' Vision & Style & The Popular Victorian Theater* (Lexington: University of Kentucky Press, 1966), pp. 110–36; James D. Barry, 'Wopsle Once More', *Dickensian*, vol. 64 (Winter 1968), pp. 43–7.

124 B. D. Bort, 'Trabb's Boy and Orlick', *Victorian Newsletter*, no. 29 (Spring 1966), pp. 27–8; R. J. Dunn, 'Drummle and Startop: doubling in *Great Expectations*', *Dickensian*, vol. 63 (Spring 1967), pp. 125–7; M. C. Kotzin, 'Herbert Pocket as Pip's double', *Dickensian*, vol. 79 (Summer 1983), pp. 95–103; K. P. Wentersdorf, 'Mirror-Images in *Great Expectations*', *Nineteenth-Century Fiction*, vol. 21 (December 1966), pp. 203–24.

125 See Deborah A. Thomas, 'In the meantime: Dickens's concern with doubling and secret guilt between *A Tale of Two Cities* and *Great Expectations*', *Dickens Quarterly*, vol. 3, no. 2 (June 1986), pp. 84–9.

126 A. L. French, 'Beating and cringing: *Great Expectations*', *Essays in Criticism*, vol. 24 (April 1974), pp. 147–68.

127 J. H. Miller, op. cit., pp. 249–78; B. Hardy, 'The change of heart in Dickens' novels', *Victorian Studies*, vol. 5 (September 1961), pp. 49–67; J. Carey, 'Dickens and the mask', *Studies in English Literature* (Tokyo, 1983), pp. 3–18; L. Frank, op. cit., pp. 151–83.

128 A. Hutter, 'Crime and fantasy in *Great Expectations*', in F. Crews (ed.), *Psychoanalysis and the Literary Process* (Cambridge, Mass.: Winthrop, 1970), pp. 25–65.

129 G. Thurley, op. cit., pp. 280, 298.

130 B. Hardy, 'Food and ceremony in *Great Expectations*', *Essays in Criticism*, vol. 13 (October 1963), pp. 351–63.

131 K. Carolan, 'Dickens' last Christmases', *Dalhousie Review*, vol. 52 (Fall 1972), pp. 373–83.

132 A. Taylor, 'Devoured hearts in *Great Expectations*', *Dickens Studies Newsletter*, vol. 13 (September 1982), pp. 65–71.

133 G. L. Brook, *The Language of Dickens* (London: André Deutsch, 1970); R. Golding, *Idiolects in Dickens* (London: Macmillan, 1985), pp. 172–84.

134 D. Van Ghent, op. cit., pp. 125–6.

135 R. M. Vande Kieft, 'Patterns of communication in *Great Expectations*', *Nineteenth-Century Fiction*, vol. 15 (March 1961), pp. 325–34. See also George Levine, 'Communication in *Great Expectations*', *Nineteenth-Century Fiction*, vol. 18 (September 1963), pp. 175–81.

136 I. Ousby, 'Language and gesture in *Great Expectations*', *Modern Language Review*, vol. 72 (October 1977), pp. 784–93.

137 M. Young, 'Distorted expectations: Pip and the problems of language', *Dickens Studies Annual*, vol. 7 (1978), pp. 203–20.

138 P. Collins, 'A tale of two novels', op. cit., p. 337.

139 G. Ford, 'Charles Dickens', in *Victorian Novelists before 1895*, Vol. 21 of the *Dictionary of Literary Biography* (Detroit: Gale Research, 1983), quoted by G. J. Worth, op. cit., p. 165.

140 P. Hobsbaum, op. cit., p. 221.

141 J. R. Kincaid, *Dickens and the Rhetoric of Laughter* (Oxford: Clarendon Press, 1971), p. 6; W. Allen, 'The comedy of Dickens', in M. Slater (ed.), *Dickens 1970*, op. cit., pp. 18–19.

142 H. Talon, 'On some aspects of the comic in *Great Expectations*', *Victorian Newsletter*, no. 42 (Fall 1972), pp. 6–11.

143 W. C. Phillips, *Dickens, Reade, and Collins: Sensation Novelists* (New York: Columbia University Press, 1917); P. L. Marcus, 'Theme and suspense in the plot of *Great Expectations*', *Dickens Studies*, vol. 2 (May 1966), pp. 57–73.

144 N. Auerbach, 'Incarnations of the orphan', *ELH*, vol. 42, no. 3 (Fall 1975), pp. 395–419.

145 J. M. Kelty, 'The modern tone of Charles Dickens', *Dickensian*, vol. 57 (Autumn 1961), pp. 160–5; A. B. Dobie, 'Early stream-of-consciousness writing: *Great Expectations*', *Nineteenth-Century Fiction*, vol. 25 (March 1971), pp. 405–16.

146 R. B. Partlow Jr, 'The moving I: a study of the point of view in *Great Expectations*', *College English*, vol. 23 (November 1961), pp. 122–31.

147 N. M. Visser, 'The temporal vantage point in the novel', *Journal of Narrative Technique*, vol. 7 (Spring 1977), pp. 81–93; M. Ron, op. cit., *passim*;

S. Connor, *Charles Dickens* (Oxford: Blackwell, 1985); W. J. M. Bronzwaer, 'Implied author, extradiegetic narrator and public reader: Gérard Genette's narratological model and the reading version of *Great Expectations*', *Neophilologus*, vol. 62 (January 1978), pp. 1–18; S. Rimmon-Kenan, *Narrative Fiction: Contemporary Poetics* (London: Methuen, 1983), pp. 95–6.

148   K. J. Fielding, 'Dickens and the past: the novelist of memory', in Roy Harvey Pearce (ed.) *Experience in the Novel: Selected Papers from the English Institute* (New York: Columbia University Press, 1968), pp. 107–31, quoted by G. J. Worth, op. cit., p. 97.

149   J. Gold, *Charles Dickens: Radical Moralist* (Minneapolis: University of Minnesota Press, 1972), p. 244.

150   H. Talon, 'Space, time, and memory in *Great Expectations*', *Dickens Studies Annual*, vol. 3 (1974), pp. 122–33.

151   M. Ron, op. cit., p. 37.

152   J. O. Jordan, op. cit., pp. 78–9.

153   D. Sadoff, 'The dead father: *Barnaby Rudge, David Copperfield*, and *Great Expectations*', *Papers on Language and Literature*, vol. 18 (Winter 1982), pp. 36–57.

154   E. L. Gilbert, ' "In primal sympathy": *Great Expectations* and the secret life', *Dickens Studies Annual*, vol. 11 (1983), pp. 89–113.

155   J. O. Jordan, op. cit., pp. 73–87.

156   P. Brooks, op. cit., p. 505.

157   C. C. Barfoot, '*Great Expectations*: the perception of fate', *Dutch Quarterly Review of Anglo-American Letters*, vol. 6 (1976), pp. 2–33.

158   M. Baumgarten, 'Calligraphy and code: writing in *Great Expectations*', *Dickens Studies Annual*, vol. 11 (1983), pp. 61–72; R. Tracy, 'Reading Dickens' writing', ibid., pp. 37–59.

159   B. Westburg, op. cit., pp. 33–71, 115–57, 159–77, 179–87.

160   S. Connor, op. cit., pp. 109–44.

161   G. Stewart, *Dickens and the Trials of Imagination* (Cambridge, Mass.: Harvard University Press, 1974), pp. 187–97.

162   L. Frank, op. cit., pp. 3–30, 151–83.

163   Quoted in Christopher Norris, *Deconstruction* (London: Methuen, 1982), p. xiii.

APPENDIX 1

The Number Division

Weekly Instalment Numbers · Corresponding Chapters · Monthly Divisions

Weekly Instalment Numbers	Corresponding Chapters		Monthly Divisions
1 – Dec. 1 1860	1–2	....	I
2 – Dec. 8	3–4		
3 – Dec. 15	5		
4 – Dec. 22	6–7		
5 – Dec. 29	8	....	II
6 – Jan. 5 1861	9–10		
7 – Jan. 12	11		
8 – Jan. 19	12–13		
9 – Jan. 26	14–15	....	III
10 – Feb. 2	16–17		
11 – Feb. 9	18		
12 – Feb. 16	19		

End of First Stage

13 – Feb. 23	20–21	....	IV
14 – Mar. 2	22		
15 – Mar. 9	23–24		
16 – Mar. 16	25–26		
17 – Mar. 23	27–28	....	V
18 – Mar. 30	29		
19 – Apr. 6	30–31		
20 – Apr. 13	32–33		
21 – Apr. 20	34–35	....	VI
22 – Apr. 27	36–37		
23 – May 4	38		
24 – May 11	39		

End of Second Stage

25 – May 18	40	....	VII
26 – May 25	41–42		
27 – June 1	43–44		
28 – June 8	45–46		
29 – June 15	47–48	....	VIII
30 – June 22	49–50		
31 – June 29	51–52		
32 – July 6	53		
33 – July 13	54	....	IX
34 – July 20	55–56		
35 – July 27	57		
36 – Aug. 3	58–59		

End of Third Stage

APPENDIX 2

Editions of *Great Expectations* during Dickens's Lifetime

I ENGLAND

1861:

Chapman & Hall:[1] three-volume edition post 8vo, 31s. 6d,[2] from the *All the Year Round* text with some revisions, not illustrated:
6 July: 1,000 copies
5 August: 750 copies
17 August: 750 copies
21 September: 500 copies
30 October: 750 copies.[3]

1862:

Library edition (Chapman & Hall): a genuine second edition with slight alterations from the three-volume edition of 1861, especially concerning the last sentence.[4] This is a one-volume edition with 8 illustrations by Marcus Stone,[5] 7s. 6d.

1863:

Cheap edition (Chapman & Hall): 3s. 6d., the same as the 1862 edition.

1868:

The Charles Dickens edition (Chapman & Hall), with slight additions and revisions by Dickens, including the addition of descriptive headlines, 3s.[6]

II ABROAD

1861:

Tauchnitz Copyright edition (Leipzig): two-volume edition following the text of *All the Year Round*.[7]

T. B. Peterson and Brothers (Philadelphia):
– One-volume unillustrated paperback, from the *Harper's Weekly* text.[8]
– A later one-volume edition with John McLenan's illustrations from *Harper's Weekly*.[9]

NOTES: APPENDIX 2

1 'During Dickens's lifetime and the duration of the chief copyrights, the only authorized collected editions issued in England were published by Chapman & Hall. These editions were expanded from time to time, and in due course furnished with introductory and critical matter': Philip Collins, 'A Dickens bibliography', *The New Cambridge Bibliography of English Literature*, George Watson (ed.) (Cambridge University Press, 1969), vol. 3, p. 783.

2 For further information on sales and profits, see Robert L. Patten, *Charles Dickens and His Publishers* (Oxford: Clarendon Press, 1978), pp. 358, 365 and 385.

3 Edgar Rosenberg writes: 'a collation of the first five issues suggests that these were all printed at a single impression and published by Chapman & Hall in the succeeding months with misleading title-pages, proclaiming them to be new editions in order to imply (and encourage) a rapid sale, i.e. Chapman may have deliberately overprinted the first edition but in view of the dubious market potential kept the publication of the early "editions" fairly small, supplying new bindings-up as the need for new issues arose', 'A Preface to *Great Expectations*: the pale usher dusts his lexicons', *Dickens Studies Annual*, vol. 2 (1972), n. 13, p. 376. On the 'flexible terminology of the time' concerning the word 'edition', see Richard Altick, 'Nineteenth-century English best-sellers: a further list', *Studies in Bibliography*, vol. 22 (1969), p. 199 and R. L. Patten, op. cit., p. 291.

4 See Walter Dexter, 'The end of "Great Expectations" ', *Dickensian*, vol. 34 (Spring 1938), p. 82.

5 Q. D. Leavis suggests that 'Marcus Stone was only engaged to do some wood-engravings' because Dickens wanted 'to provide the orphaned son of [his] old friend [Frank Stone] with a job' and considers that these engravings did 'less than nothing' for the text: *Dickens the Novelist* (Harmondsworth: Penguin, 1972), pp. 464 and 466. According to Paul B. Davis, 'Dickens seems to have given little direction to the young artist and taken little interest in the result': 'Dickens, Hogarth, and the Illustrated *Great Expectations*', *Dickensian*, vol. 80 (Autumn 1984), p. 140. Davis's essay also deals with the later illustrators of the novel, pp. 130–43.

6 Doubt has been cast 'on the extent to which Dickens *carefully* revised the 1867–8 edition': see Angus Calder (ed.), 'A note on the text', *Great Expectations* (Harmondsworth: Penguin, 1965), p. 31. Evidence of desultory work can certainly be found in the lack of consistency about capitalization in the running headlines. The author's composition of these headlines seems to have been rather unimaginative. Thus, chapter xlii receives only three tame headlines, as follows: p. 199, 'He relates his Life and Adventures', p. 201, 'He continues his Narrative', p. 203, 'The end of the Narrative'. Here are a few other examples: ch. xi, p. 47 (first encounter with Jaggers), 'I first meet a man whom I shall often meet'; end of ch. xxvi, p. 125, 'I don't like Bentley Drummle'; ch. xxxix, p. 183, 'I recognise my Visitor', p. 185, 'He explains my great mistake'. Some few headlines are faintly humorous and Pumblechook receives ironical treatment

more than once: ch. ii, p. 7 (Pip asking questions about 'Hulks'), 'The pursuit of Knowledge under difficulties'; ch. xi, p. 49 (Miss Havisham's relatives), 'Family Felicities'; ch. xxviii, p. 133, 'Pumblechook, the founder of my fortunes!'; ch. lviii, p. 275, 'The Founder of my Fortunes holds forth'. On the running head-lines, see also Rosenberg, op. cit., pp. 308–13.

7   An agreement was signed between Dickens and Tauchnitz on 4 January 1861, allowing the publishers to issue the novel in Tauchnitz's Series of English Writers: see Patten, op. cit., p. 289.

8   Peterson bought the volume rights from Harper.

9   For further bibliographical description, see George J. Worth, *Great Expectations: An Annotated Bibliography* (New York: Garland, 1986), pp. 17–19.

BIBLIOGRAPHY

1 BIBLIOGRAPHY

Stevenson, Lionel (ed.), *Victorian Fiction: A Guide to Research* (Cambridge, Mass.: Harvard University Press, 1964). The chapter on Dickens, pp. 44–153, is by Ada Nisbet.

Collins, Philip, *A Dickens Bibliography*, extract from *The New Cambridge Bibliography of English Literature*, ed. George Watson, Vol. 3 (Cambridge University Press, 1969), published by the Dickens Fellowship (London, 1970), pp. 779–850. On *Great Expectations*, p. 805.

Gold, Joseph, *The Stature of Dickens: A Centenary Bibliography* (Toronto University Press, 1971). On *Great Expectations*, pp. 167–74.

Ford, George H. (ed.), *Victorian Fiction: A Second Guide to Research* (New York: The Modern Language Association of America, 1978). The chapter on Dickens, pp. 34–113, is by Philip Collins. On *Great Expectations*, pp. 104–6.

Fenstermaker, John J., *Charles Dickens, 1940–1975: An Analytical Subject Index to Periodical Criticism of the Novels and Christmas Books* (Boston: G. K. Hall, 1979). On *Great Expectations*, pp. 199–217.

Cohn, Alan M. and Collins, K. K., *The Cumulated Dickens Checklist, 1970–1979* (Troy, New York: The Whitston Publishing Company, 1982).

Worth, George J., *Great Expectations: An Annotated Bibliography* (New York and London: Garland, 1986). Besides being the most recent, this is, and by far, the most thorough and the most useful bibliographical source on *Great Expectations*, covering the years 1860–61 to 1983 inclusive.

For titles published after 1983, it will be necessary to consult the usual annual bibliographies, the 'Dickens Checklist' regularly published by the *Dickens Quarterly* (the successor to *Dickens Studies Newsletter* since March 1984) and the 'Recent Dickens Studies' section usually provided by *Dickens Studies Annual*.

2 BIOGRAPHICAL AND HISTORICAL INFORMATION

(a): *Biography*:

Forster, John, *The Life of Charles Dickens* [1872–4], ed. A. J. Hoppé, 2 Vols (London: Dent, 1966).

Johnson, Edgar, *Charles Dickens: His Tragedy and Triumph* (New York: Simon & Schuster, 1952; London: Victor Gollancz, 1953).

(b):   *Letters, Memoranda, Reading Adaptation*:

Dexter, Walter (ed.), *The Letters of Charles Dickens*, Vol. 3 (1858–1870) (London: Nonesuch Press, 1938).

Collins, Philip (ed.), *Charles Dickens: The Public Readings* (Oxford: Clarendon Press, 1975).

Kaplan, Fred (ed.), *Charles Dickens' Book of Memoranda* (New York: New York Public Library, 1981).

Stone, Harry (ed.) *Dickens' Working Notes for His Novels* (Chicago: Chicago University Press, 1987). The book came out too late for me to consult it.

(c):   *Composition and Publishing History*:

In addition to the accounts given by Forster and Johnson, see:

Butt, John, 'Dickens at work', *Durham University Journal*, vol. 40, no. 3 (June 1948).

Butt, John, 'Dickens's plan for the conclusion of *Great Expectations*', *Dickensian*, vol. 45 (Spring 1949).

Butt, John, 'Dickens as a serial novelist', in J. Butt and K. Tillotson, *Dickens at Work* (London: Methuen, 1957; University Paperbacks, 1968).

Collins, Philip, 'A tale of two novels: *A Tale of Two Cities* and *Great Expectations* in Dickens's career', *Dickens Studies Annual*, vol. 2 (1972).

Dexter, Walter, 'The end of "Great Expectations"', *Dickensian*, vol. 34 (Spring 1938).

Dunn, Albert A., 'The altered endings of *Great Expectations*: a note on bibliography and first-person narration', *Dickens Studies Newsletter*, vol. 9 (June 1978).

Eigner, Edwin M., 'Bulwer-Lytton and the changed ending of *Great Expectations*', *Nineteenth-Century Fiction*, vol. 25 (June 1970).

Fielding, Kenneth J., 'The weekly serialization of Dickens's novels', *Dickensian*, vol. 54 (Autumn 1958).

Greenberg, Robert A., 'On ending *Great Expectations*', *Papers on Language and Literature*, vol. 6 (Spring 1970).

House, Humphry, 'G. B. S. on *Great Expectations*', *Dickensian*, vol. 44 (Autumn 1948).

Meisel, Martin, 'Miss Havisham brought to book', *PMLA*, vol. 81 (June 1966).

Nisbet, Ada, 'The autobiographical matrix of *Great Expectations*', *Victorian Newsletter*, no. 15 (Spring 1959).

Oppenlander, Ella Ann, *Dickens' All the Year Round: Descriptive Index and Contributor List* (Troy, New York: The Whitston Publishing Company, 1984).

Patten, Robert L., *Charles Dickens and His Publishers* (Oxford: Clarendon Press, 1978).

Rosenberg, Edgar, 'A preface to *Great Expectations*: the pale usher dusts his lexicons', *Dickens Studies Annual*, vol. 2 (1972).

Rosenberg, Edgar, 'Last words on *Great Expectations*: a textual brief on the six endings', *Dickens Studies Annual*, vol. 9 (1981).

Stone, Harry, 'An added note on Dickens and Miss Havisham', *Nineteenth-Century Fiction*, vol. 10 (June 1955).

Stone, Harry, 'The genesis of a novel: *Great Expectations*', in E. W. F. Tomlin (ed.), *Charles Dickens: 1812–1870* (London: Weidenfeld & Nicolson, 1969). Reprinted, with one or two slight alterations, as '*Great Expectations*: the factual matrix' in *Dickens and the Invisible World: Fairy Tales, Fantasy, and Novel-Making* (Bloomington: Indiana University Press, 1979; London: Macmillan, 1980).

(d):   *Reception and Reputation*:

Some contemporary reviews are anthologized in:

Collins, Philip (ed.), *Dickens: The Critical Heritage* (London: Routledge & Kegan Paul, 1971).

Page, Norman (ed.), *Charles Dickens: Hard Times, Great Expectations and Our Mutual Friend*, Casebook Series (London: Macmillan, 1979).

On the reputation of the novel, see:

Fielding, Kenneth J., 'The critical autonomy of "Great Expectations"', *A Review of English Literature*, vol. 2 (July 1961).

Ford, George H., *Dickens and His Readers* (Princeton, NJ: Princeton University Press, 1955; New York: Norton, 1965).

3   BACKGROUND

Bateson, Charles, *The Convict Ships* (Glasgow: Brown, Son & Ferguson, 1959).

Branch-Johnson, W., *The English Prison Hulks* (London: Christopher Johnson, 1957).

Briggs, Asa, *Victorian People* [1954], (Harmondsworth: Pelican, 1965).

Collins, Philip, *Dickens and Crime* (London: Macmillan, 1962; 2nd edn, 1964).

Collins, Philip, *Dickens and Education* (London: Macmillan, 1963).

Gilmour, Robin, *The Idea of the Gentleman in the Victorian Novel* (London: Allen & Unwin, 1981).

Hibbert, Christopher, *The Roots of Evil* (London: Weidenfeld & Nicolson, 1963).

Lansbury, Coral, *Arcady in Australia* (Melbourne University Press, 1970).

Robson, L. L., *The Convict Settlers of Australia* (Melbourne University Press, 1965).

Shaw, A. G. L., *Convicts and the Colonies* (London: Faber & Faber, 1971).

Smiles, Samuel, *Self-Help* [1859], (London: Sphere Books, 1968).

4   CRITICAL STUDIES: A SELECTION

Auerbach, Nina, 'Incarnations of the orphan', *ELH*, vol. 42 (Fall 1975).

Axton, William, '"Keystone" structure in Dickens' serial novels', *University of Toronto Quarterly*, vol. 37 (October 1967).

Barnard, Robert, 'Imagery and theme in *Great Expectations*', *Dickens Studies Annual*, vol. 1 (1970).

Brooks, Peter, 'Repetition, repression, and return: *Great Expectations* and the study of plot', *New Literary History*, vol. 11 (Spring 1980).

Carey, John, *The Violent Effigy: A Study of Dickens' Imagination* (London: Faber & Faber, 1973).

Carolan, Katherine, 'Dickens' last Christmases', *The Dalhousie Review*, vol. 52 (Fall 1972).

Chesterton, G. K., *Appreciations and Criticisms of the Works of Charles Dickens* (London: Dent, 1911), ch. 20.

Clinton-Baddeley, V. C., 'Wopsle', *Dickensian*, vol. 57 (Autumn 1961).

Connor, Steven, *Charles Dickens* (Oxford: Blackwell, 1985), ch. 6.

Craig, David M., 'Origins, ends, and Pip's two selves', *Research Studies* (Washington State University), vol. 47 (March 1979).

Dabney, Ross H., *Love and Property in the Novels of Dickens* (London: Chatto & Windus, 1967), ch. 5.

Dessner, Lawrence Jay, '*Great Expectations*: "the ghost of a man's own father"', *PMLA*, vol. 91 (May 1976).

Dunn, Richard J., 'Far, far better things: Dickens' later endings', *Dickens Studies Annual*, vol. 7 (1978).

Dyson, A. E., *The Inimitable Dickens: A Reading of the Novels* (London: Macmillan, 1970), ch. 11.

Edminson, Mary, 'The date of the action in *Great Expectations*', *Nineteenth-Century Fiction*, vol. 13 (June 1958).

Flamm, Dudley, 'The prosecutor within: Dickens's final explanation', *Dickensian*, vol. 66 (Winter 1970).

Frank, Lawrence, *Charles Dickens and the Romantic Self* (Lincoln, Nebr.: University of Nebraska Press, 1984), ch. 5, 'The house of self'.

French, A. L., 'Beating and cringing: *Great Expectations*', *Essays in Criticism*, vol. 24 (April 1974).

Gadd, W. Laurence, *The Great Expectations Country* (London: Cecil Palmer, 1929).

Garis, Robert, *The Dickens Theatre: A Reassessment of the Novels* (Oxford: Clarendon Press, 1965), ch. 10.

Gold, Joseph, *Charles Dickens: Radical Moralist* (Minneapolis, Minn.: University of Minnesota Press, 1972), pp. 241–54.

Golding, Robert, *Idiolects in Dickens* (London: Macmillan, 1985), pp. 172–84.

Hagan, John, 'Structural patterns in Dickens's *Great Expectations*', *ELH*, vol. 21 (March 1954).

Hardy, Barbara, *The Moral Art of Dickens* (London: The Athlone Press, 1970). Ch. 7, '*Great Expectations*', is a reprint of 'Food and ceremony in *Great Expectations*', *Essays in Criticism*, vol. 13 (October 1963).

Hill, T. W., 'Notes to *Great Expectations*', *Dickensian*, vols 53 (Spring 1957, Autumn 1957), 54 (Winter 1958, Spring 1958, Autumn 1958), 55 (Winter 1959) and 56 (Spring 1960).

Hobsbaum, Philip, *A Reader's Guide to Charles Dickens* (London: Thames & Hudson, 1972), ch. 19.

House, Humphry, *The Dickens World* (London: Oxford University Press, 1941; 2nd edn, 1942; Oxford Paperbacks, 1960).

House, Humphry, 'G. B. S. on *Great Expectations*', *Dickensian*, vol. 44 (Spring 1948, Autumn 1948).

Kucich, John, 'Action in the Dickens ending: *Bleak House* and *Great Expectations*', *Nineteenth-Century Fiction*, vol. 33 (June 1978).

Leavis, Q. D., 'How we must read *Great Expectations*', in F. R. and Q. D. Leavis, *Dickens the Novelist* (London: Chatto & Windus, 1970; Harmondsworth: Pelican, 1972), ch. 6.

Lodge, David, 'Ambiguously ever after: problematic endings in English fiction', *Working with Structuralism* (London: Routledge & Kegan Paul, 1981), pp. 143–55.

Lucas, John, *The Melancholy Man: A Study of Dickens's Novels* (London: Methuen, 1970), ch. 8.

McWilliams, John P. Jr, '*Great Expectations*: the beacon, the gibbet, and the ship', *Dickens Studies Annual*, vol. 2 (1972).

Martin, Graham, *Great Expectations*, Open Guides to Literature (Milton Keynes: Open University Press, 1985).

Meisel, Martin, 'The ending of *Great Expectations*', *Essays in Criticism*, vol. 15 (July 1965).

Miller, J. Hillis, *Charles Dickens: The World of His Novels* (Cambridge, Mass.: Harvard University Press, 1958), ch. 8.

Millhauser, Milton, '*Great Expectations*: the three endings', *Dickens Studies Annual*, vol. 2 (1972).

Monod, Sylvère, *Dickens Romancier* (Paris: Hachette, 1953); revised and translated as *Dickens the Novelist* (Norman, Okla: University of Oklahoma Press, 1968), ch. 26, 'Back to the autobiographical form'.

Moynahan, Julian, 'The hero's guilt: the case of *Great Expectations*', *Essays in Criticism*, vol. 10 (January 1960).

Ousby, Ian, 'Language and gesture in *Great Expectations*', *Modern Language Review*, vol. 72 (October 1977).

Partlow, Robert B. Jr, 'The moving I: a study of the point of view in *Great Expectations*', *College English*, vol. 23 (November 1961).

Ricks, Christopher, '*Great Expectations*', in John Gross and Gabriel Pearson (eds), *Dickens and the Twentieth Century* (London: Routledge & Kegan Paul, 1962).

Ron, Moshe, 'Autobiographical narration and formal closure in *Great Expectations*', *Hebrew University Studies in Literature*, vol. 5 (Spring 1977).

Sadrin, Anny, *L'Etre et l'Avoir dans les Romans de Charles Dickens* (Lille-Paris: Didier Erudition, 1985), pp. 189–240.

Schwarzbach, F. S., *Dickens and the City* (London: The Athlone Press, 1979), pp. 184–93.

Shaw, George Bernard (ed.), *Great Expectations* (Edinburgh: R. & R. Clark for the Limited Editions Club of New York, 1937), Preface and Postscript.

Shaw, George Bernard, Foreword to *Great Expectations*, The Novel Library (London: Hamish Hamilton, 1947).

Slater, Michael, *Dickens and Women* (London: Dent, 1983).

Smith, Grahame, *Dickens, Money, and Society* (Berkeley: University of California Press, 1968), pp. 169–81.

Stange, G. Robert, 'Expectations well lost: Dickens' fable for his time', *College English*, vol. 16 (October 1954).

Stewart, Garrett, *Dickens and the Trials of Imagination* (Cambridge, Mass.: Harvard University Press, 1974).

Stoehr, Taylor, *Dickens: The Dreamer's Stance* (Ithaca, NY: Cornell University Press, 1965), pp. 101–37.

Stone, Harry, *Dickens and the Invisible World: Fairy Tales, Fantasy, and Novel-Making* (London: Macmillan, 1980). Contains two major chapters on *Great Expectations*, ch. 8, 'The factual matrix', and ch. 9 'The fairy-tale transformation'.

Sucksmith, Harvey Peter, *The Narrative Art of Charles Dickens: The Rhetoric of Sympathy and Irony in his Novels* (Oxford: Clarendon Press, 1970).

Talon, Henri, 'Space, time, and memory in *Great Expectations*', *Dickens Studies Annual*, vol. 3 (1974).

Thurley, Geoffrey, *The Dickens Myth: Its Genesis and Structure* (London: Routledge & Kegan Paul, 1976), ch. 12.

Timko, Michael, Kaplan, Fred, and Guiliano, Edward (eds), *Dickens Studies Annual*, vol. 11 (1983). This issue is focused on *Great Expectations*, with the following titles: Newsom, Robert, 'The hero's shame'; Tracy, Robert, 'Reading Dickens' writing'; Baumgarten, Murray, 'Calligraphy and code: writing in *Great Expectations*'; Jordan, John O., 'The medium of *Great Expectations*'; Gilbert, Elliot L., '"In primal sympathy": *Great Expectations* and the secret life'; Eigner, Edwin M., 'The absent clown in *Great Expectations*'.

Van Ghent, Dorothy, 'On *Great Expectations*', in *The English Novel: Form and Function* (New York: Rinehart, 1953; Harper Torchbooks, 1961).

Westburg, Barry, *The Confessional Fictions of Charles Dickens* (De Kalb, Ill.: Northern Illinois University Press, 1977). Has two major chapters on *Great Expectations*: ch. 4, '*Great Expectations* and the fictions of the future', and ch. 5, '"A cobweb meant expectation": Pip and the act of confession'.

Young, Melanie, 'Distorted expectations: Pip and the problems of language', *Dickens Studies Annual*, vol. 7 (1978).

INDEX